LIBERATED
LOVE

LIBERATED LOVE

Release Codependent Patterns and
Create the Love You Desire

———

Mark Groves *and*
Kylie McBeath

ST. MARTIN'S
ESSENTIALS
NEW YORK

First published in the United States by St. Martin's Essentials,
an imprint of St. Martin's Publishing Group

www.stmartins.com

The Library of Congress Cataloging-in-Publication Data is available upon request.

ISBN 978-1-250-90895-7 (hardcover)
ISBN 978-1-250-90896-4 (ebook)

First Edition: 2024

10 9 8 7 6 5 4 3 2 1

*To our previous partners
and those who've supported and loved us along the way.*

We're all just walking each other home.
—Ram Dass*

* https://www.ramdass.org/walking-each-other-home/

LIBERATED
LOVE

Contents

PART 3: RELATIONSHIP 2.0

Authors' Note

This book explores subject matter of a kind that is most often highly personal—and at times deeply sensitive—to the involved individual(s) (men or women). For that reason, and in order to protect privacy, throughout this book, actual names and other identifying details or events have frequently been changed.

In addition, readers should note that the information in this book is not intended to replace the advice of their own physician. You should consult a medical professional in matters relating to your health, especially if you have existing medical conditions, and before starting, stopping, or changing the dose of any medication you are taking.

Introduction

When it comes to relationships, what you're doing just isn't working.

You repeat the same frustrating patterns, hitting the same walls again and again. You feel disconnected. You argue about the same old stuff. You keep attracting the same type of person. You can't seem to find someone who wants what you want and is willing to match your effort. You're told you're either too much, not enough, or some combination of both, and no matter how often you said, "I'll never end up like my parents," here you are, following tired, recognizable scripts that feel hand-delivered by your mother or father, falling in love with people eerily similar, or *desperately* trying to avoid any semblance of what their relationship looked like. Life has a funny way of delivering us what we've been trying to avoid so that we'll finally confront it.

Despite past colossal relationship blunders, here you are, still going for it. Day after day you wake up and try to connect with your partner (or at least avoid another argument); or you scroll through dating apps in hopes of finding "the one"; or you post up at bars, having meet-cute after meet-cute with what feels like an endless stream of the same kind of person.

Some may call you crazy, but really, you're just human—because if there's one thing that's true about humans, it's that humans *need* one another. And yet, it seems that most don't have the skills to create the kind of love that everyone is yearning for. No one was modeled how to love—and not just how to love but how to create long-lasting relationships that thrive. Relationships that aren't just satisfying but also healing and expansive.

It's not your fault—you were handed a faulty template when it comes to love. If you look at the history of marriage, it was never about love. Not until recently, at least. The skills that were required to keep historical relationships together were just about keeping two strangers from murdering each other for the sake of the family. How romantic! Marriage was about getting more in-laws and expanding land ownership by allying someone in the tribe next door. It was about trade and sharing resources. It was *not* about love.

No wonder all this is so hard! We're trying to keep love alive using old-world relationship skills for new-world relationship demands (cue the appropriate quote attributed to Albert Einstein: "The definition of insanity is doing the same thing over and over and expecting different results").

We're individually and collectively standing at a threshold where we must make a choice: stay in our current relationships just the way they are, or mature out of outdated survival patterns, process old emotional debris, and step onto a more meaningful, authentic, and life-nourishing path.

For us, Mark and Kylie—two relationship experts who also happen to be very much in love with each other—we now know the possibility that love can offer when we're willing to actively choose our relationships and the lessons that emerge within them with curiosity, grace, and humility. Love—when entered into by willing adults committed to transforming themselves—can be the ultimate space of healing and growth. From that place, we are no longer existing in relationships that make us feel imprisoned and that we have to stay in forever to make them work, but rather we are both *choosing* to be in a relationship that liberates us from our previous patterns and habits that prevented us from creating the type of love, life, family, and partnership we have always desired. A relationship that centers each other's souls, not fears.

We call it "liberated love" and we're excited to walk you through how to cultivate it for yourself and with others.

What Is Liberated Love?

Okay, we get it. Liberated love sounds like something you'd hear a couple of "new-agers" talking about at a vegan cafe in Sedona, Arizona. But don't worry, you don't need to join an ashram, go on a pilgrimage, eat a bunch of mushrooms, or move to the desert to understand it, embody it, or live it (although you certainly could do that). All you need is *you*—along with your courageous, curious, and open heart—to show up willing to liberate yourself.

We're regular people who have a deep passion for understanding relationships and deepening our love not just for each other, but also for the world and all the beings in it.

And we're here to help you make love blossom. We're also here to help you learn, as we've learned, to walk away when a relationship is no longer serving you. When you're willing to face your "stuff" and finally let go of old protective behaviors and patterns, you can *finally* embody and experience the love that everyone dreams of.

But don't be fooled! This isn't a book about fairy tales or a guide on how to live out *The Notebook* (although Ryan Gosling and Rachel McAdams? *Swoon*). This is a book focused on using the container of relationship to learn the necessary skills to step fully into your individual and relational potential.

We get that you will be arriving at this journey (and *oh boy, is it a journey!*) with different hopes, wounds, stories, and scars around love. But no matter how you're arriving in this moment, it's likely that you're ready for a new conversation, depth, and template for relating.

Buckle up. We hear you. And we're with you.

Love is one of the greatest instruments for expansion and liberation. For both of us, previous relational challenges were wake-up calls that forced us to ask big questions and ultimately put us on this path to liberated love. These big questions included: What's in the way of my ability to give and receive love? Why can't I figure this love thing out? Why do I feel like I can never be fully myself in a romantic relationship? Why can't I fully choose this? Why do I keep finding myself in the same type of relationships, repeating the same patterns?

These questions, and our voyage through relationships, have taken us—individually and together—to the depths of our bodies and souls. We had to get our hands dirty and dig into the deepest corners of our psyche and physiology to get to the root of what's *really* going on beneath the surface of our patterns. Trust us. We went *deep*. Carl Jung would be proud. But it was only when we got to the root of our patterns that we had an opportunity to create a new template. We call this new template "liberated love."

Spiritual teacher and social psychologist Ram Dass once said, "The highest relationship is one where two people have consciously and intentionally said, 'Yes, let's get free and let's use our relationship with one another as one of the vehicles for doing that. In order to do that, since we know that in freedom is truth, let's be truthful with one another.'"* This, dear friends, is liberated love.

Now, you might be thinking, "Well, if Mr. Ram Dass is into it, I wanna know more about it! Kylie and Mark, can you explain more about what liberated love is and what it isn't?"

Gosh, we are so glad you asked.

Here is what liberated love is, and what it isn't.

Liberated love *is*:

+ **Being able to access *real choice* in our relationships.** To be free to choose, one must be, well, *free*—free to stay in a relationship and free to walk away. When we are hooked into familiar patterns, afraid to use our voice, or under duress of any kind, then *real choice* is not available. It may appear that we can speak up or leave a relationship, but if we are afraid to hurt people or have

---

*"What Is the Significance of Truth in Relationships?," https://www.ramdass.org/truth-in-relationships/.

unexplored and unresolved relational patterns, *real choice* will feel nearly impossible, and we'll constantly wonder why we feel stuck. A feeling of "stuckness" is a big ol' sign that we're not able to access real choice.

+ **Reconnecting to the energy of love and sharing it in ways that serve and honor life.** When we're liberated, our hearts are open (thank you, healthy boundaries!) and we can bring our love and warmth into our relationships and lives.

+ **Taking responsibility for your life and how you show up in a relationship.** Responsibility is the *key* to liberation. When we jump back into the driver's seat of our lives, we return to choice. This sounds like, "I'm responsible for my life, and I get a say in how it goes and what I will and will not allow." *Ah, what a beautiful thing.*

+ **Devotion to truth.** Those who are liberated in love are devoted to being in and sharing the truth. This means when "something is up" we bring it forward. This is a devotion to living transparently.

+ **Honoring someone else's path alongside your own.** When someone expresses that they desire to grow or change in a direction that feels as if it's pulling them away from us, this is an *invitation*—an invitation to get curious, an invitation to explore our fears and their fears, and an invitation to (re)consider what's possible for us individually and together. To honor someone's path is to encourage them to trust the nudges of what they are feeling called to do and explore—no matter how scary or threatening it may feel. The wonderful thing? When we create the space to talk about dreams and possibilities, we allow that for ourselves too. It looks like honoring our own path. Trusting what is trying to move through us is also honoring and freeing another to do the same. Liberation is contagious.

+ **Practicing unconditional positive regard for both self and others.** *This is a big one—and it is the foundation for all liberated* *relationships. Practicing positive regard simply means respecting and honoring yourself and others without conditions or limits.*

Liberated love is *not*:

+ Codependency
+ Trying to control others via emotional manipulation
+ Going along to get along
+ Feeling like you're not free to leave if you want to (or feeling like you don't have a choice regarding being in the relationship)
+ Relying on another human to save you, fix you, or heal you
+ Being afraid to change or grow away from your partner
+ Trying to fix, save, or heal another
+ Denial of what is really going on
+ Contempt for another and/or yourself (treating someone as if they aren't a powerful, capable, and a whole sovereign being)
+ Verbal, emotional, physical, mental, spiritual, or sexual abuse

Now, if you just read the list above and thought, "I'm definitely landing more in the *not* liberated love camp," don't worry, we were the poster children for not liberated. We exhibited a lot—and we mean *a lot*—of codependency and denial before we embarked on this journey. *There is intelligence in our resistance.* And yet, love continually invites us to meet our edges over and over again, so that we can transmute what's in the way of its flow and fate. Or, as thirteenth-century Persian poet Rumi says, "Your task is not to seek for love, but merely to seek and find all the barriers within yourself that you have built against it."* We're excited to share a little bit more about the way love cracked us wide open over the course of our relationship journey as well as brought us to a place where we became positively obsessed with liberating others.

---

*"Our Barriers to Love: Monday's Mindful Quote from Rumi," PsychCentral, February 15, 2010, https://psychcentral.com/blog/mindfulness/2010/02/our-barriers-to-love-mondays-mindful-quote-with-rumi.

Our Story

We dated. We broke up. We matched again on Tinder. Bam. Case closed.

Okay, the Tinder thing didn't happen.

We originally met through a dating app no one talks about: Instagram. I (Mark) slid right into Kylie's DMs with something poetic, along the lines of: "Hey! I love your words. Any chance you'd wanna connect beyond the 'gram?"

We hit it off, dove deep into a conversation about love and connection, and then Kylie moved to Vancouver. The rest was *supposed* to be history. Unfortunately—or fortunately—life and patterns happened. Our old, unprocessed stuff came up and interfered with our relationship.

As much as Ky and I wanted to choose each other and walk hand-in-hand into the sunset, we found ourselves walking together toward a darkening horizon. Enter: the shadows of our previous pains and limitations.

For me (Mark), the wound that showed up in *every* relationship was, "You don't fully choose me." I loved the ladies who were *almost* ready. *Almost* healed. *Almost* all-in. The ones who *wanted* to choose me? *Boring.* Swipe left. Pass. (Sorry to those of you who tried to love me, and I ran like a scared boy because, well, I was.) I was terrified of women. Wait, let me clarify, I was terrified of an embodied, powerful woman who could choose me fully and deliver the words that called me to grow up. To be a man. To stand in my power. Of course, the ones who weren't *quite* ready were asking the same of me, just indirectly.

My wound—although triggered by Kylie's inability (you'll learn more about this in a second) to fully choose the relationship—was also empowering. I got to be a victim. I got to be the one who always said *she* wasn't ready. I got to hold that over her. I got to chase her. But eventually, that got exhausting. Because I wasn't only chasing her, I was also chasing my worth. I was chasing the idea that when she finally chose me, I'd be enough. I'd find the holy grail of love. I'd be done. No more personal growth for me! So, I let Kylie's inability to fully choose our relationship allow me to believe: *It's not me, it's her.*

Turns out, I was waiting for me to choose myself.

Okay, Ky, let's hear your side . . .

When Mark slid into my DMs, I was on the heels of a divorce. Ten or so months post-divorce, to be exact. Needless to say, I arrived at the doorstep of our relationship carrying bags of fear and resistance. My mental mixtape went something like: *Am I ready? Will I lose myself again? Do I need more time to be single and heal?* Followed by, *But this guy can "meet" me where I desire to be met. He's kind, attentive, and present. Yes, he gets it.*

For me, the pull of "yes" was stronger than any of my fearful questions. So, on we went.

Even though my "yes" was stronger, I was still psychologically split on my decision to be in the relationship. I was torn between listening to the survival instructions (which were deeply and unconsciously encoded in my nervous system) and answering the growing call of my own soul. My body's survival instructions said, "You can't do this on your own, you *need* to be in a relationship to be safe." While on the other side my soul said, "It's time to leave this relationship because the same thing will inevitably happen again."

The tension between these two polarizing parts expressed themselves in our relationship as ambivalence. Like two puzzle pieces, my wounds and Mark's wounds found each other and felt right at home. My inability to access a coherent "yes" made me feel broken. That same inability made Mark feel unchosen and unlovable. I was able to affirm my thoughts by saying, "Well, I can't fully choose him because I'm not able to fully trust myself—I am broken and split." And Mark got exactly what he wanted: someone who was *almost* choosing him.

At the end of the day, I couldn't fully choose Mark because I wasn't making the choice to stay in our relationship from a vantage of not "needing" him. As in, I was taught I needed to depend on a man, but my previous dependency had led to a loss of sovereignty. How could I choose him without choosing the same circumstances and, ultimately what I feared the most, the same outcome? But damn, did I want to be able to choose. Shame and confusion began to creep in, and I found myself riding on a nauseating merry-go-round: *Something is wrong with me, but once I heal this wound, I will be able to choose him fully. Then, all will be okay.* This went on and on and on—we're talking four years—until my physical body began to weaken, and my mental monologue became increasingly loud.

I was dancing with the wound of mistrust. I didn't trust myself, and I certainly didn't trust anyone else. Like most of us, I didn't know if there was another way to be in a relationship. So, for me, the only way to exit this codependent cycle was to do just that: *exit the codependent cycle*.

That's what I did. *We* did.

We broke up. We left each other as lovingly as we could by arriving at a sacred, full-body "no" to our previous dynamic.

But this "no" opened up space, for both of us, to find what "yes" felt and looked like within our own bodies and within our relationship. We stepped away, did some major soul searching and intensive healing work, and ten months later, we began our relationship journey again. But this time we did so from a foundation that was more integrated, anchored, and coherent.

Don't get us wrong. There's way more to this ride than: We broke up. We got back together. All was good. And we both love tacos.

The first iteration of our relationship was one journey. The "sacred pause" (what you call a breakup after you've gotten back together, and now want to call it something fancier) was a separate one. And the coming back together ("relationship 2.0," as we like to call it) is another ongoing adventure with its own twists and turns.

The pathway to liberated love is delicious, beautiful, and deep. It is filled with pain and grief and joy and all the other things that make life and love what they are (I mean, do you remember all the drama in *The Notebook*? All we seem to remember is the rain-drenched kiss!). This journey home to ourselves, our bodies, and our souls requires deep excavation. It requires a willingness to feel all the feels and move toward the potential buried in our hearts. We know this journey is good medicine because it brings us back to life. To love.

The Journey to Liberated Love

The journey—and, conveniently, this book—is broken down into three parts: Relationship 1.0, The Sacred Pause, and Relationship 2.0. It is a journey from codependence to healthy, whole-self independence to interdependence.

It mirrors the journey that we walked, and the one we've guided hundreds of beautiful souls through to reconnect with themselves and the vital energy of love again. And while we've been talking about this journey in the context of romantic love, we want you to know that this journey can be taken in any area of our lives and with anyone we are in relationship with—our family members, friends, coworkers, and, especially, ourselves. To give you a peek at the terrain, let's explore these three parts in more detail.

Relationship 1.0

To begin you'll take an honest look at the health of your relationships now. Are they thriving? Are you moving in a direction that brings you more connection and harmony, or disconnection? From there, you will discover what sits at the root of codependent patterns and attachment styles, and gain more insight into why your relationships are the way they are. After this relational deep dive, you'll be invited to get clear on what type of shifts need to take place in order to support you in breaking up with dynamics that are keeping you stuck in survival-based identities and dysfunctional relationships. Yeehaw!

The Sacred Pause

In order to change patterns and dynamics in our lives we must shift the dance by taking responsibility for how we contribute to the choreography—unconsciously or consciously. During the sacred pause you'll be creating an intentional time-bound container—a relational reset—that will support you in creating the space you need to witness, care for, and integrate the parts of you that have been driving and tolerating dysfunctional dynamics.

It is here, within the reset, that you come back into *right* relationship with your needs, your body, your desires, and your *self*—a self that is both secure *and* able to grow and change. It is a move back into healthy independence and soul-dependence—a place where you can tap into your inner authority, your soul's guidance, and rely on yourself to have your own back. As you do this work, you'll increase your capacity to be with yourself so that you can honor your body and step into deeper integrity. It's here where your soul steps back onto the dance floor, and you begin to trust yourself again.

Relationship 2.0

After emerging from the sacred pause, you'll be invited to put everything you've learned and unlearned about yourself into practice. In part 3, Relationship 2.0, you'll reopen your heart with a wider and deeper lens of awareness and inner foundation of safety. As you do this, there will be many opportunities to transform the triggers and trust your body's somatic intelligence. Here, you'll stop relying on perfected choreography and instead feel the rhythm and the movement of the steps, fully connecting with your dance partner. As we fortify our trust in self and others, we begin to open to new levels of intimacy in the form of sacred sexuality, a well-resourced community, and a remembrance of the *other-than-human* world around us. This is where we learn to stay in our center and coexist in an ecosystem of reciprocal, interdependent, and nourishing relationships.

The beautiful thing about this adventure is that while we embark on it to find love, connection, and companionship with another human being, what we inevitably discover is *so much more*. A remembrance and connection to our souls, the earth, our seen and unseen allies, the other-than-human kin, the great mystery, and everything in between. This adventure is about coming fully alive . . . perhaps for the first time in a long time.

To support us through this journey we will be weaving together a holistic—mind, body, soul—lens that brings together the work of many brilliant minds and beautiful hearts in the field of human relations. This web will include threads from attachment theory, nervous system health, somatic work, neuroscience, developmental psychology, emotional and spiritual development, energetic health, and family systems and intergenerational healing. We're going to have introspective, nerdy, soul-expansive fun getting to the root of all of this love stuff. Get ready, because we're going to take you on a ride through human evolution, love's revolution, and walk the path home together, toward what love truly is. We are going to liberate ourselves from our old patterns, understand those patterns, and heal ourselves and the world, together, one step, hard conversation, and tear at a time.

You might be asking yourself, "Is this journey for me?" This book is for you . . .

+ *If you don't feel like you can be your true self in your relationship . . .*
+ *If you and your partner keep hitting the same wall(s) . . .*
+ *If you lose yourself in every relationship . . .*
+ *If you're done playing small and minimizing your voice, needs, desires, and emotions . . .*
+ *If you're tired of settling for breadcrumbs in your relationships . . .*
+ *If you're ready to jump into the driver's seat of your life . . .*
+ *If you're ready to break generational patterns . . .*
+ *If you're tired of the same relationship outcomes and experiences, and are ready to create the relationship you've always wanted . . .*
+ *If you're not sure whether to "stay" or "go" in your current relationship . . .*
+ *If you don't trust yourself in dating . . .*
+ *If you're ready to reconnect with your body, soul, and deepest desires . . .*
+ *If you're ready to open your heart and live your sacred purpose . . .*
+ *If you're ready for a new depth of intimacy . . .*
+ *If you know there is more waiting for you . . .*

And ultimately, this book is for you if you're ready to say a whole-hearted "yes" to capital-*L* Life and to Love. As your guides, we trust in love's alchemical powers to bring you back home to yourself (and beyond) with every cell of our beings.

More than anything, we're excited to teach you all about liberated love: that magical place where our relationships are no longer a prison to our potential but rather a portal to infinite intimacy.

PART 1

Relationship 1.0

1

The Great Disconnect

We all want great love, don't we? The kind that stirs our soul and has us feeling more connected and invested in something than we ever thought was possible. The kind that takes our breath away and that can, for a moment, make us forget about the existence of time and responsibilities. The kind from rom-coms where we overcome our challenges and sail off into the sunset happily ever after.

From the outside looking in, Stephanie and Greg had *that* kind of love. They checked all the boxes under "thriving couple." They lived in a charming house, had two beautiful kids, a Goldendoodle named Doug, successful careers, and a vibrant social life.

But on the inside, unbeknownst to many, they felt trapped in a zoo of their own making (unintentionally, of course). At night, when their heads hit their respective pillows, they both wondered if that day was the day one of them would address the giant, looming, unmistakable elephant in the room.

You may know the feeling—that feeling when your alarm goes off and, yet again, you are hit with a gnawing sense that something is "off" in your life and relationship.

It might start off as a small inkling—a slight *Hmm, there's something not quite right here.* It might take years before you muster the courage to claim it, let alone address that scary feeling with others.

It's hard to know what to do with this feeling because you're not sure what's on the other side of facing it. If you're like us, you might spend every last drop of energy trying to make that elephant in the room disappear. To try to pathologize it away.

Change? No, thank you. Bring it up?! Ha. You're funny.

Instead of moving toward that feeling—acknowledging it, observing it, deconstructing it, looking at it from all angles to try to figure out why you feel this way—you repress it, minimize it, project it onto others, shame it, distract yourself, put on rose-colored glasses, and carry on your way. Joining a gym, eating well, podcasts, books, Chardonnay . . . none of them can explain or make that feeling go away.

So, you live with it. You bring that eight-thousand-pound elephant into your home and into your bed. Your partner asks why you never seem present, why you argue so much, why you don't want the same things, why you can't connect anymore, why everything feels so heavy lately . . . *why, why, why?* Meanwhile you're asking yourself the same thing. *Why am I so guarded? Why am I so anxious? Why am I so frustrated? Anxious? Overwhelmed? Exhausted? Uninspired? Controlling? Confused? Burnt-out? Depressed?*

At least that's what *we* did—and that's what Stephanie and Greg did too.

I (Mark) had been working with Stephanie and Greg for a few months. They were clients, and we had been focusing on unpacking their recent arguments and trying to get to the heart of their individual perspectives. In one session, where Stephanie had arrived solo (Greg didn't want to come that day), she burst into tears. She was desperate to figure out what she and Greg needed to do with their marriage and to know how they got where they were in the first place. *Why? Why? Why?*

I took a deep breath and asked her, "Do you want a great relationship?"

To which she replied, emphatically, "What? Of course I do."

"I'm not sure that you do."

"Yes. We do. *Obviously.*"

"Then you have to be tired of the way you are doing things. You have to want the amazing relationship more than you're afraid of letting go of what's familiar. You have to be willing to let your old relationship die so a new one can be born. You have to be willing to create new patterns and take responsibility for your side of the street. You have to be willing to explore, grow, and learn from one another and participate in each other's healing. You have to be willing to dance in the unfamiliar. You have to be *truly committed* to that vision. Great relationships don't just happen—we create them."

There was a long pause followed by a heavy sigh. I could tell that, finally, *it* clicked.

"Are you all-in for that, Stephanie?"

"Yes. I think I finally am."

We all say we *want* great love, but are we making choices that align with those intentions or desires? We are saying one thing and doing another. We are saying we want a loving and respectful relationship, yet we aren't acting in a way that creates that. We want someone we trust and someone who tells us the truth, yet we hide our own words and feelings. We say we know that communication is the key to successful relationships, yet we aren't practicing being a good communicator ourselves. We say we want someone who is available, respects our time, is honest, does what they say they're going to do, yet we stay in relationships with people who don't do any, or only a few, of those things. We *say* a lot of things, but when words aren't aligned with intentional actions, they are just that: words that align with our values but not our lives; words that invite us in a direction our footsteps never follow.

This, dear friends, is what we call *the great disconnect*.

When there is misalignment between what we say we want and what we choose, there is a disconnect. When we are in relationships that aren't aligned and supportive to our well-being, there is a disconnect. When we keep dating the same people, and repeating the same patterns, there is a disconnect. When we try meeting our needs with wants (like getting engaged to find security in our relationships or deciding to have kids when we're not ready to "keep" the relationship), there is a disconnect. When we have the same fights over and over without resolution, there is a disconnect. When resentment lives in our hearts, there is a disconnect. When we *say* we are fine and yet there's a giant lump in our throats or ache in our stomachs, there is a disconnect. When we say we're fine alone, but deep down yearn for a partnership, there is a disconnect. When we stay in work we hate, there is a disconnect. When we are afraid to bring up a topic because of the reaction we anticipate getting, there is a disconnect.

Ultimately, the disconnect is when who you truly are and how you truly feel is split off from who you're being and what you're actively choosing.

Look, we've been there, folks. If you had asked us when we were younger, "Are you great at relationships?" We would both have answered with a resounding, exuberant *yes*. In fact, we didn't just think we were great at them, we thought we were *gifted*. What exactly does "gifted" look like? Well, it ain't pretty. Like many others, maybe even you, we thought we were good at love and relationships because we were good at pretending. We thought a great relationship meant keeping the peace—going along to get along. A facade that operated under the premise that, *If I ignore all of my feelings and keep everyone else happy, no one will ever leave me*. But in doing so, we inevitably abandoned ourselves, our needs, our wants, our voice, and ourselves.

For one of us (Kylie), this showed up as being a chameleon in the relationship—shapeshifting to meet the needs, desires of partners. For the other (Mark), this meant sweeping things under the rug until there was no choice but to talk about it, being emotionally unavailable to women who were actually capable of love, and pursuing wholeheartedly the ones who were just not ready (spoiler alert: because I wasn't).

Which means we were not fully in the relationship, *our representative was*. The version of us we were told we needed to be in order to be safe and loved was present, but all the other vibrant, vulnerable, and deeper truths remained hidden—even to us.

We avoided conflict because we both lived under the naive assumption that if one avoids conflict, the relationship will then, by definition, have no conflict. It runs on the same logic that if a tree falls in a forest and no one hears it, does it make a sound? *Yes*. It does. A loud one.

The disconnect can be hard to identify when it's been normalized. When we grow up in families and a culture that pretends the hard truth doesn't exist—or fears the act of acknowledging that hard truth—we become adults who do the same. When our cultures tell us to become someone we aren't in order to be loved, valued, and to fit in, we become adults who've spent the majority of our lives being anything but ourselves.

We want to be *loved* for who we are, but we aren't willing to show up as we truly *are*. Instead, we show up as a sliver of ourselves and then feel frustrated when people don't seem to fully know or understand us.

Isn't it wild to think that you can be in a relationship, yet not *in* a relationship? You can be in a job yet not *in* a job. You can have a life yet not be living. You can be going about your business, totally immersed in checking the boxes that society tells you matter, and then, *bam*, you wake up one day to the fact that while you were checking all the boxes and attending to everyone and everything else, you have forgotten about yourself.

Suddenly, you feel in the depths of your being the unmet potential for your life: *choosing* a life and *living* a life are two *very* different things.

This raises the question: Why is it so common to be in relationships, or even just living a life, and feel disconnected from our voice, our values, our desires, and ourselves?

Just take a look at the world around you. In society, relationship status is a hierarchy. If you're married, you're better than someone who is engaged, dating, single, or (God forbid) divorced. When we're single, we're asked if we've found someone. If we haven't, we're asked, "Why are you single?" . . . as if there's something wrong with us. As if we have an ailment. As if we're not *choosing* to be single.

As a collective, we value the longevity of a relationship more than its quality, depth, and safety. We want them to last *no matter what*. We ask people, "How long have you been together?" and the longer the relationship, the more impressed we are. "Thirty years! Wow! That's incredible!"

Meanwhile, we don't stop to consider whether this couple, like Greg and Stephanie, have been holding on by a thread—stewing for almost all of those thirty years in a relationship, void of intimacy but packed with contempt. We skip right over any potential dysfunction. But imagine if, instead of learning how to develop the skills to tolerate a relationship like this, we learned how to *thrive* in it.

Perhaps the real question is: Why don't we celebrate a relationship's depth or quality?

The answer: because we've placed so much of our worth, validation, safety, and security in our relationship status that we'll do *anything* to stay *in* it, even if it's dysfunctional. Of course, challenging relationships can often be transformed when we put in the work, but because we're so afraid of our relationships ending, we avoid any conversation that might end them. The irony? These are the very conversations that deepen relationships, that liberate them.

Alas, time and time again we choose "common" and "normal" relationships over liberating ones.

But you know what else is "normal"? A divorce rate of over 44 percent.* Normal has people remaining in relationships with people they dislike. Normal contains a nasty, silent, contractual obligation: one is supposed to stay no matter what, because they have made a commitment. But this commitment to another almost never involves a commitment to oneself. In the "normal" relationship we are never encouraged to explore who we are, what we actually want, or how we can become our most authentic selves in the world through a partnership.

But we don't have to be "normal." You can say you want a *great* relationship *and* actually make choices to align with that—you can be with someone and still be yourself.

Here's the thing: Stephanie and Greg *did* want great love; they just had a competing familiar template that modeled love as self-erasure. Stephanie learned that in order to keep connection and love, she needed to get smaller and quieter. She needed to disappear. And Greg learned how to be her perfect match for this wound, and her with his. Because of this template, Stephanie, like all humans, settled for predictable and painful connection over unfamiliar and expansive love. Unfortunately, we'd often rather get what we've been taught to tolerate than step toward the mystery and miracle that is liberated love—a sacred, life-giving, intimate union with another. We would rather abandon ourselves than create relationships that celebrate our self-expression.

If you've found yourself silently agreeing with what we've said so far, then you are ready to step into the transformative power of liberated love.

---

* "50+ Divorce Statistics in the U.S., Including Divorce Rate, Race, and Marriage Length," https://divorce.com /blog/divorce-statistics/.

You are ready to be finished with the patterns. Finished with the elephant. Finished with the nagging feeling. Finished with the discontent and the disconnect.

You are ready to venture the path to empowered choice.

To get here, we must look at all of the ways we've had to disconnect from our true selves. This is where we get to hit the pause button and take an honest, humble look in the mirror. It is in this space where we drop the blame and say, "You know what, I play a role in this dance too . . ."

The Ways We Stay Disconnected and Disguised

When Stephanie and Greg realized they *both* played a role in the creation of their relationship dynamic, they were relieved. The finger-pointing stopped, and self-reflection and personal responsibility began. They *finally* felt empowered to DO something about it instead of sinking deeper into the blame game that they had been stuck in for years. They knew that if they wanted to change their relationship, they *both* would have to change. And that's just it: *a relationship we've never had requires us to become someone we have never been.*

To create a new type of relationship—one that *feels* different, lighter, and exciting—demands that we develop the skills and abilities of someone who is already in that type of relationship. It's not something we fall into or accidentally stumble upon, it's something we actively and intentionally *create.* If we keep bringing old versions of ourselves to new relationships, we'll create the same old relationship patterns. A more self-aware and integrated you—one that knows your stories, patterns, and tender spots—invites a new relationship, new choices, and new possibilities.

Through our work together, Stephanie and Greg began to see how the survival strategies they used to protect themselves prevented them from cultivating the relationship(s) they desired. They were both disconnected from themselves, and therefore felt disconnected and lonely in every area of their lives. This was made especially evident in their marriage.

To climb out from underneath these survival strategies, Stephanie,

Greg, and I explored the masks, roles, and emotional armor they had individually acquired over the years to protect themselves from feeling pain and to maintain a healthy distance from their individual underlying senses of unworthiness. For Stephanie, this showed up as being the "caretaker" and "cool girl" in her relationships. After decades of minimizing her voice and repressing her emotions, desires, and needs, her true self and soul began to push back. For Greg it showed up as being the "high achiever" and "workaholic." He felt the pressure to provide and to act as if he had zero needs and emotions. He started to lean into sharing his feelings. He too found his voice and learned how to communicate the resentments that he had formerly used to create leverage.

The relationship they once had ended, to accommodate and create space for two adults with wants and needs. This is a good thing! It was time for something to change—on the inside first, and then within every relationship they had.

The same is true for all of us: if we want a great relationship and fulfilling life, we need to look in the mirror and begin to set down the emotional armor and peel back the masks we've been hiding behind. Stephanie knew it was time to come home to her true self and all the parts that she had neglected for a very long time. She was ready to "close the gap" on the disconnect between who she thought she needed to be and her authentic self.

Closing the gap takes courage, patience, compassion, and care. While it's painful to move into the grief that exists under the armor and the unprocessed emotional debris of our past, eventually, like it was for Stephanie, it becomes the less painful path to take. You'll do anything to finally make change.

To support you in pinpointing the survival strategies, masks, and armor that keep you disconnected and disguised (from yourself and others), we've compiled a list of the most common ways we armor and mask up.

To start, we're going to shine a light on some of the common ways we emotionally armor up to protect ourselves from harm or potential pain. We come by these shields honestly. No one likes to feel pain, so we learn to layer on the emotional armor when we don't have another strategy in place to help us cope or a safe space to feel, process, and move through our emotions effectively. For some, this shows up as being avoidant, or withdraw-ing when situations become too overwhelming. For others, like Stephanie, it shows up as projection—blaming others for her pain or pedestalizing someone else's relationship as "perfect" or "unreachable." All of us, in some way or another, do this. It's when we are able to acknowledge, take respon-sibility for, and move into choice that it becomes possible for us to lay down the armor and reopen our hearts. To choose vulnerability over protection.

While emotional armor serves an appropriately protective and neces-sary function at times, it also comes at a cost. This armor, while shielding us from pain, also shields us from connection with others. When we are disconnected from our emotions we experience loneliness, because it is

EMOTIONAL ARMOR	BEHAVIOR	DEFINITION
Avoidance	"This won't work out, so I'll just not say any-thing . . ." or "There's no point . . ." "They won't care if I'm not there . . ." or constantly bailing/ghosting another.	This emotional armor keeps us distanced from the potential of pain/suffering by disconnecting us from ourselves and en-vironments that bring up uncomfortable thoughts and feelings. For exam-ple, you isolate, distance, or silence yourself in social situations to protect yourself from rejection or judgment.
Denial	"I don't know what you're talking about, I'm fine . . ." or "There's nothing to look at here . . ." "You're making a big deal out of nothing . . ." Denial quickly morphs into defensiveness when sen-sitive topics are brought forward in relationship.	To avoid emotional dis-comfort, we use this shield to disconnect from objec-tive truths and experiences that we are unwilling to accept or acknowledge about our lives. For exam-ple, when our partner says he doesn't have a problem with marijuana, but it in-terferes with his relation-ships, work, and life, he is using a shield of denial.

Spiritual Bypassing	Being the bigger person at the expense of your well-being. This person hides their attachment needs by collapsing into "non-attachment," focusing only on the positive, and raising your vibration. Over-relying on manifestation principles without looking at the impact of macro systems and unconscious imprints perpetuates self-blame and hyper-dependence.	When one is using this shield, they are hiding behind spiritual concepts. We use this armor to avoid doing the work necessary to clear emotional debris and release outdated beliefs. For example, if we label anger as a "negative/ low vibration" emotion, we're bypassing our true emotional state and the wisdom it holds.
Repression	Repeatedly says, "I'm fine . . ." when asked how they are doing. When this shield is present, it looks like a smile and surface-level interaction.	When we layer on this emotional armor, we push difficult or unacceptable thoughts out of our conscious awareness. For example, if sadness has been labeled as weakness or unacceptable, we push it down and repress it.
Projection	This sounds like, "You always . . ." "If only you . . ." "She is so . . ." "It's not me, it's you . . ." "I'm good, you're the one with the issues . . ." or, "I could never be like that, or do that . . ."	We layer this emotional armor on when there is a trait or emotion that is too difficult to acknowledge. Rather than confronting it, we blame these thoughts and feelings on other people. It's easier to blame or witness these traits in another person than confront one's own behavior. A common example is when a cheating spouse suspects that their partner is being unfaithful.

Regression	"I don't know what got into me . . ." or, "that wasn't me," or, "I'm not sure what happened there . . ."	As a way to reduce anxiety and feel psychologically safe, we put on this emotional armor and react emotionally in ways that match an earlier developmental stage. For example, after a tough conversation with our partner we find ourselves in the fetal position weeping.
Replacement	"This time it will be different . . ." "I'm bored in this relationship . . ." "I deserve more than this . . ." "She will save me and solve my problems . . ."	This is when we continue to jump to the "next best" in relationships, jobs, etc., instead of facing the reality of our situation and the emotions that are trying to arise. For example, instead of dealing with tension in our relationship, we decide to engage with someone else and eventually leave our relationship for this "next best" replacement.
Displacement	You're constantly directing your anger and frustration toward those you feel "safest" to do so with instead of toward the actual source of the frustration. You feel stuck in some dynamics, which causes you to unload (unfairly) on other people in your life.	This emotional armor keeps us focused in the wrong direction. When we use this strategy, we redirect our emotional response away from the correct person and onto another person or object. For example, when a husband and wife are in conflict and the wife doesn't stand up for herself, she may yell at her children later that afternoon.

through our emotions—our ability to be empathetic with others—that we feel connected. Not only are we blocked from connection, but we are also disconnected from the vital information our emotions provide us about our environments. Without access to this information, how will we know how to respond? We lose a valuable compass for living.

These strategies, while clever and effective at protecting us, keep our hearts encased and keep us a safe distance from others and ourselves. This shielding prevents others from knowing our true selves. Disconnection from our rich emotional world feeds the split between who we are and who we're being, preventing us from trusting ourselves and ultimately acting in ways that are aligned with our whole selves. In addition to the emotional armor we've layered on, we also learn to disguise ourselves with masks that help us compensate with feelings of lack, insecurity, and unworthiness.

One of our biggest fears is that if we show our true self to the world we won't be accepted—or worse, we will be shamed and rejected for who we are. When we don't trust that we will be loved, accepted for who we are and as we are, we locate other strategies that support us in finding love, acceptance, and belonging. We create our representative—the version we send out into the world to connect with others.

This version of us is brilliantly disguised in all of the best seasonal styles. We use humor, brilliance, or even ice-cold indifference to present the version of us we think our partners (and society at-large) will most likely accept. They fall in love with who we show ourselves to be, and then we are both committed to a lie. "Till death do us part," we suppose. When we become too fused with a mask we are wearing, we limit our ability to have authentic experiences and intimate connection. Instead of life feeling like a vibrant adventure, it feels dull and soulless.

As the poet e. e. cummings wrote, "The greatest battle we face as human beings is the battle to protect our true selves from the self the world wants us to become."* Creating space from these masks—and seeing our true self as separate from them—is how we're going to continue to close the gap

---

* Susan Sparks, "The Masks That We Wear," Psychology Today, October 20, 2015, https://www.psychologytoday
.com/us/blog/laugh-your-way-well-being/201510/the-masks-we-wear.

on the painful disconnect. As you read through the list of masks below, sit with yourself and honestly feel until you determine which masks you wear in your relationships and why you may wear them.

- **The Good Guy/Girl:** If this is your go-to strategy, not only do you want everyone and everything to be okay, you especially want to be seen as the "good" guy or girl. This kindness shows up as thoughtfulness and consideration, especially at first. But deep down it's not about empathy, it's about safety and control. This isn't ill-intended, though, it's simply how you learned to manage your caregivers and your environment when you were a child. In your relationships you have a canny ability and vigilance to always anticipate the wants/needs of your partner. You take on the responsibility of their emotional well-being and believe it is your duty to make them feel better. You shut down feelings of your own to keep the peace and not take up too much space. You tend to lack boundaries around your time, energy, and personal desires. If there was a lot of unpredictability or emotional dysregulation in your early home, you learned to keep the peace and make sure everyone else was okay to ensure *your* safety. You learned to anticipate the needs of a parent so as to minimize the possibility of them erupting or being overwhelmed. Also, you may have been praised for being the "good" child, and now, quite likely, you mistake that for love.

- **Ms./Mr. Independent:** Not only is your theme song something by Beyoncé, you pride yourself on being the lone wolf. You protect yourself from vulnerability by taking on life and all the responsibilities that come with it by yourself. You are seen as successful and competent by others. You "don't need no (wo)man," and you sure as hell don't need to ask for help from anyone for anything. You pride yourself on being "all good" and not needing others. In relationships, you struggle to share your emotions for fear of being weak, incompetent. You tend to need a lot of space and feel overwhelmed by emotional intimacy and commitment. This mask often comes from experiencing emotional neglect and a lack of emotional attunement from caregivers. You might have learned at a young age that you can't trust others, and that your safest route in life is to figure it out on your own. Maybe you saw one of your parents lose themselves and their autonomy or perceived that they never had it, and you thought, "That will *never* happen to me." And it hasn't. But neither has openness and/or vulnerability.

+ **The Perfectionist:** The perfectionist is always caught in the ever-evolving pursuit of the ideal. If this is your strategy, you like to be seen as put together. You source validation and security from presenting as if everything is picture perfect. Grades? Straight As. Style? On lock. House? In order. Your social media? Selfie central. In relationships, you spend a lot of energy managing what other people might think of you. Since there is so much energy being directed into looking a certain way, your relationships lack emotional depth and intimacy. You are often so busy trying to control everything that it robs your relationships of flow and ease. In your pursuit of the "perfect" relationship, you may have run from some of the most amazing people because of fear of judgment or because you judged them. You believe people love and value you because of how perfect you are, so you disconnect with any part of you that you don't perceive as acceptable and desirable.

+ **The Savior/Rescuer:** Gosh, you're basically Jesus, aren't you? As the savior, you love to rescue others from pain. You love the wounded duck, the comeback story, the standing-outside-the-window-holding-a-boombox moment (who doesn't?!). You spend a lot of your energy care-taking others and managing their emotional needs. You *love* to "save" people from dysfunctional relationships, catching them *just* as they get out of a relationship and need help healing from their heartbreak. You take on the coaching role in your relationships and have all the tips and tricks to teach them how to get better, be better, and crush life! The downside is that you often only feel loved and safe when other people need and depend on you. You will often find yourself with people who depend on you and are needy (although you kinda like that!). You struggle to honor yourself and your boundaries because you feel responsible for others. You can't possibly prioritize yourself, your needs, and the ways in which you need to grow because then who will be in charge in the relationship? You construct an unconscious hierarchy in the relationship, and this is so that people can't actually meet you eye to eye in love. Why? Because your value might be taken away. You don't trust other people to be competent to handle their own things. Ultimately, you focus on other people's pain to avoid your own pain. And this is all likely due to having taken on a similar role as a child. Your parent(s) likely parentified you. They perhaps had an addiction, maybe a chronic illness, or were emotionally immature themselves, and it required you to grow up fast and take care of everyone and everything.

- **The Jester/Performer:** You got jokes? Humor is one of the greatest relationship skills for a masterful partner, except when one uses humor to avoid intimacy, depth, and vulnerability. If this is your strategy, you love making people laugh—and while it may be fun and authentic, it's also getting in the way of you opening your heart and being seen. You likely have a lover, friend, and/or family member who's asked you, "Why can you never be serious?" or "Why do you always have to be sarcastic?" Well, it's because you're *really funny*—and it wasn't safe for you to feel all your feels as a kid. So, as an adult you feel most comfortable when you are performing and shifting the vibe of any environment to laughter and humor. In your childhood maybe you learned to lighten the mood of the family or tried to keep your parent(s) laughing so that there wasn't as much pain. In your relationships you bring a lot of laughter and joy, but when this strategy is rooted in the avoidance of emotional pain or vulnerability, it limits the depth of intimacy available.

- **The High Achiever/Workaholic:** Did you win another competition? Are you still number one?! Well done! You know who you are! You like to be at the top. You will put a lot of things and people second so you can be first. You are competitive with others, and especially yourself. Failure is your worst nightmare, and you do anything to avoid it. In relationships, you find value and security through being validated and celebrated for your achievements. It can be a challenge for you to slow down, soften, and surrender. You may also struggle to show vulnerability and your emotional side, so you stay busy and focused on your next goal. In relationships, you feel that people stay/value you because of your success. Maybe this is your value as a provider, your status in a job, the letters behind your name, or simply the value of your bank account. Either way you likely got here because you got rewards and love as a child for winning competitions or striving to do so, so that your parent would (finally) notice you. Those with this mask experience fragile relationships because there's a lot of approval-seeking and a fear of failure. Healthy conflict requires getting comfortable with surrendering—not just surrendering the need to "win" an argument, but also lovingly surrendering to vulnerability and opening up to love. This level of vigilance mixed with performance makes it so you can never arrive and relax into your relationship. You don't get to exhale and unwind, so your relationships oscillate around tension.

+ **The Damsel in Distress:** Well, if this isn't the fault of Disney and the countless old-school rom-coms that say you gotta need to be saved so a knight in shining armor can come save you. If you're not broken, how's someone going to feel needed? You're tied to the proverbial train tracks hoping someone will notice your struggle so you can be saved. Maybe you can't pay rent. Maybe you present as incompetent with life and need a savior to walk on water and save you from drowning in your responsibilities. You come by it honestly, though, because if this is your strategy, you love the thought/reality of being saved. You believe that someone will come into your life and make it all better. You source security and safety through fragility or feeling "broken." In a relationship, you constantly seek reassurance and emotional support from your partner. You present with your problems up front, likely overshare on first dates, and are just waiting for the "right" person who will just "get" you. You blame yourself for relational difficulties and think that things are hard because you feel broken or something is wrong with you. You live this role when you've never seen someone close, perhaps your mother, step into her power—so you don't either, and you keep a healthy distance from your inner authority. (Hello, patriarchy!) This plays into someone feeling bad for you and wanting to rescue you—and ensures they stay with you. Healing and becoming "whole" would require the dissolution of the strategy that keeps you connected to people, so it feels almost impossible to let go of.

+ **The Martyr:** If this is your strategy, you find yourself spinning in your latest woe. You always seem to be suffering or feel like you must sacrifice your desires/well-being for someone else. You're constantly complaining that there are no good potential partners out there and wondering, *Why do I always attract the same kind of person?* You think your online dating program must have a virus because you get all the duds while your friends are matching with Ryan Reynolds or Gal Gadot, and *no one ever seems to want to love me.* In relationship you take on a lot at the expense of yourself, and then use this to try to guilt others into doing things for you. You love trying to save the unsavable and find yourself in relationship dynamics with people struggling with addictions of all kinds. This victim mentality does not negate an experience that may have caused someone to wear this mask, but rather calling out living in this state allows you to source power from it. You likely learned this as a child from a parent who modeled the same behavior.

+ **The Playboy/Playgirl:** No matter your gender, this one shows up as the one who's the smoothest, most charismatic, slick, desirable, and mostly unavailable mask out there. You may present as wanting the greatest love, but somehow you are unable to move beyond the pursuit of novelty and orgasms. Maybe you hide in poly-amory (not all polyamorous people wear this mask, of course), get bored easily with the same people, keep getting "avoidant" on your attachment-style quiz, or love a good "friend with benefits." Not only do you source validation through being desired, you also likely correlate your worth to your looks, your body, and your cha-risma. These strategies protect you from *true* intimacy and others from *really* seeing you. Through this mask you control the depth your relationships can go to mitigate your risk of abandonment and rejection, so you don't have to confront your deep sense of unworthiness.

- **The Spiritual One:** Sorry, you probably can't hear us through the sound of gongs and the smell of patchouli. If this is your strategy, you live in love and light. You love learning and exploring spiritual concepts and desire ascension. Your chakras are constantly align-ing, and you live your life by your horoscope. So, your relationship outcomes aren't your responsibility; it's that damn Mercury in ret-rograde! In relationships, you may use these spiritual concepts to avoid the full range of human emotion by minimizing what you spiritually deem as negative or low vibration. Emotions are just your "pain body" (a term used by Eckhart Tolle), and when people give you feedback, you tell them they need to raise their vibra-tion and practice breathwork (breathwork is great!). This keeps your relationships limited and disconnected from reality because in the desire to avoid conflict and real feelings, you don't get to experience the realness of your own emotional brilliance as well as the brilliance of your partner and the feedback your relationships are generating for you. You may have had your feelings bypassed by religious/spiritual parents and/or found value in escaping the feelings of your traumas and childhood by just calling those things "karma" and believing they all happened *for* you so you can just move on and go to another ashram. This is not to minimize the spiritual, because we both love the spiritual, but rather to see where we use this mask of "ascension" and enlightenment to avoid the descent into the realities of life, love, and the complexities of the heart.

We're a dynamic bunch of humans, right?

These masks and the brilliant strategies that come with them are the exact ways we stay disconnected from our *real* selves—feeding the fear that who we are underneath it all isn't good enough, lovable, or worthy. This is the tricky part about wearing masks—the more we build our world and relationships around them, the stronger we grasp to them for fear of losing those we love and care about the most. They bind us to others while blinding us (and others) to our essence. Challenging, right? Don't worry, in the coming chapters we'll support you in safely peeling back these masks and revealing your *true* vibrant colors. Remember, we are the ones who put the masks on, so we can always choose to take them off.

Bridging the Gap

We ask you:

Are you willing to do the work to cultivate a great relationship?

Really, are you? Are you willing to take the masks off in service of yourself and love? Are you willing to put down the emotional armor and stand courageously (and shakily, of course!) in *your* voice, *your* desires, and *your* truths? *Bridging the gap with another begins with closing the gap within.* To do this, it takes work. It also takes courage, a continued commitment to growth, and a supportive network of humans who are here to champion love, truth, and liberation alongside you.

Before we embarked on this journey together, we didn't know a different relationship—one filled with ease, intimacy, freedom, truth, and reverence—was possible. We're happy to report that doing the work *works*.

You may wonder what happened with Stephanie and Greg? Or what might happen to your relationship if you step deeper into this work? Or, if you're single, will someone be able to meet you in *all* your gloriousness?

We didn't write this book to keep people together or promise anyone the "perfect love." We wrote it with the promise of you finding yourself and then bringing that whole version of yourself to the world and your relationships. Because this is what it takes to have and cultivate great connections.

Deep down, we believe that all of our souls, whether we're conscious of it or not, yearn for someone to see through our strategies, masks, and armor. We are desperate for someone to call us out on the ways we run from love. As terrified as we are of it, we want to be witnessed in our entirety. We want to be naked and safe. And at the core of our human hearts is not just a yearning to be loved but also a need to be seen and witnessed in all of our messiest parts.

This need can be summed up in one word: intimacy. (In-to-me-see— see what we did there?!)

Intimacy means closeness, and closeness means being able to see it *all*— the good, the bad, and the ugly. Whether it's mommy issues, daddy issues, body issues, trust issues—being in a sacred union with another human being shines a light on every dark corner of Pandora's box and brings every single unresolved issue out of the shadows.

This is a very difficult thing, *and* it's also a very good thing.

We *all* want love—that amazing rom-com, fairy tale, kissing-in-the-rain-as-Adele's-version-of-"Make You Feel My Love"-plays kind of love—*so* much so that most of us are willing to do anything and everything for love . . . even if that means taking responsibility for ourselves, acknowledging our pain, and making a change. Our deep desire for union is the alchemical force that pushes us deeper into our pain so that we can peel back the masks and soften the emotional armor that prevents us from experiencing love and union with ourselves and others.

Always remember, you can only meet someone as deeply as you've met yourself.

EXERCISE
Closing the Gap

As we explored in this chapter, as a way to protect ourselves from pain, we split off from our essence and become who we need to be in order to survive. This is where our representative (along with the armor and masks) is born. As a way to support you in illuminating the internal tension between the two sides of this split—who you're being versus who you truly are—we're going to put pen to paper and take a peek at what's happening in your internal world. Grab your journal and explore these questions:

- *What masks have you layered on to get your needs met and to source love and safety?*
- *What wound is underneath this mask (abandonment, neglect, rejection, unworthiness, etc.)?*
- *What stories—when triggered—keep you hidden beneath the armor and masks?*
- *What does this mask/dynamic protect you from?*
- *When you wear this mask, how does it impact you? How does it impact your relationships? What does it keep other people from seeing within you?*
- *What possibilities in life and relationship does it prevent you from opening yourself up to?*
- *What does this part of you that lives below the mask need in order to soften its grip and open more fully and be seen (e.g., a boundary, more safety, ability to access your voice)?*
- *If you had to integrate and let this part of your identity die, how would you be invited to expand?*
- *What other identities might be available to you? What does it feel like to try these on?*
- *What would it feel like to live a life free of masks? Where would you direct that energy instead?*

2

The Root of Codependency

Most of us have deeply embedded patterns in our relationships that we'd like to change. Whether it's minor frustrations, reactivity, choosing the same people, being boundaryless, not advocating for our needs, or constant feelings of unworthiness, we're *so beyond tired* of hitting the same wall and repeating the same patterns over and over again. To get to the root of these patterns and transform them, we need to look at our origin story. We learned these things somewhere, and that "somewhere" is—you guessed it!—almost *always* childhood.

We come into this world being 100 percent dependent on our primary caregivers for survival, which means we are 100 percent vulnerable in the first couple of years of our lives. Because of this vulnerability, over time, if our developmental needs aren't met (or we experience trauma), the big curious eyes, open hearts, and creative spirits we were born with are molded into who we need to be in order to fit in, belong, and survive. And, for good or ill, the seeds of our relational patterns are planted.

To better illustrate this, we'll follow the life trajectory of a tomato plant when placed in two different environments.

First, let's take that sweet, innocent tomato plant and place it in environment numero uno. This garden is a lonely place without any other plants, has limited sunshine, and lacks water and minerals. Imagine a desert wasteland with a tumbleweed blowing across, and our lonely little plant just sitting there all alone. No friends. No water. No tomatoes. You wouldn't be surprised if we told you this plant is having a hard time bearing fruit, would you?

Now, let's take this very same plant and give it a new home. In environment number two it feels like the song "Stayin' Alive" is on repeat. This garden is like a daytime brunch club. There's an abundance of warmth from the sun, soil rich in nutrients, daily watering, and a network of friends (microbial and beyond) that support and love on the tomato plant. Now, you better believe that tomato plant is making delicious little tomato babies.

Let's carry this idea over to our cultural garden bed. This time, *you're* the tomato plant.

If you're planted in a garden bed with abundant access to resources (food, water, sunshine, shelter); receive warmth and love from a rich relational ecosystem; are invited to weave your gifts into the tapestry of life; live close to the Earth, have rituals, a connection to your ancestors; are invited to explore your relationship to your soul; and are encouraged to reach for the sky, you'll likely blossom and bear fruit. Right?!

Now, let's take a journey to a different kind of garden bed. One we might call the "Western way." If you're planted in a garden bed where your needs are minimized and/or neglected; where you don't receive an abundance of love; where you aren't encouraged to grow and expand; where you struggle or compete to find resources (as well as attention!) and have to prove your worth in order to survive; and where you don't feel a lot of trust in yourself or others—you'll likely want to crawl back into the soil from where you came. You'll probably want to become numb. We get it. Heck, we've done it. It's not that you don't *want* to thrive, it's just that you don't know how. These conditions aren't conducive to rich, vibrant, and fulfilling ecosystems . . . or humans.

Humans are just like that tomato plant. The environments we are raised in matter. When we struggle to bloom into our potential, it's not supportive to blame the plant for its lack of development. Instead, what we need to do is look at our environments and ask: Is this environment conducive to growth, love, connection? What does this plant, this child, need in order to grow and blossom? As children, we don't have the rational faculty to ask these questions and examine the soil we were planted in. We don't understand that when our needs aren't met it is because it is an *environmental* failure (and cultural failure), not a *personal* failure.

Instead, in order to preserve our primary attachment bond (to our parent or caregiver), we assume that *we* are broken, unlovable, and unworthy. It is far too destabilizing to believe that Mom and Dad are flawed and not trustworthy. We aren't able to understand why our mother let us cry for two hours, why we were punished, why our father left us, why we were criticized, why we were told to stop crying, why we weren't held more, why Mom and Dad screamed at each other, or why our baby brother got all of their attention.

We didn't have the rational faculty to tell ourselves in that moment, "Mom is doing the dishes so she can't hold you, but she still loves you," or "Dad has to work to make sure the bills are paid so he can't spend more time getting to know you," or "Mom is too stressed right now to pay attention to you." Without the ability to zoom out and understand the full picture—the garden bed from which you were required to grow—and when these ruptures in connection occur repeatedly and without repair, we experience deep-rooted emotional pain. The young, undeveloped mind can't understand *why*. To the child's mind there are simply the questions, "Am I enough for my parent(s) to choose me, love me, protect me, and take the time to understand me? Am I safe to feel all my feelings and be curious about the world?"

The pain or neediness these relational ruptures bring into our hearts stems from feelings of abandonment and rejection by those from whom we crave love, attention, and belonging the most. As time passes and we grow from child to adolescent to adult, our unmet needs become the tender spots and wounds that we carry into our current lives and relationships.

The impact of these early ruptures on our relationships goes by many names in our culture today. To name a few: trauma bonds, narcissist/empath dance, insecure attachment, toxic dynamics, immature love, overfunctioner/underfunctioner, and love addiction. While all of these terms overlap in numerous ways and share a similar root system—that of disconnection and dysregulation—in this book we're going to explore these relational dynamics through one of the most common (and most difficult to untangle) manifestations of these dynamics: *codependency*.

Codependency, as defined by Rachael Maddox in her book *ReBloom*, is "when one person takes responsibility for another's difficulties or emotional experiences in ways that block the other from the opportunity to rise into their own growth, resiliency, or resourcefulness—and does so in a chronically disempowering way. Codependency is a means of subconsciously controlling uncomfortable realities." This dynamic isn't limited to the romantic realm of relationships; it has the potential to show up in any/all of our relationships, especially with family, because, of course, that's usually where we learned this dance. Codependency requires that we stay small or artificially inflated and stuck in adaptive survival strategies to keep the relationship(s) going. We seek our safety through giving and taking care of people, or staying "broken" and needing to be taken care of. Or as neuropsychotherapist and author Britt Frank puts it, "Codependency is an effort by our inner child to rescue someone else's inner child." Phew. Let that land.

Here are a few ways a codependent dance begins to manifest and create unhealthy patterns in our relationships:

+ Prioritizing others' needs over your own or being overly available
+ Overfocusing on others' achievements, addictions, activities
+ Putting your partner on a pedestal (or yourself on one)
+ Applying pressure on a relationship to go somewhere quickly
+ Creating perceived alignment with a partner (or anybody!) by censoring yourself (prioritizing their passions, beliefs, desires, and values over your own; minimizing your needs to appear needless and not be "too much"; pretending you want what they want in order to give the illusion of shared desires; being more concerned with matching with a person to create the perception of alignment than true alignment with ourselves)

- Isolating in a relationship, withdrawing from friends and family
- Quitting your self-care routines (no longer hanging out with friends, going to the gym, meditating, etc.)
- Controlling or manipulating others (trying to influence the behavior of others in order to lower the risk of them leaving; trying to get what we want by using things like money, sex, and gifts to get them to "choose" us)
- Feeling threatened if your partner develops or continues to honor their self-care routines and passions when you don't (this looks like when they are going to the gym, eating well, doing personal growth, etc., and because you haven't been honoring yourself, you attack their rituals instead of getting into integrity with your own)
- Practicing obsessive behaviors (searching phone, social media, emails, etc.)
- Overanalyzing messages, emails, conversations (sitting and lamenting about the meaning behind every word that is used and getting stuck in rumination and catastrophizing)
- Engaging in harmful physical habits (unhealthy food, alcohol, drugs, lack of movement)
- Losing yourself ("I don't know who I am or what I want.")
- Becoming confused or overwhelmed when asked about needs ("What do I need? I have no clue. I've never thought about that.")

Listen, it might be hard to see yourself in this list of behaviors and patterns. And while it's not always easy to look at and turn toward the ways we've shown up in our relationships, everything you do that is seemingly not helpful in relationships or gets in the way of creating the love you know deep in your soul that you want was put into practice to protect you from being *hurt*. So, these patterns must be honored. We must turn toward them with grace. At the same time, we can look at these patterns and recognize that they are no longer useful or moving us toward the life and relationships we want and crave.

So, with grace, we recognize that at the root of these codependent patterns is the desire for *safety and security*.

Which is why, in our work, we expand and deepen the definition of codependency to include the *core pattern* that drives it. Here's our definition of codependency:

> Codependency is a relational dynamic where we **source safety** from someone or something outside of ourselves **at the expense** of our own needs, sense of self, and overall well-being.

Key words being "at the expense of." Unhealthy, codependent patterns occur when we place the needs of the other, or the relationship, *ahead* of ourselves. It's a survival strategy that attempts to get core needs met at the cost of ourselves. Connection to the other comes ahead of everything and anything, especially us. Essentially, we forget about—or even lose—ourselves in service of the relationship and the familiar wounds that drive it.

Digging Deeper

Imagine your partner walks into the house from work and you sense that something is "off." It's not obvious that there's something up, it's that you just happen to be highly attuned to shifts in mood. You pick up on their mood because at some point your safety depended on your ability to read the room and the people in it. You assume that this "off" feeling could be about you and worry that it could potentially lead to disconnection or pain . . . because at some point in your life that's exactly what "off" feelings led to. When you were young maybe you walked on eggshells around your parent(s). Maybe a parent's emotional dysregulation led to aggression, yelling, abuse, and/or unpredictability.

Even though your partner might be quite safe emotionally to communicate with, you still have the unconscious and intuitive need to fix the situation and make sure they feel happy *now*. You might not be sure why, but their mood makes you anxious, so you try to appease them, nervously asking, "What's wrong?" and "Are you okay?" in an attempt to make their mood feel less unsafe for you. This presents like empathy—and it is similar, in that you're *really* good at picking up on what someone else is feeling—but unlike empathy, it's rooted in fear. Your concern is really a bid for safety. If they're okay, you're okay. And with codependency, if they're not okay, well, you do the math. You'll spend your entire day letting your partner's not-okayness consume your thoughts, and you'll have a hard time attending to anything other than trying to fix *their* stuff.

Therapist Tory Eletto said, "Codependency wires us to balance the system versus learning to balance ourselves." When we're disconnected from our center and a felt sense of safety, we feel like we have to walk on eggshells to manage and balance the system around us.

When we don't have enough evidence that connection and the world are safe, we tend to operate in a state of hypervigilance—we respond to these situations by becoming guarded and on edge to control the external environments and relationships we find ourselves in. However, when we examine this dynamic through the lens of our earliest imprinting with our caretakers, it opens us up to compassionate witnessing and curiosity. If you're an eggshell walker, ask yourself: Why don't I feel safe around others? Whose needs did I have to predict/attend to when I was younger? What does my system (mind/body) believe about connection? The world?

On the flip side, if you use moodiness and emotional dysregulation to prompt people to emotionally accommodate you, look for how you create emotional reactivity to subconsciously source safety and control. If you're an eggshell user, ask yourself: Where did you learn that having a need to be fixed or a feeling to be soothed allowed for your need for connection to be met within your early childhood/family? A possible response to this may be: You learned that by doing this you could be seen, heard, and tended to in ways that you deeply craved. Wise move. Your earliest environments and relationships imprint you, constantly shaping how you think, how you behave, and what you believe about yourself, others, and the world.

To get to the root of these patterns we're going to zoom back to your childhood (the soil you were raised in) and look at your primary attachment bonds. These are the earliest relationships you had with your mother, father, and/or your primary caregivers. They laid the foundation for how you relate to and connect with others today.

Childhood

In early childhood, to avoid disconnection and ensure survival, we learned to orient ourselves around our primary caregivers' needs *at the expense* of our own. The cornerstone of this behavior? "If I can make them okay, then I am going to be okay." So, we continue to scan the environment and live out the questions, "Mom/caregiver, what do you need?" and "Dad/caregiver, what can I do?" And so we give, repress, give, manage, give.

When we have endured emotional or physical neglect, trauma, and/or a lack of caregiver attunement, our nervous system adapts and seeks to find regulation and safety at all costs. One of the ways we do this is through a hyper-socialization response (aka the people-pleasing/appease/fawn response), which is an embodied self-protective response our nervous system deploys to appease others and manage our environments in order to diffuse anxiety, minimize potential conflict(s), and feel more secure in our relationships.

Adolescence

In adolescence, this core pattern from childhood creates the foundation for codependency to thrive in our romantic relationships. In one of my (Kylie's) sessions with Mark Wolynn, therapist and author of *It Didn't Start with You*, he expanded on the expression of this pattern, saying: "To avoid or attempt to control the pain of loneliness, abandonment, emotional neglect, betrayal, and unmet needs, we pull others close: 1) making them want us, 2) intuiting their needs, 3) making them feel good, and 4) drawing them closer [at the expense of the self]."

The cycle continues, and we do the same thing we learned to do in early childhood—we leave our center and psychically end up in other people's fields, intuiting what they need until there is no sense of self. We live with the questions "What do they need?" and "Who do I need to be, or what do I need to do to make them okay so that I can be okay?" As this pattern continues to play on, our energy diminishes, and our bodies begin to shut down as resentment rises and our life force shrinks, sometimes dropping to zero. We get physically sick and are met with an autoimmune response, digestive issues, or a diagnosis that pops up seemingly out of *nowhere*. We get anxious or sad. Eventually, if life is left unexamined, we find ourselves at a rock-bottom moment, and either we implode, our sense of self withers away, or our relationship blows up. Sometimes it's all three.

What's tricky about this core pattern is that when we find ourselves in this dynamic, we often can't differentiate between true intimacy and the high we get from this familiar cycle of love infused with dysfunction. We feel the high of love when we experience emotional connection after feeling its absence. We go from nothing to something and this feel-good feeling is labeled as love, and we get hooked back into the dance—chasing the soothing we receive when connection is reciprocated. We anesthetize our pain with arousal and continual small affirmations of being chosen.

Gulp. Read that again.

Adulthood

André was a client I (Mark) had who felt unsafe when communicating with his partner. He was successful in his work, and a great communicator with his friends and at his workplace, but with his partner, he would become overwhelmed and freeze in conversations, unable to find his words.

His partner was quite reactive. Her nervous system would go into "fight mode" whenever they had a disagreement. When trying to navigate conflict together, he would start to express himself, but because he could sense her activated nervous system, he would take a long time to find his words. The more time he took to respond, the more she reacted. Eventually, things would erupt with her, feeling overwhelmed, yelling at him. He'd mumble and eventually collapse, telling her whatever it was she was upset about that day wasn't a big deal, and she was right. When they reached out for support, they were both frustrated and wanted to change this pattern.

When we looked at André's childhood, we discovered that not only was his father an emotionally cold and harsh man who used to hit him if André displeased him, his mother was also distant and reactive. Neither of his parents offered him tenderness, and no one celebrated his sensitivity or taught him how to have boundaries or honored his feelings. Anger, because of his father, was dangerous to him. He disconnected from his own anger to maintain connection with his parents. In order to maintain what little connection he could with his mother and father, he hid his voice. He went along to get along. Eventually, he did the same with his partner, becoming everything she needed so that he could make sure she was okay.

He didn't have access to "no." He didn't know how to create a safe space in dialogue with his partner because before he even consciously knew it, his nervous system was saying, "Be quiet! Stay small! Don't do anything to upset her more or you'll be abandoned or hurt."

This pattern of withdrawing and shutting down triggered his partner, whose core wound was feeling emotionally neglected and abandoned. She didn't know where she fit in in her childhood with her parents, and she had been told that she was "too much." When there was distance in her relationship with André, she felt anxious and unsafe. When André was quiet and took a while to respond, her nervous system read that quiet as a signal that he might leave. She used her anger and reactivity to try to feel control, clarity, and, ultimately, safety. And because of his walking on eggshells to accommodate her emotional dysregulation and reactivity, they both established the exact same patterns from their childhoods in their adult relationships. Unconsciously, they didn't trust each other, and they didn't trust themselves in relationship with each other.

Their conflict and relationship patterns were the key to their liberation, and when they finally realized this, they could turn toward their challenges (and origin stories) with curiosity, understanding, and compassion. When *both* people in a relationship hold the intention to change, grow, and create a relationship where the question shifts to "What are we being invited to look at and heal together?," they move one step closer to blossoming—individually and together.

Hello, liberated love.

The Codependent Body

In addition to "seeing" and living out these patterns in our relationships, we find them beginning to show up in our health and well-being. When we're spinning in this codependent dance, these conditioned patterns begin to manifest in our physical, emotional body in various ways—letting us know that we, the environment, or the relationship(s) we are in need to shift. Pronto.

The disconnect from the body, our feelings, our voice, and our sense of agency begins to show up as:

+ **Burnout, overwhelm, and exhaustion from hypervigilance.** Constantly being on guard to protect ourselves from rejection and/or abandonment is exhausting. Checking our phone, wondering what they're thinking—these behaviors are taxing and eventually break down our bodies due to chronically high cortisol (a stress hormone).

+ **Increased anxiety due to disassociating from your body and your emotions.** When we disassociate (disconnect from our body), we disconnect from our embodied experience and our emotions. This "gap" shows up as anxiety.

+ **Disconnection from (clean) anger, intuition.** When we're connected to *clean* anger, we're connected to the emotions that honor, place, and protect boundaries. Clean anger is constructive and says, "No, I am not okay with that." It is expansive because having access to our "no" calms our nervous system and creates safety. Unclean anger, on the other hand, is destructive and often appears as aggression or abuse. When we're not connected to our clean anger, we're not connected to our bodies or, in turn, our intuition. (We'll dive deep into this in chapter 8!)

+ **Lack of healthy self-protective boundaries.** When we don't have healthy boundaries, we don't trust ourselves to stand up for ourselves and what we value.

+ **Depression and feelings of apathy, fragility, and loneliness.** Think of the word "depression." To *press down* our feelings. This feeling of helplessness disconnects us from our hearts, bodies, and passions.

+ **Lack of sexual and creative energy.** When we're looping in survival mode, creation energy goes offline—and embodied intimacy goes along with it.

+ **Frustration and resentment.** Resentment shows up with others when we don't show up for ourselves.

+ **Digestive issues, sleep issues, autoimmune responses.** The body can't digest food well or think about healing if we're constantly putting energy toward others. When the body is in a constant state of vigilance, it's not able to rest. This depletes every bodily system, including the immune system.

When we lack a felt sense of inner safety and struggle to self-regulate due to unprocessed trauma, it interferes with our ability to connect with ourselves, our feelings, and others in authentic and enriching ways. As in, *if we don't trust ourselves, we cannot authentically and safely trust and connect with others.* It isn't until we get to the root—to the core experience(s) that led to this way of relating—that we begin to see a light at the end of the codependent tunnel.

In chapter 1 we explored how we cope with the *disconnect* from self through armoring up and layering on the masks. Here, we're going to expand on the impact that these early environmental failures and traumas have on our bodies, self-perception, and relationships. To do that, we're going to take a good, hard look at your nervous system.

To begin, let's all jump onto the same page by defining "trauma." Bestselling author and trauma expert extraordinaire Bessel van der Kolk, MD, provides a perfect definition of trauma, saying: "Trauma is not the story of something that happened back then, but the current imprint of that pain, horror, and fear living inside [the individual]."

Trauma is not a single event. It is the overwhelm of *ongoing* activation as the result of the event(s). Some examples of trauma include being a parentified child (having to prematurely take care of the emotional and/or physical needs of a caregiver), systemic oppression, lack of caregiver attunement, physical or emotional abuse, not getting your physical/emotional needs met consistently in childhood, and conflict in the home.

While painful experiences are a fact of life and many of us move through them without scars, when we lack the necessary resources—like a calm and secure other person to comfort us, and the safety our systems need to process the traumatic energy after the event ends—the trauma becomes stored in our bodies. To cope with the overwhelm, our autonomic nervous system (ANS)—the part of the body that is responsible for managing automatic functions in the body like your heartbeat, digestion, and body temperature—comes in to protect us and subconsciously responds in various ways to lessen the threat and ensure survival.

When the answer to the question "Am I safe?" is "yes," your ANS can soften, and you feel regulated, open, safe, and available for connection with others. When the answer is "no," and your body senses a level of danger greater than its capacity to cope, it calls on support from the other parts of your autonomic nervous system to kick into gear. We've mentioned a few of those responses already, including the hyper-socialization and hyper-vigilance response, but there are a few other brilliantly designed responses that our system has on hand to navigate the difficulties of life. Here is a list of these embodied self-protective responses:

1. Hyperarousal Responses
   » The sympathetic nervous system is called in and comes to our aid when the body senses that it *can* win against a real or perceived threat. These include:
     * **Hyper-socialization/Fawning:** orienting around another's emotions, needs, behavior in relationship to maintain safety. This looks like over-accommodating, people-pleasing, and appeasing to not "rock the boat" or upset another. For example: when you say yes to go to an event with your partner when you really want to say no, you're appeasing him and operating from fear instead of from truth.
     * **Hypervigilance:** when your guard goes up, you're walking on eggshells, and you experience a state of height-

ened alertness in relationship. For example: you notice your partner seems "off," so you close up and ask her, "What's wrong?"—over and over (and sometimes that repetitive hypervigilance is only ever spoken one or two times, but the internal rumination goes on and on).

* **Fight:** when fight mode is activated, we metaphorically (or literally) raise our fists and move toward the perceived or actual threat with intensity, speed, and aggression. For example: when we are in a conflict with a friend, and we move into defensiveness and amplify our voice to prove our point.

* **Flight:** when the flight mode is activated, we quickly move away from the perceived or actual threat with fear, anxiety, or concern. For example: when you feel overwhelmed in a relationship, you tend to bolt out of the environment without communicating.

2. Hypoarousal Responses
   » The dorsal vagal complex is called upon and comes to our aid when the body senses that it *cannot* win against the real or perceived threat. These include:
   * **Freeze:** when the freeze response comes to our aid, we feel a numbness and heaviness fall over us and experience immobility, difficulty speaking, and a dissociation from our bodies. Our ANS calls on this response to lessen the emotional or physical pain we're in. Freeze has many levels and many manifestations including immobility, silence, depression, and feelings of shame.

When stored trauma is activated—when our system codes something as dangerous—our ANS calls on these responses to protect us, which triggers the self-protective patterns we've been playing out for decades and a dysregulated nervous system. These traumatic imprints interfere with our nervous system's ability to move fluidly between hyper- and hypoarousal states and come back, eventually, to safety. When your nervous system is regulated, you have the flexibility to move freely between feeling safe and becoming activated when necessary.

Accessing this flexibility within our nervous systems becomes harder to do when our embodied self-protective responses start looping, sending us signals of danger—"Fire! Fire!"—when there is no fire or smoke present. When we don't have the wiring to self-regulate—because it wasn't cultivated within our earliest relationships—we lack the capacity to deal with the ebbs and flows of life. Without this resilience in our system, we more easily find ourselves looping in hyperarousal states (like walking on eggshells 24/7)—or dropping down into hypoarousal states (like collapsing into a depressive state).

These traumatic imprints, what happened *back then*, interfere with our ability to be open, vulnerable, and connected *now*. And that's just what trauma does ... *it wires us for protection, instead of for connection*. As Peter Levine, trauma educator, teaches, "Trauma is about broken connection. Broken connection to the body, broken connection to our vitality, to reality, and to others."

The autonomic nervous system's job is to keep us safe, alive, and connected. And it's wired to do that by any means possible. This is why, when we're activated, we time-travel to a younger version of ourselves and respond in the same way we did when we were younger. We do now what we did back then ... because it worked.

It's like an automated script that kicks in when being safe, *now*, is the priority. When experiences like receiving care, setting a boundary, intimacy, and being seen are coded as "dangerous" to our systems, when we move toward this in our relationships we will be met with resistance. This is normal. It takes time to build the evidence that what wasn't safe historically is safe now. While our minds logically know something is "safe," it isn't until we work with our bodies and process the stuck survival energy in our systems that we will experience this safety in our bodies as well. Only then will we be able to move forward and make the long-lasting changes we so desire. Until we do this work and become aware of how our ANS is responding in any given moment—we will continue to stay in historical loops of behavior, never really allowing a new experience of love and connection to be created. A liberated one where we can put down our shields and strategies and exhale into each other's presence.

Gosh . . . if only it were that easy, right?!

Keep in mind that grief is a normal response when we learn about how our automated patterns are created, but in the same breath there is an exhale because we don't have to keep doing it the way we have! Instead of the old ways that we used to respond in conflict and to intimacy . . . we can now create more space and, in turn, a different way of relating.

Big exhale.

Where and How We Source Now

Okay, let's go over what we know so far. Codependency is the dance we find ourselves in when we're stuck in self-protective mode and don't feel safe, and then do our best to try to find or create safety through the various survival strategies we've mentioned—the emotional armor, the codependent dynamics, and the masks. These strategies are manifestations of our nervous system doing its thing. For example, underneath the "good guy/good girl" mask that many of us play out in codependent dynamics is a mixture of the hyper-socialization/hypervigilance response. This mask isn't just a role you play, it's a strategy that your wildly intelligent body has used to keep you safe and alive (thank you, body!). This is why the key to accessing more agency and authenticity begins with coming home to yourself and tending the needs of your nervous system.

This work matters because the more we depend on a relationship as a source of safety and homeostasis, the more negotiable our sense of self (our needs, desires, thoughts) becomes. As in, the more our safety and security depend on the relationship, the more malleable we are and the more likely we are to continue to agree even when our bodies—and hearts—tell us not to.

This reminds me of a client I (Kylie) had named Jasmine. She started working with me because she wanted to feel more confident in her life. Through our work together we illuminated a dynamic within her family system that was feeding her belief that she was incapable and incompetent. Jasmine received financial support from her family but it came with a huge emotional cost. She started to realize that by taking this money and support (sourcing safety), she couldn't honor *her* needs, *her* voice, and *her* path.

Instead, there was a covert agreement in place: "We will give you this, but you must put the family ahead of yourself, listen to us, and not challenge how we do things." It was a way—intentional or not—to manipulate and control (through pseudo-altruism). Although deeply unconscious, this dynamic fed into her narrative of feeling like a "damsel in distress." For Jasmine to shift this dynamic, she needed to become aware of all the places she was sourcing safety and security—and at what cost to herself.

The support she was receiving wasn't *clean*—it wasn't free of expectations—and while support is theoretically wonderful, it doesn't feel wonderful when it costs us our ability to express ourselves. The implicit agreements needed to be made explicit. She needed to renegotiate the relationship free of masks. If the truth costs the financial support, then the support must be let go of in service of self-expression. Eventually, after choosing to take aligned action and create financial security for herself, Jasmine was able to thank her family for their support, releasing the obligation to be or do anything and becoming her own source of safety.

Work like Jasmine's is what we are all being invited to do when unhooking from codependency. Exploring the ways we source safety and security externally—and at what cost to ourselves—is the first step out of a codependent dance. Because, like we mentioned earlier, *true safety is an inner job*. When we can be with ourselves, feel and honor our emotions, and set healthy boundaries, we experience a felt sense of safety. This sense of safety emerges from being able to move/act based on choice (in the present moment) instead of on adaptive survival strategies that are rooted in the past.

When we know ourselves and are rooted in our values and our worth, we make choices that are aligned with who we are and what we want *now*. Instead of constantly seeking safety, security, and support from others, we can source it from ourselves. Instead of adapting to the world at the cost of ourselves, we make the world adapt to us, in service of our self-expression and the individual self-expression of those we're in relationship with. No longer do our relationships require us to play small—we invite our relationships to grow into our own bigness.

EXERCISE
Where Do I Source?

In this exercise you're going to begin to see where you source safety and security from and at what cost to your mental, emotional, physical, spiritual, relational, and financial well-being. This isn't about shaming or blaming yourself for where you're at on your journey; it's about compassionately and honestly naming what is, so that you can step into awareness and begin to see how these codependent patterns may be showing up in your life. Grab your favorite beverage and carve out some time to sit with yourself, your journal, and these questions:

- *What am I sourcing externally? (validation, safety, security, worthiness)*
- *From whom/what? (relationships, men, women, work, sex/intimacy, money, beauty, social media, etc.)*
- *At the expense of? (my wholeness, my voice, my sovereignty, my truth, my soul, my health, etc.)*
- *Is this dynamic sustainable for me? (energetically, financially, emotionally, physically)*

3

The Mother/Father Threshold

Ah, memory lane. Many of us avoid (or, at minimum, are incredibly overwhelmed by) the idea of taking a trip down its winding way. Sure, that lane can be paved with delightful moments of more innocent times, our childhood home, or cherished time spent with our siblings or parents, but it can also be dusted with a whole lot of pain and hurt.

Either way, the trip is *necessary*—this pilgrimage to our origin story is vital for healing.

To grow and liberate our relationships and lives—to get to the next level—we have to dismantle and learn from our former roadblocks to intimacy so we can continue our journey to liberated love. Note: *This isn't about desecrating what was in the way. It's about loving what's been in the way, because what's been in the way has served the beautiful purpose of protecting us from experiencing that homegrown hurt again.* As we love who we've been, let's explore how we are shaped in our relationships *developmentally*. Let's look at *why* you do what you do and *where* all those patterns came from.

So, pack your baggage (pun intended) and buckle your seat belts. We'll be your friendly tour guides and copilots to get you to your destination safe, sound, and, most important, secure.

However, we can't promise it won't be a bumpy ride.

The Attachment Journey

When we ask our clients about their childhood experiences and how they view their parents and primary caregivers today, we usually hear something like: "My childhood was great and my parents were caring!" or "My parents are the reason behind the pain I feel and limitations I experience."

On one side we hear denial, and on the other side we hear blame. Underneath both sides of this spectrum—denial and blame—live the grief and anger we feel when we come face-to-face with what was and what never was in our childhoods. This work of witnessing and excavating the grief, shame, and anger makes space for what can be . . . when we're ready.

Ready?

Great. We're right there with you. Let's start with attachment theory.

Attachment theory is how our core attachment bond with our mother or primary caregiver in childhood impacts our ability to connect and relate in adult relationships today. The gravity and importance of attachment work finally landed for us when we realized that until we healed our imprints from early childhood, we would continue to unconsciously choose and attract partners that mirror and replicate our childhood experiences.

For my (Kylie's) client Anita, she chose partners that resembled the dynamic and patterns she had with her mother. This replicated a lack of boundaries, a disconnection between her genuine feelings and herself, and merging with her partners' energy and preferences, in the same way she did with her mother—to seek safety. In the midst of her own sacred pause, her life changed in hearing about a session I had with Mark Wolynn when he looked me square in the eyes and said, "Our partner shines a light on what's unresolved in our early relationship with our mother." Until you do the attachment work, you'll continue to find yourself in similar dynamics repeating similar patterns.

Gulp.

We don't know about you, but nothing lights a fire under our tails like being told that we'll continue to attract unfulfilling partners, codependent relationships, and familiar and unwanted dynamics in our lives if we don't do this healing work. *Quickly buys all books on attachment*

Whether you hold a skeptical view on attachment theory or you're a firm believer in the healing power of attachment work, we welcome you to cross what we call "the mother/father threshold."

The mother/father threshold is the journey back to our primary attachment bond(s) with our mother/father/primary caregiver and the blueprint that was formed from these earliest relationships. It is here, within our core attachment bond, that our relationship to life, nourishment, safety, mother, other, and self was imprinted and shaped. Understanding these attachment styles gives us more context and compassion for why we show up the ways we do in relationship and connection.

As we explored in the last chapter, children are born 100 percent dependent on their primary caregiver(s) to tend to and meet their developmental needs. One of the most important needs we have in early childhood is a secure, attuned, and regulated caregiver who can support us to regulate our own nervous system since we can't, as babies, make ourselves feel better on our own. If we have a caregiver who is attuned to our needs, consistently supports us to regulate our own nervous system, and provides us with a safe, loving environment, we develop a secure attachment. When we have a secure attachment, our nervous system codes closeness with someone, and space away from someone, as safe. We learn (and experience) through this primary attachment bond that we are safe in connection, safe in the world, and safe to be our whole, autonomous, and authentic self. When we have a secure attachment, we experience more ease in our relationships and can communicate our needs, ask for support when we need it, lean into vulnerability, and embrace intimacy.

Doesn't that sound nice?!

Alas, secure attachment is not the norm today. This could be for many reasons: unprocessed generational trauma; neglect; lack of presence, support, and protection; isolation; insufficient co-regulation in early childhood; family turmoil; medical procedures; environmental conditions (war, oppression, poverty); a culture that doesn't honor the importance of Mom or Dad being available and attuned to the child; toxic adult relationships; and the reality that many primary caregivers aren't in the driver's seats of their own nervous systems. When our caregivers struggle to regulate their own nervous systems, a child doesn't receive the consistent or sufficient co-regulation that is necessary for them to learn and be able to self-regulate—a secure attachment is inhibited and an insecure attachment is formed.

When we have an *insecure* attachment, we learn and experience that it *isn't* safe to trust the world, ourselves, and the people in it. As you can imagine, this makes relating with others as adults stressful and challenging.

Think of your attachment system as a radar that is constantly assessing the safety and security of your relationships. It's constantly asking, "If I need you, will you be here for me? Is this person safe?" Our attachment style is how we respond to these questions.

There are three styles the attachment system has to express itself when insecure: the anxious attachment style, the avoidant attachment style, and the disorganized attachment style. Let's expand on each of these styles a tad more and learn how each is formed.

First up, secure attachment (our goal!).

Secure Attachment

A secure attachment is formed when we grow up in an environment that is filled with lots of love, skin-to-skin time, and consistent care from regulated and nurturing caregivers. When we have an emotional/physical need and reach out, our parents respond appropriately to that need. As infants, our needs, of course, are preverbal. When a parent is attuned and present to us, on some level they not only can identify what we need but are also intent on trying to meet that need even if they don't understand what we're asking for. In a secure attachment, we trust our parent and don't need to protect or take care of them. From this space, as we grow up, we are more confident to explore the world, take risks, and fully express ourselves. We know that our parent is there for us if we truly need them. As adults, we feel safe to express our needs and share what is coming up for us. We are okay being alone and enjoy connection with others. We don't need to avoid conflict because we can manage conflict well. Through our disagreements we grow and deepen the trust and the connection.

Anxious Attachment

An anxious attachment forms if we had a caregiver who was inconsistent in their ability to meet our needs, attune to us, and provide safety, regulation, and connection. The data our nervous systems received was: "Sometimes my caregiver is reliable and loving, and sometimes their reactions weren't appropriate to the stimulus we provided (e.g., a parent who yelled every time we cried, shamed/bypassed us, or hovered over us fearfully every time we were sick in bed)." *Cue walking on eggshells.* There are many reasons why an anxious attachment style might form. For example, maybe our caregiver was dealing with their own anxiety, had financial struggles, and/or had their own unprocessed trauma, resulting in a lack of presence and reliability. Because of this lack of predictability, an anxiously attached child learns to behave in ways that keep their caregiver (and eventually their partners) close. The script running this attachment is: "I'll do whatever I need to do to keep them close, because I need them close to be okay." This attempt to keep others close might show up as emotional outbursts or as caretaking behaviors. For those with an anxious attachment style, any connection is better than no connection.

Avoidant Attachment

If we had neglectful caregivers, incapable of meeting our developmental needs, or we experienced regular rejection from our caregivers, we develop an avoidant attachment style. Within this early environment, our emotional needs were shamed or neglected altogether. Perhaps our parent didn't have the capacity to be with our emotions, so they were not only unavailable to meet our needs but couldn't even hear them. Perhaps our parents got divorced, lived apart, and were overwhelmed with their own emotions so they weren't present for our experience and what was going on in our lives. Like all children, avoidantly attached children crave intimacy and have an inherent biological need for connection, but quickly learn that connection isn't safe and/or is unreliable. The data our nervous system receives is that connection is unsafe and/or leads to pain. That if we need something or someone, they won't be there for us, so it's easier to just not need them, or pretend that we don't. To cope with the acute state of dysregulation from not having our needs for safety, attunement, and connection met, our autonomic nervous system shuts down to numb the pain and terror we feel. The lack of evidence for safe connection makes it very challenging for those with an avoidant attachment to get close to another and receive care. Avoidantly attached children become adults who feel safest when they are on their own island, a tolerable distance from others.

Disorganized Attachment

A disorganized attachment forms when our caregiver(s) are sometimes a source of safety and other times a source of danger. For example, maybe our caregiver was kind and loving one day, and the next day after a few drinks they were the source of emotional or physical abuse. The data our nervous system receives is: "Connection eventually leads to my pain, and harm." When our primary caregivers are sometimes safe and sometimes harmful, we never know what to expect, leaving us split between meeting our need for connection and meeting our need for survival and safety. The script running this attachment style is: "Come close, but not too close!" and "Come closer; get away from me." This lack of trust in others creates an internal and external push-and-pull dynamic, where our system never feels safe enough to fully lean into intimacy. As adults, disorganized-attached children feel frustrated by their inability to receive and give love with ease.

Secure, anxious, avoidant, disorganized. Which one feels the most resonant to the way you are currently showing up in relationships?

Now, just because we have a tendency toward *one* of these styles does not mean it is determinative. It is possible to experience a combination of multiple attachment styles—shifting from one to another depending on the relationship you're in, the attachment style of the person you're inter-acting with, and which parts of you are being activated.

Often when we first learn about attachment theory, we will use language like "I am anxiously attached." But really our attachment style is how we respond to what our radar (nervous system) codes as unsafe or insecure re-lationally. Instead, we like to say, "I am prone to responding anxiously." That way you give yourself space to also respond in other ways. You are a human. You are complex. You are dynamic. Best of all, just because your system leans toward one of these styles doesn't mean you are stuck there forever. YOU CAN CHANGE YOUR ATTACHMENT STYLE! (Sorry, we had to yell that so you hear us!) That's right, our systems are malleable and can heal. This is the beautiful thing about attachment work—it offers us a pathway to heal and move into what is called an "earned secure attach-ment." Earned secure attachment is when we move from an early insecure attachment to a secure attachment later in life through healing and safe relating. Suddenly, we have a solid sense of self and a good balance between healthy dependence and autonomy.

Alright, now for the really juicy part—the *how*. How do you move from insecure attachment to earned secure attachment?

Doing the Attachment Work

You might not be surprised to hear this at this point in our journey, but attachment work is—*wait for it*—nervous system work. To illuminate the interrelatedness between attachment theory and the nervous system, we're going to weave in some basics from polyvagal theory. Polyvagal theory, introduced by Stephen Porges, is an evolutionary and neuropsychologi-cal exploration of the vagus nerve's role in emotional regulation, the fear response, and social connection. When we understand what's happening in our bodies, we can begin to provide ourselves with the regulating re-sources, nourishment, and care we need to reenter a space of regulation and embodied safety (aka feeling calm and relaxed). As polyvagal educator and somatic experiencing practitioner Sarah Baldwin reminds us, "What's happening in your body tells you the story of your attachment."

So, let's explore what's happening in our bodies when each attachment style is activated. In addition to building our somatic literacy, we're going to share some tolerable steps based on each attachment style to move in the direction of an earned secure attachment. That's right, the story in your body can be changed by taking manageable steps that your system can tolerate. Steps that feel doable to your system. You might notice that, at first, these steps don't feel good or comfortable, because our autonomic nervous system will try to step in and slow us down by saying, "STOP. This is not safe." Taking these tolerable steps supports our systems in moving out of previous attachment scripts (this is not safe) and creating new ones rooted in regulation and security (this is uncomfortable but I can stay here).

Attachment Styles and the Nervous System

When we are securely attached, our autonomic nervous system can rest. We can exhale. In polyvagal theory, this rest state happens when our ANS is in a ventral vagal state. When we're hanging out in a ventral vagal state, we feel safe, at home, regulated, in our center, and capable of experiencing the joy of intimacy, pleasure, connection, and the present moment. Because we received the proper wiring to self-regulate through healthy modeling of co-regulation with our primary caregiver, we're able to deal with the ebbs and flows of life with more ease and trust in ourselves, and we find it easy to ask for support when needed. You can continue fostering secure attachment in yourself and with others by amping up skills like deep listening, having a gratitude practice, and practicing presence, empathy, and repair.

When our early-attachment bond(s) lead to the formation of an anxious attachment style, our ANS calls upon the sympathetic response. As you may recall from the last chapter, the sympathetic response mobilizes us into doing what needs to be done to ensure our connection to our primary caregivers and, eventually, to our partners. For those hanging out in a sympathetic response walking on eggshells, heightened levels of anxiety, and managing the external environment and perceived needs of others is the norm. For those with an anxious attachment style, their autonomic nervous system needs a caregiver/partner close to feel okay. This hyper-reliance on external regulation disconnects them from their center, sense of self, and their needs.

Working through Anxious Attachment

Those with an anxious attachment style didn't receive the consistent foundation of safety and co-regulation they needed to trust themselves with their own emotions/needs/choices and others, making self-regulation (the ability to come back to center) a challenge. Instead, the anxiously attached try to survive and cope with their relationship anxiety by constantly reaching out to others for safety, love, and connection at the expense of the connection they have to themselves.

For Jenny, this was the case. In one of our sessions, she shared with me (Mark) her frustration in not being able to trust her partner when he was traveling on business. When there was space between them, her mind constantly played through the worst-case scenarios that sounded like: *He's cheating on me; He's not coming back; I'm going to get left behind.* The louder these stories became, the more intense her need was for relief: proof that he wasn't cheating and that he wasn't going anywhere. This led Jenny to do things she wasn't proud of, like going through his emails without his consent and texting him constantly to check in on where he was and what he was doing. She was exhausted and tired of feeling anxious and insecure. Her partner, while compassionate to her fears, also wished she could trust him more since he had never done anything to betray her trust.

When our reactions don't match the circumstance at hand, it's a clue that our younger parts are being activated and running the show. The physical distance in Jenny's partnership activated a younger part of her—the part that thinks that what is happening now is like what happened in the past. That space isn't safe. That space leads to pain, and possibly rejection and/or abandonment. To her younger self and autonomic nervous system, having distance and space felt like a life-or-death situation, because in early childhood Jenny experienced a significant amount of birth trauma and was separated from her mother for the first three weeks of her life. Every time there was a space or disconnect from her primary caregiver, she was worried that she was going to be abandoned. Jenny wasn't needy, she was scared.

For Jenny, and anyone with an anxious attachment style, building capacity for attuned co-regulation and embodied self-regulation is the key to healing. She needed to learn how to connect and be with others in a way that feels relaxing and safe—which meant opening and trusting the goodness and care she received from others—and she needed to learn to self-soothe and increase her capacity to sit with herself and her own discomfort. What Jenny was seeking by going through her partner's emails and the incessant texting and checking in was what somatic experiencing practitioner Sarah Baldwin calls a "survival connection."

We seek this connection when we feel so dysregulated that we need another human to be okay. (e.g., "Where are you?!" "Come home now!" "What are you doing?" "Call me!").

This survival connection is different than attuned co-regulation, where we have the capacity to be present with another and receive the regulation their nervous system is bringing to us in this moment. Instead, for us anxious-attachment folks, the chaos our bodies feel renders us unable to *be* with and present with someone who is trying to bring us the gift of calm. You might notice this in your own experience when you have a hard time trusting when things are perceivably safe. This often makes us want to kick up some dust and bring in some chaos—jealousy, complaining, hypersensitivity—because chaos feels familiar. This happens because as much as the anxiously attached desire connection on one hand, they don't believe it's possible on the other. Because we expect to be disappointed, hurt, or rejected—we don't allow ourselves to receive the goodness that is right in front of us. Instead, we stay in the familiarity of the wound.

A tolerable step we can take when we are anxiously attached is the practice of attuned co-regulation with another. For example: Can you notice what's arising in your body in someone else's presence? Can you soften into the present moment with someone and receive their kindness, energy, and regulation? Can you name what is going well? Can you receive 1 percent more goodness from this connection?

Another tolerable step you can take to increase your capacity to self-regulate is to do a self-soothing practice. This might be turning on your favorite playlist and letting your body move, taking a five-minute pause to ground yourself into your body, or taking a walk in nature by yourself. It might sound simple, but these steps provide our ANS with proof that we *are* safe when we are on our own and that we can move through the discomfort that space and distance bring in our relationships. We are building experience and trust in ourselves that we can face life and handle it on our own. That when we say we're going to do something, we do it. This recognition that *we, ourselves* are reliable is everything! That we honor our own limits, keep our own word, and can depend on ourselves. It is through these tolerable steps that we begin to fill our database with new experiences that lead to more safety and trust in self and others.

Working through Avoidant Attachment

When our younger self faces constant neglect, isolation, rejection, and a lack of presence within our earliest attachment bonds, it calls on the most extreme form of self-protection we have. In polyvagal theory, this self-protective response is called our dorsal vagal complex, and, as you may recall, it is when our ANS calls on a complete immobilization response. We move into dorsal vagal when we can't protect ourselves through fighting back or fleeing. So instead we shut down and disassociate to numb the terror and dysregulation we feel from not having our needs for safety, connection, and love met. Those with an avoidant attachment style commonly feel a sense of apathy and overall disconnection from their bodies, life force, and sense of aliveness. Avoidantly attached folks learn to survive by disconnecting from themselves and disconnecting from others.

Clark knew this experience well. After the end of his most recent relationship, Clark, having hit what he called his "emotional rock-bottom," booked a session with me (Kylie) to discuss why he struggled to receive, give, and keep love in his life. He didn't use these words, though; instead, he led with, "WTF is wrong with me?! Why do I keep pushing love away?"

He was beginning to see that he was the common denominator in every one of his relationship challenges, whether it be at work, with close friends, or in his love life. Instead of sinking deeper into shame and isolation, he reached out for support. Hallelujah! In one of our sessions, he shared how his previous partner told him that she didn't feel like he was open or willing to go deeper with her, and that every time she tried to get closer and have conversations with him regarding their future, he would pull away. She wanted someone who was ready to go all in. After asking Clark about how his body responds to moving closer and deepening into commitment, he said, "I shut down, collapse ... and it's hard for me to find words." It's not that parts of him didn't want this too, it's just the thought of getting closer and moving in together overwhelmed his system. *Will this closeness lead to pain? Will I lose myself?*

For Clark, the key to opening and deepening into intimacy was two-fold: he needed to learn how to self-regulate without numbing, and also to increase his capacity for co-regulation. Which meant, he needed to learn how to feel (move through) stuck survival energy in his system that made him want to run and find pathways of *embodied* self-regulation—feeling all the feelings—instead of numbing/disassociating. Which brings us to the distinction that there is a difference between *regulating resources* and *survival strategies.*

Regulating resources, like spending time in nature or calling a supportive friend, are things we bring in that tell our ANS that we are safe when we are activated. These resources help increase the capacity we have in our nervous system so that we can process what is activating us through regulating with nature, our friends (co-regulation), and ourselves (self-regulation). Resourcing allows us to shift out of the familiar, autopilot response and into regulation and empowered choice.

Survival strategies, while beneficial when we had no other strategies available to us, are things we do to numb our activation energy because we don't know what to do with it. These strategies help us disconnect from stress and overwhelm, yes, but they also disconnect us from our body and center. Some examples include watching TV, shutting down, scrolling on social media, shopping, workaholism, escaping into a substance, etc.

Regulating resources check us in, while survival strategies check us out.

A tolerable step that Clark could take instead of numbing his activation through working all the time could be going for a walk every evening instead of checking his emails and scrolling the internet. For those with an avoidant attachment, space is necessary for them to self-regulate. The key, however, is to learn how to increase our capacity to be with the activation instead of numbing/disconnecting ourselves from it. We have to learn that escaping/avoiding isn't the only way to navigate activation. That we can, with support, learn to be with the discomfort/intensity we feel. If we don't do this nervous system work, our autopilot response(s) will continue to move us away from intimacy and closeness.

Another tolerable step those with avoidant attachment can take is to increase our capacity to be in connection and co-regulate. This can be as simple as making plans to catch up with a friend and noticing any internal desire to pull away from closeness. This practice of self-attunement— noticing and being with our internal sensations and feelings—is a skill that allows us to stay with whatever is arising for us while simultaneously holding connection with another. If we notice the urge to push away and disconnect, instead of disassociating and disconnecting, can we consciously sit with this discomfort and activation for five more seconds? Can we share what's coming up for us in the relationship? How does that feel? Notice what comes up. Witness it. Honor it.

Working through Disorganized Attachment

To cope with having a primary caregiver who is a source of love and care one day and a source of harm the next, our ANS calls on our freeze response.

The freeze response activates both our sympathetic resources (mobilized state) and our immobilized (dorsal vagal) complex. On the outside, those with a disorganized attachment might look calm, blank, chill, and reserved, but on the inside, they are experiencing high amounts of arousal and activation energy. The reason for this mismatch between what's happening for them internally and how they are presenting externally is because it wasn't safe for them to defend themselves and mobilize their fight or flee response in early childhood. So instead, the dorsal vagal complex (immobilized state) was activated, and they disassociated to protect themselves.

When Maria learned more about the disorganized attachment style in our (Mark's) work together, she was relieved. Finally, there was language that described her internal experience and fear of getting too close to another. She shared that in previous relationships, whenever she started to get close to someone, she would pull away and come up with a story as to why this relationship wasn't going to work. It wasn't until she met Rafael, her current partner, that she wanted to explore this pattern—and, hopefully, work through it. After some digging, Maria shared a fear that lived between her and intimacy: "How do I know that they won't turn on me, or that this relationship is even real?"

For Maria, connection equaled harm. Her wise system decided that if she didn't get too close, then she could protect herself from the impact of this impending harm. She knew that this push-pull dynamic—her need for connection was at odds with her need for safety—was draining and preventing her from creating the family she desired.

Maria was ready to move into deeper intimacy. To support her system in untangling her survival instinct from love and attachment, she needed to move out of freeze mode and complete the stuck survival responses in her system. To do this work, she began meeting with a somatic therapist to practice co-regulating with a safe person as she moved into opening to new levels of intimacy.

A tolerable step those with a disorganized attachment can take is to let people close and choose when to create distance. For example, Maria can share with Rafael, "I notice that every time I get close, my nervous system wants to push you away because it doesn't feel safe. At times this closeness can feel overwhelming to my system, causing me to disassociate and check out. When this happens, I might need to take some space to be able to regulate my nervous system so that I can be more present for you, us, and this conversation." This puts Maria into the driver's seat of her own nervous system, which increases self-trust that she can protect herself in ways she didn't have access to in early childhood.

Becoming the owner/operator of your own nervous system begins with coming home to your inner child and understanding the language of your body and nervous system.

Tending Your System and Inner Child

The journey of coming home to wholeness is the process of turning toward the parts of us that we had to leave behind. Just because we didn't have the childhood we deserved doesn't mean we can't gift ourselves that now. This doesn't mean we time-travel and try to change the past or our childhood. No, it means we become the one who tends to and gives ourselves what we didn't get but deeply craved and needed as children.

What was it that you needed? What was it that you craved? It is through the process of reparenting—of going back to our younger parts and imprinting *new* experiences—that we begin to reshape our nervous system and create an internal secure attachment. We not only create new, better memories for our future but also a new template and a new way of being and relating.

Our challenges in relationship invite us to do this work. We can choose to heal, grow, and become who we always needed to be. This step is a major reclamation of our power and worthiness. *When you stand up for yourself, you communicate to every part of you (past and present) that you are here, you are safe, and you matter.* You stop chasing others trying to convince them of your significance. You treat yourself as significant. You stop waiting to be chosen. You choose yourself. When you have compassion for yourself and these younger parts—instead of self-directed anger and internalized shame—you communicate that it's okay to be human, make mistakes, that you are worthy of being taken care of, and that your emotions are important.

Compassion, though it might seem like a small exercise in the present moment, feels incredibly big through the eyes of our scared inner child. Accepting compassion is often a tender process. The process of reclaiming and reconnecting can open us up to the original pain of not being seen, loved, or nurtured in the way we hoped for. We must grieve this truth and give ourselves the permission to love all of us in ways that others couldn't. But we can't run from the truth of our pain anymore. Although as children our adaptive strategies help us cope with painful truths, as adults the work is to turn toward these often painful truths. To love these painful truths. Which is not to bypass the experience of our pain but to compassionately accept and move through our pain. Ultimately, our wounds deserve the attention we seek from others.

For some of us, it will take time, warmth, and care to rebuild and reconnect with the parts of us that we've had to repress, minimize, and exile into the shadows. Like any child who experiences this neglect, it will take time for our inner child to warm up and trust that we are here *now* and that we aren't going anywhere. And we get to embody that truth.

When we notice our system moving into activation (feeling anxious, pushing away, shutting down), we can hit the pause button and imagine our kind, deeply loving inner parent holding our inner child with care and ask them these questions:

- How are you feeling? What do you need from me in this moment?
  » Some examples: validating emotions and experiences with compassion and care, reassurance about who I am, to know that I'm going to be okay, etc.
- I sense that you are feeling _____. Would you like to talk about it? What would you like to do right now? How can I support you?

As we open and move toward new experiences of safe connection, care, and love—both from ourselves and from others—our bodies receive the deep imprint that we are loved, and that we are not alone in the world.

Through this reconnection, and internal/external co-regulation, our trust is restored—along with a sense of centeredness.

This work of healing and reconnecting to our inner child allows us to grow up, mature out of the masks and protective ways of being, and ultimately become adults in relationships. This means showing up as our full selves with access to the wisdom derived from our pain. The healing of what has previously been avoided and/or protected facilitates access to our hearts and our power. It is how we learn to trust ourselves.

You are so damn worthy of the love and life you crave. Doing this work reinforces that truth. We see you and acknowledge you for taking the trip back to ol' memory lane.

EXERCISE
Evaluating Patterns in Attachment Styles

Ask yourself the following questions and consider writing the responses in a journal:

- *What did I want most as a child and didn't get? (This is usually what we long for in our adult relationships too.)*
- *What feelings did I have over and over as a child? (These are usually the feelings we find ourselves having consistently in relationships today.)*
- *What childhood frustrations and responses come up as you journey down memory lane? (List all you can think of.)*
  Example:
  Frustration: My dad worked a lot and wasn't available.
  How I responded to this frustration: I sulked and constantly complained.
- *What are your current relationship frustrations and responses? Do they mirror what occurred in your childhood?*
  Example:
  Frustration: My partner is never home because he's working.
  How I respond to this frustration: I withdraw and sulk.

Notice the attachment style that goes with the responses and how our adult frustrations and responses tend to mirror our childhood ones.

Remember, below every frustration is an emotional need. For each frustration you have, what emotional need (to be understood, to feel considered, feel safe, feel loved, feel heard) is not being met?

What is a way you or your partner could meet your need in those moments?

4

Getting Right with Reality

We were six months into our relationship, and I (Kylie) was nervous about deepening into another committed partnership. I was fresh off the heels of a divorce and knew I needed to build an inner foundation of self-trust and an external foundation of self-reliance and financial independence if I didn't want to lose myself in a codependent dynamic again. I was terrified of repeating the same pattern and ending up in the same place.

The adult part of me was clear: "You have work to do!" But the younger part of me wasn't convinced on taking this solo path of individuation. To minimize the tension I felt, I reconciled the split by telling myself, "I can build this foundation from within our relationship." Clear sailing ahead, right? Unfortunately and fortunately, my subconscious had something else in mind. Literally.

One night, I woke up from a dream trembling in a pool of sweat. The dream was simple. Mark and I were in a burning house, and some far-off voice stated, clearly, "It's time to go."

I lay awake for hours. I couldn't shake myself free from the vision of this burning house and the intensity of the message that came with it. For days it destabilized me. Was it time for me to go? Were Mark and I going to go up in flames if I didn't? Was this my soul speaking to me or my trauma interfering with the relationship? What was I being asked to do? What was true? Was it all just a dream? Was I just afraid of commitment?

Without the capacity to face this dream and the messages it held, I labeled it as "trauma" and stuffed it as far as I could into the depths of my subconscious where I didn't have to touch it, look at it, or do anything about it. That is, until it came back.

Here's the kicker. Just because we repress feelings, dreams, fears, and truths doesn't mean they disappear and don't impact us in small and big ways. The burning house lived in my body, and in the ether between Mark and I, controlling the depth of intimacy and level of closeness that was available to us. So why didn't I bring it forward? The reason I believed I couldn't discuss this dream with Mark was because I feared that it would be the end of our relationship, and with it, my source of safety. But if I could not acknowledge and explore the messages of the dream and share it with Mark, how could I loosen its grip, make space for truth, and be open to the possibility of change? The reality is I couldn't.

I know I'm not alone. We all hold back truths that can impact our relationships. Sure, sometimes we'll explore for a moment the fact that we're not a great communicator, or we may think we have a challenging relationship with alcohol, but that's all it is, a momentary thought. Here and then gone. We continue just as we were. The burning house goes from being a terrifying, urgent truth to being dismissed as "trauma" and "just a dream."

The truths you can't hold are holding you hostage.

The tragedy?

It *could* have been the moment everything changed—the moment where we stopped running from the truth, and instead chose to learn to orient around it.

What is required for change to take place, whether it's relationally or personally, is a deep commitment to radical responsibility for the life we are creating. It isn't until we can honestly sit with ourselves and say, "This is exhausting me," "Something is in the way," "I am split," "I don't like who I am becoming," or "I don't want this," that there is an opportunity to shift out of it and make lasting change. But if we cannot accept the truths of our lives, we cannot change. Why? We're not in a relationship with *reality*.

Blind Spots

If we've learned anything so far in this book it is this: we humans are *really* good at protecting ourselves from pain and blocking out information that threatens our sense of safety and security. Remember that brilliant and beautiful nervous system of yours? Our system is *so* wise that it will block out and intentionally blind us from anything that destabilizes our version of reality, our sense of safety, and the pillars of belief that uphold it.

We call these our blind spots because they inhibit us from moving into any emotion or action that feels unsafe or overwhelming to our system. In addition, these blind spots prevent us from seeing ourselves (and others) as whole, empowered, and sovereign beings.

When we lack the capacity to acknowledge truth and the potential pain that comes with it, we cling to narratives that keep us stuck in our adaptive roles, identities, and codependent dynamics.

Let's take the burning house dream for example . . . Instead of accepting the message "It's time to go," I repressed that directive and moved into the loop of shame: What is so wrong with me that I can't receive this love?

When we see ourselves as "broken" or as "victims," it becomes easier to sit in loops of blame, shame, and guilt than it is to grow, grieve, and heal. These mental and emotional loops keep us split and block us from integrating the lessons reality (which can be painful!) can teach us. If we opt to feed the disempowering *beliefs* we have about ourselves, it makes it almost impossible to see beyond the story we've told ourselves for so long. Instead of maturing, we remain developmentally suspended in an early-adolescent state psychologically, spiritually, and emotionally. In this suspended state, we internalize the parent-child dynamic and play out the "bad girl/boy" or the "good girl/boy" narrative. When we are replaying these scripts, we don't have access to the energy or self-esteem needed to make real change in our lives.

Loop-de-loop-de-loop.

In an effort to escape the cycle, let's take off the blindfold and explore eleven blind spots that keep us from seeing reality more clearly.

Blind Spot #1: Shame

Shame says: *I am broken. I am unlovable. I am unworthy. I don't matter. I am incompetent.*

The *shame core* develops when toxic energy is directed at us from family members, coaches, teachers, siblings, media, or culture—for example, when a teacher says to a child, "You're not very good at that." If we lack a strong sense of self, or a loving, protective adult in our lives, we internalize this message and instead of seeing the *environment* or *interaction* as broken, toxic, and dysfunctional, we begin to believe that *we* are broken.

We minimize our own intuition and emotions. Instead of acknowledging and bringing up what is true for us out into the open, we account for this "off" feeling by saying there is something wrong with us. The more toxic energy we internalize from our environments and relationships, the larger the shame core becomes. To a young mind, absent of a wisdom-wielding adult, criticism and traumatic experiences become a failure of the self, not a failure of the environment or just opportunities to learn and grow.

There are two main ways we dance around, and cope with, the shame core. We either move above shame and take on distorted identities of superiority/grandiosity (Savior, Ms. Independent, Mr. Good Guy), which sounds like, "I'm not going to let them shame me ever again." Or we move below it and collapse into narratives of inferiority and feeling less than (Damsel in Distress, Martyr), which sound like, "They are going to reject me, what's the use? I'm not good enough anyway." Both strategies—whether it's moving above shame or moving below it—inhibit us from experiencing the core emotions (anger and sadness) that live underneath shame.

Shame was my (Kylie's) go-to for the first thirty years of my life. After my divorce, which served to amplify my feeling of brokenness, I went on to hide behind the cloak of shame for years. I was young (twenty-four) when I got married and divorced, but it wasn't my youth that was a problem, it was my expectations for what a union with another person could provide me. Divorce amplified and affirmed the loops in my head that repeated that I was broken, a disgrace, a sinner, and that no one would love me for who I was. Ah, gotta love internalized religious doctrine! These narratives felt familiar and safe to me because they fed into my survival identity of being helpless, incompetent, and worthless. I knew how to relate to and navigate the world as a small, powerless person.

Here's how this feedback loop played out: *If I'm broken and incapable of coping on my own, then I must stay in relationship 1.0 with Mark. Mark is my savior; I am the one who needs fixing.*

It wasn't until I was having lunch with my friend Christine who said, "You're free to come out of the cage now, you can stop hiding," that I realized just how comfortable I had become hiding in this cage of shame and smallness.

So, I had to find a way to break through the confines of the cage of shame to get to a place of personal liberation.

How? I am so glad you asked!

The way through shame:

+ We must move from seeing any parts of ourselves that we or others/culture have deemed "worthless" to seeing them as simply the parts that have been wounded. You are not worthless, you are wounded (and your wound can be tended to and held). Begin to acknowledge where we hold shame and know that we weren't born feeling this way. Shame is learned, and it's not your fault.
+ Hand it back. It's time to externalize what we've internalized and hand the shame back to its origin point—the person who originally shamed us. This way we can tend to the grief—anger and sadness—that exists underneath the shame.
+ Go from silence to sharing. Shame thrives in secrecy. For shame to loosen its grip, we must bring it forward. We must begin or continue to find safe spaces, places, and people to share and own our story so it doesn't own us.

Blind Spot #2: Guilt

Guilt says: *This is my fault. I did something wrong. I am selfish. I should be punished. I am responsible for their pain and well-being.*

Guilt is the belief that you did or are doing something wrong. Some of the top areas we experience guilt are:

1. Not spending enough time with partner/family
2. Prioritizing your needs, desires
3. Saying "no"
4. Not being the "perfect" friend, parent, daughter/son
5. Spending money on yourself
6. Placing the responsibility of your partner's (and anyone's) happiness on your shoulders
7. Taking personal feel-good time
8. Disappointing your family/friends

This reminds me (Mark) of a client I worked with named Rachel. She came to work with me because she felt stuck and wanted to move forward in her life, relationship, and job. After I asked Rachel what she desired, she clearly stated, "I want a committed partnership, a leadership role at work, and one day a family of my own."

Beautiful! This is a woman who knows what she wants.

I then asked Rachel about the status of her current relationship, and she replied, "Well, I've been dating the same guy for four years, but he isn't interested in a committed relationship or building a family of his own."

Interesting . . . So I asked her, "Why are you choosing to stay in this relationship with him when he doesn't desire the same thing you do?"

After taking a pause and shifting her gaze, she replied, "Because I'm worried about what will happen to him if I leave the relationship. I don't know if he will be okay."

Oof. A few things were happening here. Rachel was taking responsibility for his emotional well-being and didn't trust that he would be okay without her. She felt guilty about potentially hurting his feelings and feeling contempt for him (a lack of belief in his sovereignty and maturity). Guilt and contempt were preventing her from getting right with reality and moving forward.

In the end, she got to blame *him* for *her* not getting what she truly desired. Brilliant! (And don't worry, we're looking at blame in a second.)

The way through guilt:

+ Release the shackles of "should" that keep you bound to yesses that are really nos. For example, Rachel needed to release the "should" that stood in between her healthy desires and her current reality: "I should take care of him." "I should lower my standards." "I should be okay with this."

+ Which brings us to the next BIG step in moving through guilt. It's time to drop the bags of other people's well-being on their doorsteps! To clarify, this doesn't mean we don't care and operate with love in our relationships—it means we're no longer overriding our own capacity, truth, and well-being to accommodate others. This isn't love, it's obligation. Making them feel okay with themselves is not your responsibility!

+ Sometimes guilt emerges when we have done something that's harmed another. This is where we get to make honest amends, forgive ourselves, and commit to doing better moving forward.

+ And lastly, it's time to up the ante and give yourself permission to become and create every little thing that guilt is holding you back from.

Blind Spot #3: Regret

Regret says: *I ruined my life. I messed up. If I hadn't done that, I would be better off.*

Regret, guilt's sister, also prevents us from being in the present moment and moving forward. When we feel regret, we stay firmly planted in the past, ruminating on what happened and punishing ourselves for something that occurred some time ago. We become imprisoned in a loop of self-punishment and believe that if we hadn't done X, then there would be an alternate reality we'd currently be living that is better for us and/or for them. The tricky thing about regret is we can't know what would have transpired had we taken another path—even though our minds like to think they do know for certain.

The way through regret:

+ Identify the lesson. When we make choices that we later regret, it is usually an invitation to learn a lesson. Get curious and ask yourself, *Why did I make that decision?* Was it because you were afraid? Was it because you didn't see another choice in the moment? Whatever it was, begin to dig up the deeper reason you went one way when you wish you would've gone another way.

+ Forgive yourself. When you know better you'll do better. Offer yourself grace for what you did or didn't do back then. Lean into faith. Your soul isn't concerned with what's right or wrong; it only cares that you are walking your own path, learning the lessons you came here to learn, and that your soul is alive. Can you have faith in your path? What is meant for you will not pass you by.

Blind Spot #4: Blame

Blame says: *It's their fault. Life isn't fair. They are the reason I am this way. This is my fault.*

Blame works as a defense mechanism, inhibiting us from moving into the core emotions underneath it. When we're looping in blame, we see ourselves as powerless to someone or something outside of us. While someone can certainly be at fault and responsible for hurting us, blame can keep us stuck in the past. It's how we hold blame that determines its blinding effect. I'll never forget a message I (Mark) received from my client Susan about the power of self-blame. She shared in a post-session reflection, "Grief is painful. But I'm noticing and learning that my tendency to blame myself for things [childhood stuff] has blocked my ability to access the grief. How can I grieve something that's my fault? I discovered that for me to move past the self-blame/shame, I had to work through a few negative beliefs which eventually led me to giving my 'little self' compassion. And it's the compassion for my little self that shifted things, ultimately allowing me to release a lot of grief!" This shift out of self-blame and into self-compassion allowed Susan to access the grief that existed underneath the blame. She was able to see her childhood clearly, and eventually move out of the self-blame that kept her feeling small and powerless.

The way through blame:

+ Name the blame. Explore the roots of your blame story. Where are you placing blame (internally or externally)? How do you punish yourself? How do you punish others?

+ Explore the emotional underbelly. What core emotions (sadness, fear, anger, excitement, disgust) exist underneath the blame? Fill in the blank: *Blame is preventing me from feeling* _____.

+ Take responsibility. What is yours here? What isn't yours? Once you are clear on what's yours and what isn't, it's time to move from being powerless to empowered. What boundaries do you need to enact (internally or externally) to feel safe, empowered, and in choice (you are free from any obligation to be or do anything that isn't aligned with your whole self)? For example: I will no longer beat myself up, or be someone else's emotional punching bag.

Blind Spot #5: Anxiety

Anxiety says: *What if (worst-case scenario) happens? I'm terrified of the unknown. This isn't going to turn out well. I am going to lose everything.*

We experience anxiety when multiple core emotions collapse in on one another. For instance, if we're feeling grief, anger, and fear all at once, we will likely experience this as anxiety. That is, until we tease apart and sit with each core emotion.

Anxiety is also an inhibitory emotion, or an emotional stop sign. Anxiety blocks our ability to see what's happening right in front of our eyes and within our bodies because we are so focused on the future—worrying about *what could happen*—that we don't address what is happening *now*.

Angela was, like many people, stuck wanting to leave yet not wanting to hurt her children through the divorce. She was in the ambivalent condition of neither going nor actually staying. There are many core emotions blocked in the staying: *anger* about having to stay; *despair* in not being able to choose oneself and move forward in a way that feels liberating; *fear* about hurting the children; *grief* because of the experience of watching and feeling her potential not be realized (which may be reached by leaving a relationship that no longer feels aligned); *excitement* about what is possible for her life.

Although divorce certainly has an impact on children, so does staying and not living truthfully. We have to ask ourselves, *What do I want to teach my children?*

Interestingly, Angela's mother also stayed married to her father out of fear of judgment and the impact it would have on the children. Her mother spent her entire life suppressing her truth to maintain a relationship that required her suppression. This is what Angela knew. Her anxiety was asking her to acknowledge her truth, get in contact with her emotions, and make the choice that was best for *her*, which is the choice that is best for her children as well.

The way through anxiety:

- Tease out core emotions. Are you feeling fear? Anger? Sadness? Disgust? Ask yourself: *What core emotions are being blocked, and if I expressed/embraced those emotions, how would my life be asked to change?*
- Explore your momentum. What story/life are you cocreating that doesn't feel in alignment with your values? Where are you saying yes (or nothing at all) that doesn't feel good, or "right," in your system?
- Work through worst-case-scenario thinking. Make a list of each scenario you are afraid of happening. *What if I'm "too much" and he leaves me? What if sharing this dream ends our relationship?*

What if I never find someone else? What if I'm alone forever? Now flip the script and move your thoughts into a more balanced and harmonious loop. For example, let's flip the script from *What if I never find someone else?* to *What if I never invite in the "yes" that's in my future?*

Blind Spot #6: Trauma

Trauma says: *Is this trauma or is this truth? What is wrong with me? This is all my stuff.*

Often we become stuck in the tension of trauma versus truth. Here we're suspended in the mental realm constantly trying to figure out if the root of our feelings is based in trauma or truth. No matter where it is based, it is real because we are experiencing it. I (Kylie) stayed suspended in this tension for years, labeling my burning house dream as "trauma." Instead of investigating it and trusting it, I feared it, repressed it, and wished it would go away—only furthering my tension and disconnect from self. I knew that if the dream was truth, that I would have to face the decision to leave . . . and that wasn't something I was ready to acknowledge.

The way through trauma:
- *Name* what is present without labeling it as trauma or an absolute truth. For example: *I had a dream that really shook me that I'm afraid to share.*
- Validate somatic experience and the corresponding story. For example: *I'm noticing a lot of activation in my system and the story I am telling myself is I need to go, and that my relationship is over.*
- Hit the pause button. Do a regulating activity (take a cold shower, go for a walk, breathe, give yourself a hug), or co-regulate (call a friend, snuggle a pet) until you feel less activated.
- Find a safe space. Share your experience with someone who can hold the complexity and sometimes contradictory truths with care, curiosity, and non-judgment.

Blind Spot #7: Familiarity

Familiarity says: *This is just how things are. Change isn't possible. This is how it is for me.*

When we play the scripts above, we feel defeated. There is a strong sense of apathy in saying, "This is just the way things are." Change and possibility diminish into the shadows when this reaction runs the show. When the pain of opening to possibility feels too much, we stay in an immobilized state instead. Hope feels too distant and we don't want to be disappointed, so we acquiesce to living in a dulled sense of reality.

Sheila found herself here a lot in our (Kylie's) sessions. When invited to talk about her desires and needs in her relationship, she collapsed. We explored this a bit more in our work together and discovered a few core beliefs that anchored her firmly in the land of familiarity and kept her frozen. Her core beliefs were, *I don't deserve more. This is as good as it gets for me. I should be grateful I even have a relationship.* With these core beliefs driving the show, it's no wonder Sheila didn't feel confident to share her desires and needs.

The way through familiar:

- Exploring our core beliefs. What core beliefs do you hold around self-worth, receiving, goodness, and possibility? Fill in the blank: *When I believe these thoughts, I prevent myself from experiencing* _____ .
- Opening up to grieve. Tending to our grief softens the blinding effect of familiarity as we open to possibility and life again by grieving what did happen. What core emotions live under these beliefs? For example: Underneath Sheila's "I don't deserve more" was sadness and anger for not being seen, supported, and honored.
- Increasing capacity for the good. Can you open to and begin to find and feel the good in your life? Allow your system to reorient toward small wins by asking, *How good can it get? What else might*

*be available for me if I open myself to possibility, and the great mystery
of life?*

+ Tapping into play, creativity, and imagination. Invite more of these
into your life. Go somewhere you've never been (whether that's a
faraway trip or a new coffee shop), take a class to learn something
new, put on a song and move your body in whatever way feels
right. This supports your mind in reorienting toward possibility,
novelty, and joy again.

Blind Spot #8: Dependence

Dependence says: *I need him. I need someone to feel happy. I need someone
to tell me what to do. I can't survive without her. How can I trust myself when
I can't feel what's right and wrong?*

The more we depend on others for our sense of security, the harder
it is to step into self-honesty, especially if a feeling or truth threatens the
relationship. Instead of standing in our authentic response, we merge with
others and allow them to be the authority over our lives. We become dependent on their wisdom, their direction, their competency, and, in turn,
minimize our own.

Without a strong connection to his center, Matt always found himself
getting lost in his partner's energy, path, and needs. He shared in one of
our (Mark's) sessions, "She is so sure and clear about us that I don't question it." After digging and getting clear on his own authentic experience, he
was able to name his apprehension and lack of clarity. He wasn't sure about
the relationship and where it was headed. It's not that Matt didn't want to
be in the partnership, he just wanted to make sure his authentic response
was present and alive in their dynamic as well. This required him to stop
following his partner's lead and discern for himself what his true feelings,
needs, and desires were in the relationship.

The way through dependence:

+ Name the dependence. For example: *I am depending on them for
a sense of stability, direction, safety, worthiness, love, and validation.*

When I am sourcing this from them, I am doing so at what cost? For Matt, the cost was big—losing himself, his voice, and his own well-being.

• Come back to self. Notice where you are taking on someone else's energy or giving too much of yours away. Check in with yourself before connecting with others and after. *How did I feel before? How do I feel after? Do I feel drained, depleted (giving energy away)? Or did my mood shift to match and mirror their mood?* For example, "They were sad, so now I am sad" (taking on someone else's energy). Ask yourself: *What's mine here? How can I build my inner foundation so I don't have to rely on another for my sense of stability and worth?* (We'll get there in the next chapter!) Continue to bring your energy back into your body, and release what isn't yours.

Blind Spot #9: Survival

Survival says: *Stay in line and you will be safe. I know what's best/safest for you. You will be abandoned if you do this or if you do not do this.*

Our deepest need is to belong, and our deepest fear is exile. When we believe that our connection to others and our relationships will be threatened by something true in our lives, we struggle to step forward and share those deep desires. When our desire for change has us oscillating around new values that will move us away from our friends, our family, our community, or even our culture, the fear is real. Usually we surround ourselves with people who live how we live and choose what we choose. To change risks exile.

Nicole was terrified to step into her power and create a life on her terms. For her this looked like leaving her career of eight years to start her own business, and creating some boundaries with her mother. Every time Nicole went to have the conversations she needed to have to make those changes, she noticed that her nervous system became activated, her hands clammy, and her voice nonexistent. Naturally, this frustrated Nicole. She asked, "Why can't I move toward the things I say I want?" To which

I (Mark) replied: "Because your system doesn't trust that it's safe for you to step into your power and risk losing the connection you have with your mother." It was time to look at the survival instructions etched into her nervous system and cells.

The way through survival:

+ Tend your younger parts. Notice what fears are present for you when you think about taking up space, stepping into your power, or setting boundaries. *If I do this, I am afraid _____ will happen.* Whose fear is this? (Is it yours, cultural, passed down through your lineage?) Process any grief around the loss of connections, exile, lack of belonging, etc., from embodying your authentic self.

+ Tend your system. Reaffirm that you are safe by doing something that brings you back into regulation. Call a friend, take a walk, book an appointment with your body worker or therapist.

+ Find an "expander" (as Lacy Phillips, teacher and manifester extraordinaire, calls them!). Expanders walk a path we desire for ourselves. It can be so helpful for our minds to see someone like us who is doing something we desire to do for ourselves. It shows us that what we desire is possible and safe! A mentor, brotherhood circle, or aligned community does wonders for our nervous system when we are venturing into truth.

+ Locate supportive allies and community care. We need other souls who champion, celebrate, and support us as we climb out of survival strategies and cycles. *Find them stat.* Do activities you love and you'll meet people who are doing what they love too. Join book clubs, go on retreats, go to conferences, meetups. Seek out a coach, therapist, group classes, or join a CoDA meeting (a twelve-step codependents anonymous recovery program). Authenticity may move us away from people, but it is always moving us *toward* others. This is the community that will celebrate our new way of being.

Blind Spot #10: Fantasy

Fantasy says: *They will change. Their potential is so great. They weren't seri-ous when they said* _____. *He will save me. I will be better off with her.*

When we are in fantasy land, we trade in present-moment truth for the *potential* of a different reality in the future. We see this trip to fantasy land show up in various ways—from believing in someone's potential (in-stead of who they are being now) or disconnecting from the discomfort of a current relationship by fantasizing about our life with someone else (e.g., the hot yoga teacher). So often we fall in love with potential by trading in our own.

Eminent social psychologist Caryl Rusbult studied the impact of fan-tasizing about real or imagined alternatives to our relationships and how this was predictive of infidelity. Basically, the moment we enter this fantasy world, it is the beginning of the death of our relationship.

Tim was a pro at living in fantasy land. Whenever he would reach a limit in his romantic relationship, he would call me (Mark) and start talking about his *potential* life with so-and-so. He would expound, say-ing, "I'm bored in my relationship . . . I need some more excitement." One day, after listening to Tim share, I stopped him and said, "I think you use fantasy as a way to distract yourself from the discomfort in your current relationship." It was time for Tim to look in the mirror, leave fantasy land, and plant his feet firmly in reality.

The way through fantasy:

+ Acknowledge fantasy land. For example: Tim needed to acknowl-edge that he was spending a lot of his mental and emotional energy fantasizing about a new relationship instead of directing energy into his current one.
+ Evaluate what's really here. Discover which core emotion(s) and belief(s) exist underneath the reaction that sends you to live in fantasy. *When I am in fantasy, I am avoiding feeling/facing* _____. *When I am in fantasy, I feed the belief that* _____.

+ Come back to reality. Instead of leaving reality and dreaming about another, it's time to name what's present for you in your current relationship—honestly, and openly, with someone you can trust and work through it with.

Blind Spot #11: Hope

Hope says: *I hope that he/she will change eventually. I hope that we will get back together.*

Hope is a beautiful thing. It's when hope blinds us from what is true that it begins to get in the way of our ability to be in reality. Can you walk with hope *and* be grounded in reality? Can you hold a prayer of possibility *and* still be with what is currently true? This is key.

After deciding to go on an intentional break from her relationship to do some healing work, Colleen had hope for her and her ex's future. When they reunited after their sacred pause to explore their connection, Colleen was excited. As she and her previous partner explored their connection, Colleen realized that some things hadn't shifted, and that this relationship was still not a "yes" for her. Instead of being blinded by hope, she was invited to place her hope on the unknown path that lay ahead of her. She was invited to place her hope in the future instead of the past.

The way through hope:

+ Stay in your lane. Allow hope to take up 10 percent of your mind space. Focus the other 90 percent of your energy on moving in a direction that is aligned with your soul's purpose, desires, and needs.
+ Explore the edges of hope. Fill in the blank: *Hope is preventing me from seeing/facing _____. Hope is preventing me from grieving _____. Hope is preventing me from releasing _____ and opening to _____.*

Reconnecting with Reality

As we face what's real and present within ourselves and within our environments, we begin to reconnect with what is real and restore trust within ourselves.

This restorative journey starts small, with one question: *What is true for me in this moment?* For me (Kylie) this was the very question that invited me to differentiate the past from the present, hit the pause button, and begin the trek back home to reality—one truth at a time.

The more I resisted the truth that lived in my cells and showed up in my dreams, the deeper I sunk into shame, anxiety, and guilt. The blind spots grew bigger and bigger with each new morning and eventually I felt altogether blind. My close friends, family, and Mark could hear the struggle in my voice and see the sadness in my eyes. I was sick and my body was struggling to cope with the tension—the gap—that lived between my survival programming telling me to stay small and in the relationship.

My soul, on the other hand, was saying, *It's time to go.*

I remember one conversation with my friend Jordan as I was lying on my couch doing my best to avoid the emotional and physical pain I was in. Jordan is one of those friends who has walked through many fires of her own—a friend who cuts right through the rationalizations and gets to the core.

I was giving her an update on Mark's and my relationship, telling her how I was struggling to be "all in." She looked me right in the eyes and said, "Ky, nothing else matters but truth. What do you know to be true right now?"

I took a deep breath and sighed. It was the most relaxed my system had been in a long time, and with equal parts relief and fear, I responded, "The truth is I need to leave."

This was the first time I disclosed this truth to *anyone,* even myself. And while I felt relief in finally acknowledging what I knew to be true deep down, I was still afraid of it because I didn't know what existed on the other side of it.

From that conversation forward, the question *What is true for me right now?* became my lighthouse. As I slowly disclosed deeper truths to myself, and eventually to others, my system started to feel relief. I was no longer denying myself. I was no longer moving in a direction that opposed my soul. I was no longer hiding. I was no longer lying.

The restoration of truth in your life is a sacred journey.

This restoration is about gently—and not-so-gently—being willing to eat that giant piece of humble pie and take the first step toward moving through the world without the weight of lies on your shoulders. And although these lies are often subtle, protective, and appear normal and even good to the outside observer, inside we are torn and split. The soul calls us to land firmly back into reality, while our coping strategies and addictions attempt to quell the tsunami that reality is about to bring down upon us. Whether we want to listen is up to us for a while. But eventually we don't have a choice.

Remember, it is *normal* to abandon our true self for "love." It is *normal* to hide our dreams and desires and live a life that will bring us a sense of security and safety. It is *normal* to live the life you were taught to want and check the boxes that everybody checks to ensure they are doing life "right." It's even *normal* to be anxious, overwhelmed, depressed, addicted, and disconnected.

Eff normal. Normal is a lie.

Getting right with reality means standing in the face of the fire and not settling for self-deception. Truth has an uncanny way of liberating you from anything and everything that isn't aligned with your authentic path. On the other side of honesty and self-disclosure is a world where you get to decide what you want to create and who you want to be. Being connected to reality allows us to actively shape what is happening in the now. So, we bring you back to the questions: What do you want to create? Who do you want to be? How do you want to be remembered? You are responsible for creating the life and relationships you desire. Are you ready?

Great. Let's get real.

EXERCISE
Getting Right with Reality

As a starting place, let's create a compassionate and loving space to be with *what is*. To get right with reality without needing to change or do anything at all. That's right, you don't need to do anything with the information you disclose; in fact, naming something honestly and vulnerably shifts you back into integrity with yourself. Regardless of whether you do anything at all, restoration of integrity and reconnection to your internal world is a win. *Name it to tame it.* It moves the adult you back into the driver's seat of your life—choosing to stay when that feels right, and to shift when it doesn't anymore.

- *What blind spots are you hanging out in?*
- *What are they preventing you from seeing or hearing?*
- *What are they preventing you from facing?*
- *What truths are you avoiding in your life?*
- *What are you done pretending is okay?*
- *How does acknowledging those truths make you feel?*
- *How would your life change and what would become possible if you fully aligned your life with all the truths you know but haven't (fully) accepted?*

5

Breaking Up with Normal

When you begin to face the truths that live within you individually, as well as between you and your partner, it forces you to ask the difficult question: *Can we do the work to create a new dynamic together, or is it time to break up?*

Rachel and Dylan were asking themselves this same question when they reached out to work with me (Mark). They had been together for four years—the last of which had been rocky. I could sense the tension, sadness, and exhaustion in the air when Rachel, at the end of her emotional rope, asked me, "Is it supposed to be this hard?"

Rachel and Dylan aren't alone here. When our protective patterns are looping and we can't seem to break through to the other side of a conflict or disconnect, it's normal to feel defeated and deflated. This may sound like: *What are we missing here? What happened to the good ol' days? Why can't we seem to get past this issue?* This can be because of an acknowledged misalignment of futures, values, and deal-breakers. But it can also be because we're stuck in a loop of unhealed wounds. Both Dylan and Rachel were unable to see how each one's individual and unique set of survival patterns was keeping them locked into a familiar yet unfulfilling dynamic. This is a common place to find ourselves in post-honeymoon phase. And while it can feel disheartening to find ourselves in a similar place relationally *again*, when we orient toward these blocks and limits with compassion, care, and curiosity—together—we have the potential to heal the parts of us that yearn to be seen, witnessed, and held by another.

Before we continued our work together, I asked Rachel and Dylan, "Are you both committed to this relationship, and to doing the work individually and together that is required to move through these limits?" They both, with equal parts hope and fear in their voices, looked at each other and said, "Yes." Rachel was ready to stop blaming Dylan for their struggles, and Dylan was ready to stop collapsing into a familiar loop of apathy (*This is just how it is*). They were both ready to meet their edges and everything that came with it.

Unlike Rachel and Dylan, sometimes there isn't a shared desire and a mutual commitment to evolution, growth, and a healthy relationship. When this is the case, it's hard to say which way to go or what path to take. What we can say is this: when you choose growth and liberation, those around you and the relationships in your life will shift.

Why?

Because *the next level of love and relationship requires everything to go to the next level too*. It requires that who we were as a couple and as individuals dies with the old relationship. This doesn't always have to mean the dissolution of the partnership (although it certainly can mean that) but it does require the death of old patterns. It requires *breaking up* . . . but that breaking up starts with who we were in the previous dynamic.

In partnership, sometimes you are reluctant to take the full leap into a new dynamic because you and/or your partner are not both *all in* on taking that deeper dive. Our reluctance can sometimes be because of our lack of trust in our partner to be there when things get hard. A lack of trust that they are leaping too. But do you see that this is still part of the same imprisoned, unliberated pattern? "I need to know you'll go there so I can go there. I need to know you're courageous and willing to go to the vulnerable place so I can too. *So I won't be alone there*."

This is the trick, though. *When you let go of familiar patterns and break up with what was, even if your partner and/or the relationship doesn't survive the leap, you will.* When you decide to enter a healing process wholeheartedly, you will be free of the *need* to make sure that others will

join you. Through leaping you are committed to both love and liberation. What finds you on the other side may not be your partner, but it
will be aligned.

When you stop trying to do everything you can to stay together, and
instead focus on bringing out each other's light and celebrating each other's truth, no matter how much it hurts, love is truly shared and honored.
Hiding ourselves and playing small (by diminishing ourselves) to keep a
relationship is not love. It is not in service of the relationship. It's in service
of not being too big or too much. It's in service of keeping the relationship
together over keeping our integrity intact. It's in service of fear.

Would you want anyone to be in relationship with you if it required
that they hide themselves and their heart? That they had to walk on eggshells or believe they're broken so you can stay together and get another
medal for checking off another anniversary and acting like everything is
okay and great when it's not? How is that in service of love? Who benefits
from that?

If you wouldn't want that for anyone else, why would you accept it for
yourself?

Really, truly ask yourself in this moment: Are you ready to break up
with "normal" and move into something greater? Love is about two people
in relationship learning to orient themselves to the truth. To build a self,
and then a relationship. When we do this work, we're no longer collapsing
our energy or matching the energy of the environment by doing what we
think we need to do in order to not rock the boat. Instead, we find our own
authentic truth and let that coexist with another's authentic truth. Your
relationship becomes a container that celebrates both of you as individuals,
and the container expands as both of you do. This is what it means to be
both free and *in* love.

If a relationship doesn't have space for you to be yourself, you don't
want it. And if one person is doing the work of both, you don't want it. Just
remember that any relationship you've been in that doesn't celebrate you,
you've *agreed* to be in.

Can you accept that truth?

Okay, good. Now let's break up with normal.

Resourced and Well-Equipped

What exactly does "breaking up with normal" entail? And what does this process require from us? When we are breaking up with normal, we're breaking up with the roles we've played and the survival strategies we've layered on in order to protect ourselves.

For example, if you took on the role of caretaker in your family system, you learned to over-function emotionally and take on the emotions of those around you. You did what you could to keep the peace and keep everyone else okay. As you wake up to this role you've been embodying, and the strategies that have traveled with you over the decades, you begin to realize that you've likely been playing out the same dynamic in all of your romantic relationships. You realize that you've oriented to all of your previous partners in the same way you oriented around your father—recreating the same dynamic over and over again.

This awareness—first and foremost—of your core wounds, roles, and strategies invites you into the work of breaking up with normal.

For much of this book, we've focused on the mental, physical (somatic experience), and the emotional. Now we want to focus on the wildly practical—specifically what you might need to do in order to break up with normal (whether that means within your current relationship or outside of it). To ground back into reality and match your outer reality with your inner truth, you may need to take some preliminary steps to support yourself so you feel comfortable and confident to act. Remember, *our capacity for change is dependent on our capacity to hold everything that comes with change.*

It would be a lot for us to go from one extreme—keeping the peace and relying on one person for everything (financial security, safety, community, worth)—to another—leaving with no plan or foundation in place. In fact, it would be unlikely that the thought of *really* leaving would even cross our minds. Instead, we would likely be sticking around in ambivalence, feeding our blind spots: minimizing the truth, gaslighting ourselves, blaming someone else, or labeling the idea of leaving as terrifying. Of course, this is a perfectly wise move when we're not well-equipped. Unconsciously we are protecting ourselves and ensuring our survival. But it's important to note as well that *just because it's wise on one level from a survival-based perspective doesn't mean that living in ambivalence isn't harmful on another.*

So, how do we begin to expand our vision and take responsibility for our lives? *How* do we break up with normal and step into the wild adventure of realignment?

To access more agency and choice in our lives, we need a strong inner foundation of self-trust, self-esteem, and self-competency. Doesn't *that* sound nice?! Well, if we've spent however many years without those things, having that foundation can feel like a distant dream, can't it? The work to achieve that level of self-trust and groundedness is worth it not only because of the results we'll get in our lives and our relationships but also because of how it impacts our health, our emotional state, and our general well-being.

In other words, *to be centered in oneself is to be free.* (And it is available to anybody at any time!)

It can take time, energy, and resources to build the inner foundation necessary to reach the point in our lives where it feels safe and possible to respond and act in healthier and authentic ways.

Take the subject of money. We can't deny it—in our world money equals food, shelter, and safety. For me (Kylie) taking responsibility for my financial well-being was a massive step in being able to trust myself. Before getting into right relationship with money, I relied on my family and romantic partners to support me when I couldn't make ends meet. I stayed in this cycle for years . . . and for me, it wasn't an easy one to break. I wasn't ready to trust myself with choice and power, even though I desired it with every cell of my being.

I remember one "aha" moment vividly. I was nearing the point of *almost* standing on my own two feet. My coaching practice was full and my debt dwindling. I was feeling good and empowered. After months of this growth my body began to slowly shut down as the emails, the holding space, the responsibility started to build.

I didn't realize I was stuck in an all-too-familiar codependent loop: in order to receive this support, I needed to give all of myself away. I was indebted to my business now instead of to my family or partner. So, I kept on giving, giving, and giving until I had nothing left to give. I burned out, and collapsed under the weight of it all. Feeling hopeless and afraid to recreate the same dynamic again within my work, I hit the pause button and turned to Mark and my family for support. I was stuck in freeze mode and didn't know how to step forward in my life and business with boundaries.

At first, I found myself back where I began. Even though it felt support- ive to receive this aid in finding balance from my family and Mark, eventu- ally it enabled my smallness and energized the part I was trying to break free from (the Damsel in Distress). If I receive support from my partner/ family, then I must do what I think they want me to do, say, and be. Enter: loops of obligation, expectation, powerlessness, and boundarylessness.

As time passed, my conscious awareness of this codependent dynamic grew, and I knew I needed to take *full* responsibility for my own finances if I desired more choice in my life. So that's what I did. I sat down with my family and Mark and declared: "Thank you for your support, but it's time for me to break through this cycle of dependence and rely on myself financially."

I didn't jump from being hyper-dependent to feeling like a self- competent boundary boss babe in one day, and I certainly didn't do it all on my own. That's not how sustainable change happens. We all need the right people (guides, mentors, therapists, friends) in our corner and the skills (emotional attunement, nervous system regulation, boundary work, com- munication strategies) to support ourselves to get over the speed bumps that show up along the way.

This is where healthy resourcing comes into play.

What does it mean to resource? We resource so that we can "go inside" the body and stay grounded while experiencing uncomfortable sensations, emotions, or memories. Resourcing is bringing in anything that supports us in feeling safe, nourished, and supported. This ability is critical—especially when we're moving out of conditioned habits and stepping into change. Resources may be internal, such as having daily routines that support us, or external, such as having a supportive friend. Here are a few resources one might need to feel safe in making a major change:

Inner Resources:

+ Self-trust (*honoring your own limits, boundaries*)
+ Internal boundaries (*keeping your commitments to self*)
+ Daily routines (*honoring your needs for food, hydration, sleep, movement, rest*)
+ Nervous system regulation (*attuning to your nervous system's needs*)
+ Self-esteem (*embodying worth and knowing inherent value*)
+ Inner strength (*resilience and being okay no matter what happens*)
+ Emotional regulation (*listening, processing, and honoring emotional impulses*)
+ Core values (*values that support alignment*)
+ Permission to be human (*grace around making mistakes, freedom from blame and shame*)
+ Honoring your own needs (*taking care of self before taking care of others*)
+ Self-love (*inner self-talk and boundaries that are loving, protective, and caring*)
+ Self-consent (*living attuned to self, first and foremost, regarding body, needs, and emotions*)

External Resources:

+ Community (*other people to be loved by and to love*)
+ Financial security (*agency to make choices aligned with values, self*)
+ Supportive friends, family members (*to depend on and to give to*)
+ Ancestors (*to call on for guidance and support*)
+ A loving pet (*extra cuddles, co-regulation, and companionship*)
+ Therapist/practitioner (*a place to reestablish trust in connection*)
+ Consistent care and validation from safe people (*a place to reopen your heart and be seen*)
+ Physical location (*a place that nourishes and supports you*)

+ Being honored and celebrated for who we are (*a place to embody your true colors freely*)

We cannot stress enough how important being well resourced is for change, especially sustained change (so important that we included an appendix in the back of the book!). To take big leaps we need to know there is a net to catch us when we fall.

As we create, find, and establish these resources and meet our needs, something magical begins to happen—we begin to reconnect with ourselves and disconnect from people, habits, and environments that aren't nourishing and conducive to living well. Because we're setting a high standard with ourselves, we start to hold that standard for everything and everyone in our lives. And, damn, it feels good. And scary. And good.

Relationally this may sound like, "I notice that I've been hiding my true self, desires, and wants from you. I've taken on the role of caretaker in our dynamic and I am tired and done minimizing myself and my own needs. From now on I am committed to bringing my authentic self forward and I would love your support in this process. I'm thinking we can create a weekly ritual where we have a check-in to assess what needs are present for us both and relationally, and how we're both feeling? How does this feel for you?"

What would your life look like if you started saying, "I'm done playing this role and feeding into this dynamic with you. I'm ready to go deeper with you. What do you say?"

This is what it looks like to take responsibility and courageously choose a new path.

Radical Responsibility

"Responsibility" comes from the Latin word for "response." Yep, this means our actions are our direct response to what life is asking us. The irony? We rarely take time to assess where our lives are headed. Sure, this is partially due to how busy, overwhelming, and stressful life can be, but it's also because we don't always *want* to know. When we look at the future we're creating, it might not be where we want to end up. Instead of taking the steering wheel of our life, it's easier to bury our heads in the sand and blame (and trust) fate to either bring us where we want to go or somehow save us when we get there.

But this only works until it doesn't.

So, we'll explicitly ask you: Where do you want to be in twenty years? In ten years? In one year?

If you let your life continue to direct itself and everything stayed the same as it is today, where are you likely to end up? Would you be okay with that?

Pause for a second.

Take a deep breath.

Okay, now imagine if you decided today to shift your life and align with your power and your deepest calling—where could you be? How would that feel to declare and to hold?

This recognition of what is currently true may be heavy, but it is also incredibly liberating. Why? Because you no longer get to be the spectator watching your journey. You have the right to be happy! You have the right to be fulfilled! You're allowed to prioritize and choose yourself! Shocking, we know!

What do you need, and what step can you take right *now* to access more empowered choices in your life? What needs to end? What needs to begin? What would life feel like if you stood in the truth of these answers and decided to claim the potential you're leaving on the table not just for your relationships, but also for your life?

To step into the fullness of ourselves and our lives requires immense courage. It requires a willingness to make our way into the unknown. Due to our family patterns, the masks we wear, and our adaptive strategies, we're wrapped in the patterns that insulate us from feeling our pain, and the power of presence and choice. You can't live a full life and love with your whole heart if *you* are not fully *here*.

Changing established patterns and removing masks is far from easy. You might wonder why it's so hard to use your voice? Why it's so challenging and paralyzing to lay a boundary for the first time? Why it feels almost impossible to say goodbye to that "friend with benefits," or whatever type of relating that is not in service of your deepest desires? Why does all this sometimes feel so difficult? Why does the body seem to feel stuck? Or why does our voice just not work when we need it the most?

Look, if you're changing a relationship pattern, you are likely changing generations of established behaviors. It is in your relational DNA! It's woven into the fabric of how your family system operates. And, often, our cultures and religions have only reinforced our masks and roles. There's *a lot* of momentum moving us in the direction opposite of liberation. There's a lot of perceived (and historically validated) safety (read: certainty) in continuing to choose the same things. You're going to ruffle feathers. You're going to face resistance. And that resistance will come from within as well as from those you're in relationship with.

When you break up with who you've been, you're healing your lineage. You're changing your family tree. You're altering your destiny. You're healing your "stuff" so your kids don't get handed the baggage you got handed. And if you've already handed some baggage down, have no fear, it's never too late to heal and take your baggage back and turn it into deeper trust and connection. Yup, this is what radical responsibility looks like. Taking ownership for your side of the street.

Radical responsibility means claiming our truth, telling the truth, and being willing to disappoint others. Who, when, and how much do we disclose? This all comes down to discernment. What is appropriate will depend on the specific dynamic and the intention you hold. To "tell the truth" we need to check in with ourselves and ask what conversations we have been avoiding and why we are avoiding them. Living a life where we are free from lies, in whatever capacity, is liberating. Discernment is learned one conversation at a time.

Responsibility also requires growing up—to cross the developmental threshold from adolescence to adulthood requires us to move out of the traps that blame, shame, and guilt keep us stuck in. These blind spots are like anvils ... that weigh us down and hold us back from stepping into integrity. The old story that dies as we break up with mediocrity is that we're not worthy of more. That we're not worthy of love. And that our self-worth depends on if people love and approve of us. Instead, ask yourself: *Do I love and approve of myself? Do I like my choices? Do I actually like who I'm being? Am I living my life in alignment with my values?* Ask yourself these questions daily! Pin them to your wall, for heaven's sake! These are your check-in questions to determine if you are consistently showing up for yourself, acting in alignment, and taking radical responsibility for your life and your choices.

Remember, if you don't love your choices, you won't love yourself. If you're living a life misaligned with your values, you won't value yourself. It is *you* who must claim this. It is *you* who must say, "*Enough!* No longer will I stand for this. No longer will I allow myself to play small. No longer will I blame others for why I don't get to have the life and love I want."

Leaving with Love

You've made the shifts, you've had the hard conversations, and you've given it your all to heal and work through the blocks you're facing—individually and within your relationship. And yet, despite your devotion and energy, something still stands in the way. When this is the case, as it was for us, sometimes the most loving thing we can do is break up.

We didn't arrive to our ending lightly. How could we? We had built a life together—had a beautiful community of friends, a home, and shared dreams and desires for our future. Yet, when we arrived at the end of relationship 1.0, we were half dead and heartbroken.

Sitting across from each other at our kitchen table, we held hands and looked each other in the eyes. I (Mark) said: "I am going to create a family and a beautiful life with someone, and I would like that someone to be you. If you can't do that with me, for whatever reason, that's okay. If you can't choose this, for whatever reason, that's okay. I still love you. And I will always have love for you. But I can't continue to build something in the wrong direction. If this relationship requires that you believe you're broken to be in it, then I can't consciously choose to be in this relationship with you either. A relationship should never be a prison. You are free to go if you need to."

My (Kylie's) tear-filled response? "You're right . . . something has to change." Defeated, and with no more energy to keep trying to force something that couldn't be forced, I knew that I couldn't keep moving in this direction either.

After months and months and months (and months) of denial, terror, fear of the unknown, grief, and questions (*Will I find another person who cares for me in this way? Will people think I'm broken because I couldn't make it work? Will I ever be able to create the life, family I desire? Will I be alone?*), finally, we had arrived at a turning point.

This turning point was the place where both of us stopped running from our lifelong patterns and finally faced the most terrifying possible truth: that two good, well-intentioned people who loved each other dearly were not meant to be together romantically. We accepted a truth that had been trying to make itself known for a while. We suffered in the denial of it. We tried to therapize it. We tried to coach it. We tried to do anything but face and choose the thing that demanded to be faced and chosen.

The choice we thought would bring our destruction ultimately brought our liberation and the opportunity to meet and cultivate a love—one free of control and manipulation—that we would've never found had we kept living by our same codependent scripts: "I need you to be okay." "I need you to choose me to feel worthy."

This is the magic of release (and endings) that we are all being invited to trust over and over again on this human journey. To release the grip on what was—and who we were—so that something more authentic, aligned, and fulfilling may emerge.

EXERCISE
The Art of Letting Go

If you're ready for liberated love, then you're ready to face endings with your heart open. Which means instead of running from the pain (while also not ignoring it!) you acknowledge that you can't go back to behaviors that are not in alignment with your soul's desire for liberation and love.

Ask yourself:

- *What are you done doing? What habits and behaviors no longer serve you and what you want to create?*
- *Who are you done being? What masks are you done wearing?*
- *What blind spot(s) are you done with? What choices/behaviors could you implement that would liberate you from your blind spot(s)?*
- *What do you want more of?*
- *What habits/rituals do you need in your life?*
- *What are you committed to creating?*
- *What are you breaking up with? Who are you breaking up with? (Think of any relationship where you must wear masks and participate in patterns that shrink the possibility between you and them.) Remember, this isn't about leaving everybody behind, it's about rising and inviting them to rise too, with you, if that feels right for you and them.*

PART 2

The Sacred Pause

6

Liberation through Limitation

Within every caterpillar is a set of imaginal cells—a blueprint of something beautiful and exquisite to come. We believe you, like the caterpillar, have seeds of potential within you. Seeds that hold the template for something more true, aligned, and beautiful to come. Seeds that will guide you in a process of metamorphosis, a process of becoming . . . when the time is ripe.

For centuries, our ancestors who had a deep connection with and reverence for the Earth knew the power of ritual containers—cocoons, if you will—to support us in maturing developmentally (emotionally, relationally, psychologically, and spiritually) and *remembering* our own unique place in the world. Without these traditional rites of passage, most of us don't step into the chrysalis of transformation consciously or willingly. In fact, like the caterpillar, most of us are forced by some external event (a breakup, diagnosis, loss) into the chrysalis—a dissolution process—that leaves us with two options: rot or become. Grasp the past or release. Clutch to rigid frameworks or open to possibility. Reject reality or accept it. Continue to project our pain or take responsibility. Control or surrender. Stay or soar.

What if, instead of crawling along, waiting for something to happen, we grabbed the reins to life and said, "You know what?! I need to *do* something. I need to stop what I'm doing, turn inward, and find myself. I need a cocoon."

When we consciously accept the chrysalis, we are trusting the cyclic nature of death and rebirth—we are accepting the challenge and invitation to become. Like the caterpillar, these times of intentional withdrawal—of becoming biological and proverbial mush—are crucial for transformation. Which is why, in this chapter, we're going to support you in creating your cocoon. It's time to reconnect with your inner mystery and come home to who you truly are.

The practice of liberation through limitation—of creating an intentional time-bound container in order to redirect our energy into the present, activate our potential, and deepen our relationship with our true self—is an ancient one. We've seen these types of practices take place all over the world and in certain religions for centuries. Some believers in containers fast (abstain from food for a period of time) with the intent to purify and connect with God. Others, like some monks in monasteries, take vows of silence for months and sometimes even years. And then, of course, you've got the Catholic nuns and priests who have made a vow to a lifetime of celibacy . . . talk about some serious devotion, right?

The practice of conscious limitation shows up in more modern expressions too—from sober January, meatless Mondays, digital detoxes, and even dark retreats where people limit light, connection, and sensory stimuli.

Taking intentional space—what we call a sacred pause—is some of the most effective medicine available to us on the planet. It is through the creation of this space from "normal" or what has been—whether that's drinking cocktails, eating cheeseburgers, doom scrolling, or bingeing Netflix—where we begin to separate from old patterns and dynamics and observe our internal world, differentiate our true self from distorted identities, and *finally* tend the younger parts that yearn to be met in healthier ways. As we engage in this work, we cultivate the capacity to be with ourselves and process the accumulated trauma we've been carrying in our bodies. When we slow down, it becomes easier to witness our unhealthy responses to life, and we are no longer left at the unconscious whim of deeper patterns and imprints.

Which is why, after our breakup, I (Kylie) needed a relational reset.

Four months after our breakup, I began a three-month journey consciously taking space and limiting myself from dating, seeking, having sex, and relating with men. My commitment to myself was to not text, date, social-media creep, be intimate with, or engage romantically with men, including and *especially* with Mark. Little did I know that this would bring me to the depths of my fears, the truest longings in my heart, and painfully reconnect me to my own body.

Right after I chose the start date (January 12) and end date (April 5) for my container, my nervous system went *full tilt*. To put it lightly, I was, uh, FREAKING OUT. Some of the dialogue and stories that emerged from the depths were: *I'm not capable of doing this work. I am going to die. I am going to lose him forever. I can't survive on my own. I need men in order to know who I am. I'm worse off than I ever was. I should be doing something useful. If nobody loves me, I won't exist. WHO AM I?*

Becoming primal muck—caterpillar goo—is an agonizing process filled with confusion, pain, and more questions than answers.

The intensity of this fear response initially shocked me. *Why am I so terrified to be alone? Why is my system so activated?* As we create space and enter an intentional time-bound container, we'll be interfering with deep neurobiological grooves, habits, and dynamics that have been a source of safety and regulation for a *long* time. The choice to limit something that we rely on for safety and regulation shakes our systems, both internally and externally ... and that's the whole point! To shake it up and push the neglected parts of us forward to be witnessed—the parts that drive unhealthy dynamics from outside our conscious awareness.

During this time, I was brought back to the core of codependency and the corresponding beliefs that held this dynamic in place. If we've learned to source safety through our romantic relationships, it's going to be a groundbreaking shift for our system when we say, "Nope, we're not going to source safety from men/women/another for the next three months." We are going to source it from ourselves. No longer are we pleasing others or performing in any way to be loved. No longer are we denying our genuine feelings and our inner mystery.

No longer are we trapped *in* the pattern.

BAM. That's the ticket.

Now, granted, when we make these declarations, we're going to run into many different flavors of resistance. Here are some of the common fears and beliefs that we've seen pop up as clients engage with this work:

+ *I am going to be alone forever.*
+ *No one will be there when I'm done with this work.*
+ *I'm not capable of doing this.*
+ *This is too much.*
+ *I am being selfish, unproductive.*
+ *This is a waste of time.*
+ *This won't work for me.*
+ *I don't need this.*
+ *I am going to die.*
+ *I don't need to do this work; I just met someone and they might be The One.*

When we limit any behavior we've relied on, be it smoking, drinking, social media, sex, sugar, dating, we will begin to give ourselves many reasons why we shouldn't be doing this work—any reason that prevents us from facing reality and moving back into the grief that lives underneath our habitual patterns. This is our mind/body system's attempt at moving us back into safety by redirecting us into dynamics, habits, and behaviors that we know, that are familiar and "normal." Being prepared for and understanding the root of this resistance allows us to meet it with care and tend the younger or deeper parts of us that are afraid of change. The parts of us that don't trust that there can be another way.

My container was how I was able to shift back into empowered choice—no longer chasing and orienting around someone else for my safety and sense of security. No longer pleasing, performing, or shapeshifting. I was anchored in my body, genuine feelings, and instincts, and I finally felt clear, connected, and centered in *myself*.

One of the main reasons we're turning to a practice of conscious limitation—of orienting inward—is because it is extremely challenging to focus on the self when there is someone else. The work of shifting out of core patterns in an environment or relationship that is constantly triggering our core wounds and survival programming is not easy and sometimes feels impossible. Hence the call for space, a sacred pause, and a relational reset.

So,

If you're in a dysfunctional relationship . . .

If you're separated . . .

If you're in a cycle of breaking up and getting back together . . .

If you're single and seeking . . .

If you're single and longing . . .

If you're human, looking to create more peace, love, and choice in your life . . .

We invite you to explore what taking an intentional reset and creating a time-bound container could look like for you at this time in your life. Curious about where to start? We invite you to begin with these two questions:

What people, places, things, and habits in your life feel heavy?

What people, places, things, and habits in your life feel light, easy, and joyful?

Next, go through the "heavy" list and get really real with yourself. What would need to shift to make the relationship to this person/place/thing/habit feel lighter? Can you, in good conscience—prioritizing the intention of growth and restoring *your* wholeness—stay in relationship with this person/place/thing/habit? What boundaries would you need to put in place? Do you need to bid them/it farewell?

Of course, how this sacred pause looks will depend on your specific situation and what feels the most aligned for you at this time, but we'll share a few pathways we've seen our clients take and tell their stories to illuminate how this could unfold for you.

Creating Your Container

As you can imagine, shifting out of core patterns requires an immense devotion to our individual path. It requires a commitment to a destination no matter the circumstances—a north star. Something that matters to us more than our fears and the comfort of our patterns.

So, step number one to creating your container, no matter your circumstances, is to ask yourself: *Where am I now? What feels off? Where am I out of alignment? What am I sick and tired of?* This may sound like: *I am done losing myself in relationship. I am done putting myself last. I am ready to shift out of my toxic work environment.*

Where do you want to end up on the other side? This may sound like: *I want to feel confident, and secure in myself and relationships. I want to know myself. I want to reconnect to my body, instincts, and intuition. I want to release the past and trust myself. I want to feel safe, whole, and empowered.*

The purpose of your time-bound container is to shift out of survival programming, which is akin to a superhighway in our system. It's to step *out* of the pattern so we can both observe and change it. These survival strategies are well-traveled, offering minimal resistance to our mind/body system. They are what we *know.* The roads not so well-traveled are the new patterns, actions, and beliefs that we're shifting into. Taking these dirt roads requires more awareness, more mental and emotional energy, and a more intentional focus on our part—until, eventually, they become more fortified through continual right action and a recoding of safety in our system.

In neuroscience there's a saying, "Neurons that fire together, wire together." The container allows us to leave the old road behind and begin building a new one. One that serves who we truly want to be and what we truly want to create.

The destination? *You are directing your inner GPS toward wholeness, integration, and the creation of the experience of liberated love.* This liberation means making intentional choices of what roads you will build and how you're going to get to where you want to go. However, this sometimes requires us to take a break from driving to learn new maps and new possibilities. To pull into a dusty motel and rest for the night. To milk the metaphor as much as possible, think about the sacred pause as choosing to suspend your license until you're truly fit to drive.

Which leads us to step number two. Create your speed limits (sorry, had to).

Whether it's simply taking space from the old ways of doing things ("For the rest of this year, I am devoted to telling you the truth, taking the space I need, and honoring my needs"), removing or limiting daily distractions (taking a month off from social media, TV, shopping, alcohol, workaholism, etc.), or taking intentional time away from relationships that aren't supportive of your healing journey (deciding to skip out on the holidays or not see a particularly hurtful friend for a few months), the best way to set yourself up for success is to provide limits not only around how you are acting but also around the amount of time you are deciding to do it.

And step number three? Mark your calendars. Set the clock.

Time is a sacred ingredient in any transformation process. If our containers aren't long enough, we risk a premature exit and interference with the transformation that was underway. If we become too comfy in our containers, they become cocoons of comfort and avoidance. Determining the length of time necessary that is supportive for your growth becomes a question for you, your partner (if you're in a relationship), and your body to live into and explore. Tune into your body; what amount of time feels right to you? Is there an amount of time that feels on the edge of scary, yet possible? The beautiful thing about setting our limits around time is we can always check in with ourselves and assess. *Do I need more time to do this work? Do I/we feel ready to end this? What is my motivation for ending/ extending my container? Do we/I still need more space?*

When it comes to relationships—whether you're in love, fresh out of love, or looking for love—the subject brings with it unique containers. What your container looks like is solely up to you. We recommend that everyone creates their own container even if they are doing this work in partnership to focus on what patterns and specific behaviors they are looking to explore and shift. Remember, these containers are about coming home to self first . . . so that we can bring an "I" with genuine feelings and intact instincts back into our relationships. Before we move on to some examples of what this might look like, we want to remind you that there is a powerful technology at work in consciously and intentionally (co)creating these containers. Our souls and cells respond when we set a clear intention and create the space to be worked on—in every way.

In Relationship

It is possible to create a sacred pause while still staying in your relationship—to "break up" and still stay together—but let us be the ones to tell you that it can be *incredibly* difficult.

When Ella came to work with me (Kylie), she was adamant on making it work with her partner, Ben. She had moved countries, and created a home, community, and a life that she was terrified to let go of. Instead of moving too fast into a conversation around breaking up, they wanted to give this relationship their all—they wanted to leave everything on the table so that if there was an ending (eventually) they would know they gave it everything they had. For them, this looked like taking an intentional period of celibacy—to disrupt their pattern of soothing and avoiding through sex—so that they could get to the deeper issue of insecurity in their relationship. In addition, they decided to see a couples therapist every week for four months to support them in working through their relational blocks and entrenched patterns.

The only way to move forward intentionally in this space is to allow all possibilities (and one of those possibilities, whether you like it or not, is ending the relationship). The commitment of the intentional container is in service of love, truth, and what is best for *both* souls, as well as the souls of your children, should you have any. The greatest lesson to children does not come from two parents who stay together no matter what—it is two parents who are dedicated to love, growth, and liberation. We say all of that and acknowledge the fear this might bring up for you and your partner.

The biggest prerequisite to doing this work is that *both of you have to want to do it*. If one of you already has your foot out the door, then this container cannot be shared. You can be afraid of a potential ending. You can feel like that might be the answer. But you have to be open to other answers. The baseline you want to come back to as you lovingly and openly enter this space of individual and relational self-discovery is to allow yourself to be surprised by what you find.

So, what could creating a container in a relationship look like?

- *Create Space from Your Partner*
  - » Travel—Going on a trip or adventure that allows you to have space to nurture yourself and reground.
  - » Get a separate place for yourself—Moving out for a period of time to reevaluate the relationship and reconnect to yourself.
  - » Separate bedrooms—Finding a space for you to come back into your own energy to feel, process, and be with your internal world while you both do this work.
  - » Conscious celibacy—Most of our wounding cycles show up in the bedroom. Sex is often used as a placebo for healing. If celibacy is already happening due to disconnection, this is about explicitly naming that reality and engaging in this choice consciously. *It shifts the energy when the limitation is coming from choice instead of avoidance.*
  - » Pull your energy back—Stop trying to change, fix, control, push, or prod your partner (energetically, verbally, behaviorally). No one *likes* to be treated in these ways.
- *Enter an Intentional Healing Dynamic*
  - » Decide to work with a therapist, guide, or mentor for a specific amount of time to explore what's coming up in your relationship. Bringing a neutral third party in can be incredibly supportive when working with entrenched patterns and dynamics.
  - » Take a course or read a book together to better understand your dynamic and learn new relational skills.
  - » Examine your relationship. Ask: How is this going? How are you feeling? Then cocreate new agreements. Set a time to check in weekly and see how both people in the relationship are feeling.
- *Break Up*
  - » Separate for a period of time. Sometimes, breaking up is the most loving gift we can give each other. This space can be especially healing for you and your relationship if you've

been in an on-again, off-again dance for years. If breaking up seems like the best option for you and your relationship, explore what this time apart might look like. *Are we moving out and putting in a no-contact policy for three months? Are we separating, focusing on ourselves, doing our own healing work, and connecting weekly to see where we're at?* There is no right way to go about an intentional separation, but in our experience, it helps to have clear agreements in place. For example: During this time, we are devoted to self-work. We will not date or "open" ourselves to other people at this time. Let's agree to have a monthly check-in to see where we are both at. Sit down with your partner and get curious about what feels good and supportive for both of you.

We want to honor the anxiety that might come up in discussing and navigating these options and exploring what a container looks like for you and your partner. This is normal. This is healthy. Create agreements that allow this fear to come forward and to be in service of what is best for both of you as individuals, and for the relationship, whatever that looks like.

Single and/or Dating

It has been four years since Sarah's last serious relationship, and she came to me (Mark) *ready* to find a man and be in relationship again. She, like many of the women we've worked with, was tired of dating unavailable men. But we all know people like Sarah, who say they're tired of unavailable and toxic relationships, and yet keep finding themselves in those relationships. Why is that? Well, being tired of a behavior or choice doesn't seem to be enough to fully stop it, right? It takes more than desire and exhaustion; it takes making intentional choices about what we want to create in our relationships.

When Sarah heard about a container that was about healing—which meant no dating and no intimacy for three months—her first reaction was, "Uh, nah. I need to get into a relationship now! It's been four years!"

What most people don't realize until they're *in* the container is that the container is what allows us to feel into our power, and also where we give our power away.

When we're trying to change a partner-selection pattern, we need to take a break from relating because it allows us to feel into what we were previously unconsciously drawn toward. Usually, this pattern comes from being drawn to a familiar tension that was imprinted early in our lives and associated with love. You know the drill. This tension is usually an unavailable parent, unreliable caregiver, or perhaps neglect or abandonment.

When you're ready to change your partner-selection pattern do this:

+ Become hyper-observant of the person/people you're desperately being drawn toward. Who looks like the embodiment of all your past relationships (signs of unavailability, self-absorption, bending the truth, etc.)? This is your kryptonite and an invitation to break your patterns. Make a list of these characteristics and stay. Away. From. Them.

+ Have a friend on call who is ready to support you in avoiding whom your chemistry is drawing you toward.

+ Get ready to be uncomfortable! Change requires the unfamiliar. The unfamiliar is scary, even if it's in the direction of healthy. Have some self-care practices on deck.

+ You might not find your new reliable, boundaried, respectful partnership template hot . . . *yet*. When we can trust ourselves with whom we choose, reliability becomes a deadly, sexy, delicious aphrodisiac. *Wild*, right?! Get ready, because someone who texts you back and does what they say they're going to do is going to have your loins tingling.

The container is imperative to healing patterns because it allows the space you—yes, you, yourself, and *just* you—need to relate to the world without that pattern being activated. Most people who jump from relationship to relationship are afraid of sitting in this too. They need the constant stimulus of the wound in order to avoid the grief and pain in the wound. Ironically, of course, this pattern has us living in it. In short, the container allows you to stop choosing others over yourself.

What it looks like to choose yourself:

* Committing to choices that expand you. If something is keeping you the same, or shrinking you, it's not for you anymore. Be done with that. YOU HEAR US?! DONEZO.
* Choosing health.
* Choosing growth.
* Choosing love.
* Committing to being uncomfortable.
* Celebrating your wins.
* Enlisting a cheering squad who supports you becoming your best and highest self.
* Increasing your capacity for hope and possibility.
* And finally, *choosing conviction* (creating what you most desire) over convenience (Lisa Nichols said this once to me [Mark] and it completely shifted how I live).

When I explained this to Sarah—and that on the other side of the container was a woman who would be able to smell unavailability the moment Tinder sent a notification—she was *all-in*, excited to put this pattern behind her.

"This container sounds like a detox," Sarah remarked.

It's exactly that. We must get sober from all of the things that pull us away from ourselves. By entering the container, we are saying "no" to previous patterns of love that have been infused with dysfunction. We no longer are drawn to those who can't choose us because, for a specific amount of time, we have chosen to hold our integrity and intention for transformation. In other words, we have demonstrably chosen *ourselves*.

When Sarah completed her container, which was filled with test after test, she reentered the dating world committed to what she wanted. She trusted herself in relation to others because throughout the container she was the living evidence that what she wants matters. She moved through previous patterns and opened herself up to *receiving* love instead of chasing it.

What was available to Sarah through this work is available to anyone. And if you're kinda thinking maybe this would be good for you, follow that call.

Whether you are fresh out of a relationship or have been single for some time, here are some ways for you to create that much-needed space for yourself:

- Remove yourself from the dating scene (bye-bye, Tinder!)
- Stop seeking a partner
- Place a no-contact boundary with previous partners (potential partners)
- Zero booty calls and intimacy
- No more stalking exes or potential partners on social media
- Stop interacting and messaging and using *all* your strategies to get attention and feel desired
- Start saying "no" to the things that drain your energy
- Take intentional space from friendships, relationships that drain your energy (e.g., nonreciprocal and codependent)

If you've been single for a while, the thought of intentionally creating space from dating and seeking a partner can feel counterintuitive and straight-up backward. Echoes of "I've already been in a no-dating container for the last *X* years" spring to mind. But, for all of our single friends out there, we want to remind you that when you intentionally *choose* not to date or seek out a partner—even for a short amount of time—you begin to realize how much of your energy actually went toward finding one. As this energy frees up, a powerful reset can occur that shifts years-old dating patterns—like choosing unavailable partners and settling for crumbs.

When conscious choice is involved, everything shifts.

Navigating Choice Points and
Boundary Violations

Throughout your time container you will have to choose repeatedly: stay the same or evolve. We call these moments on the path choice points, and they are the crossroads we all stand at in certain moments of our lives when we must choose to repeat a pattern or use a new way of responding. A choice point can look like many things, such as choosing to text the guy you're taking space from when you've had a hard day, choosing to say yes out of obligation to a family event because you're afraid of what might happen if you don't go, or, alternatively, honestly expressing and honoring what feels supportive and loving to you.

Just because we create an intention to limit something doesn't mean we won't be confronted with a million choice points along the way. Remember, you are moving in opposition to the deepest, oldest grooves in your system. If you've ever tried to cut out sugar, alcohol, or social media from your life, you know exactly what we're talking about. Our minds are superstars at finding the reason it's okay this time or the reason that justifies us breaking our own boundaries and commitments. When we find ourselves at these crossroads, it helps to have a visual reminder, an anchor, that reminds us of our intention—our *why*—behind doing this work. This can be an altar you create to honor this work, a written message on your mirror, or a reminder you set on the home screen of your phone.

I (Kylie) remember an awareness I had when I realized I was going to a specific spin class to try to get the attention and validation of the male instructor. This was early on in my no-man container, and I was seeking a hit—an "I matter, I still exist" hit. *Who am I without the male gaze? Do I matter or even exist anymore?*

It was a choice point, and I had to decide between: a) meeting and soothing these fears and needs myself through healthier pathways, or b) continuing to seek this external validation from the spin instructor. This time, I chose to meet and tend to my needs instead of chasing the validation I craved. That time, I chose to honor my container and limits. Which wasn't the case always . . . and brings me to the time when I broke every agreement of my no-man container.

I was a couple of months into the journey, and I was beginning to regain trust and strength in my body, a place I dreamt about reaching for years. That is, until a sneaky fear entered my system and took over.

The fear said, "If you don't reach out, you're going to lose him forever."

With this fear in the driver's seat, I replied to one of Mark's Instagram stories. Suddenly I found myself sitting face-to-face with Mark, and eventually going all the way with him. I thought to myself, moments after (and even during), *HOLY high heavens, how did I get here?!*

This boundary violation rocked me to my core. And it stung even more because it was *all on me*. I immediately collapsed into shame spiraling, heartbreak, and embarrassment. I couldn't believe that I had done that to myself and to Mark. Because I was afraid to lose him forever, I broke my container and my word.

Boundary violations, whether they are made by self or by someone else, are going to happen as we do this work. These ruptures of trust are prime opportunities for learning, and the way we do that is through a process of repair. This is where learning becomes healing.

So, what are the steps to repair the violation?

1. *Notice where punishment blocks reconciliation.* Are you a pro at giving the cold shoulder, turning the other way, ignoring texts, and punishing others when they've hurt you? Do you shame and berate yourself for making a mistake? Explore how punitive consciousness blocks repair attempts from others, and with self.

2. *Acknowledge the rupture with compassion.* In relationship, this may sound like, "I'm sorry I hurt you and didn't operate from a space of kindness and respect. I should've stepped back. I want to move past this and come back together with you." With yourself this might sound like, "I'm sorry I didn't honor or listen to you . . . I know that hurt you, and I promise to do better next time."

3. *Process shame, grief, blame, sadness with self and community.*

When we experience a big rupture in our life, having an empathic witness—someone to hold, process, and reassure us that
it's okay to make mistakes and that we are still loved—is necessary medicine.

4. *Reassess commitment.* Is this limit or boundary supportive, sustainable, and doable for me at this time? Is there a more loving
   and achievable boundary I/we could put in place instead?

5. *Adequately resource.* What do I need to stay grounded in my center, and to move forward with more clarity, kindness, and consciousness? For example: a support group, friend, or ritual that
   brings you back to your center when activated.

6. *Recommit to your devotion, intention.* Remember the "why" underneath it all. For example, *I am devoted to love, my authentic path,
   and soul.* This clarity is what keeps you moving in the direction of
   wholeness and healing.

This boundary violation showed me that I hadn't fully let go and grieved
the ending of our relationship. Gah, grief and endings are so hard! I knew
I needed to *let go* of Mark regardless of which direction we both decided to
take at the end of my container.

The truth is Mark could've moved on, and that was a truth I needed to
accept and be okay with. I needed to meet the fear of losing him head-on
so that I could shift out of fear and into trusting myself. Imagine the difference between orienting to a relationship from a place of fear (*I'm going to
lose him!*) versus from a place of trust (*If this is meant to be and is in highest
alignment for us both, it will be!*). When we move from a space of trust, we
feel empowered, connected, and clear.

I needed to reconnect with the embodied truths: *I will be okay no matter
what happens. I trust that what is meant for me will be.* To reconnect and
ground yourself into these truths, I had to release the childlike belief that
someone was going to come save me from my pain, and from my confusion.
I needed to release the fantasy and say hello to reality: *No one is coming
to save you.* Facing this truth catalyzed my journey into healthy dependence—a space where I was dependent on my own instincts, intuition for

guidance (over following others, or doing what Daddy/Mommy says), my own sense of inner safety and security (over outsourcing it at the expense of self), and my own sense of worth (over pretending to be someone else or proving myself). This soul dependence opens the door for true choice to emerge. And it all happens to us alone, in a cocoon of our own making.

Soul Dependence

It can be easy to romanticize the process of becoming, of maturing, of rebirthing ourselves. Without knowing what goes on in the caterpillar's cocoon (it's gnarly) we simply see the metamorphosis from caterpillar to beautiful butterfly. But in reality, as much as it's beautiful and relieving on a soul level, it's a painful process of dissolution on the human level.

The cocoon is both a coffin and a portal—a coffin for the previous version of you and a portal into the next version of you. It's accepting the challenge to grow and the agony that comes along with it. To ripen into adults and become soul dependent—where you can be free from fickle dependencies and rest in who you are, what you want, and what you know to be true from the deepest recesses of your being—we're invited to meet our fears, release control, cherish and inhabit our bodies, welcome home the neglected parts of ourselves, release the past, and grieve what was (or what wasn't). A process where we learn to sit with ourselves in the longings and the aloneness. It is a process of stripping away the armor and the masks—of becoming that primal goo—for the sake of evolution. And it's a solo journey that only you can take for yourself.

Even if you choose not to create a container, our ultimate hope for you is that you *transform*. It's that you answer the call your relationships are inviting you toward. Changing patterns is hard, but creating these intentional time-bound containers is one of the best ways we know of to initiate this change without life having to force you to. These containers facilitate the movement from unhealthy dependence to healthy dependence and, eventually, interdependence—of healed and authentic individuals coming together in community. Because here's the deal: As adults we can't go back in time and recreate childhood and expect another adult to guide us and meet every need we have. This isn't realistic or empowering, to say the least. Instead of going backward, we're inviting you to move forward by taking responsibility for your life, needs, and energy in the present moment, and begin the process of reconnecting with your own soul as your north star and deepest ally.

In other words: Create a damn container. *Now.*

Say it with us: "I'm done with these patterns and dynamics, and I am ready to MAKE a shift and do something about it." As you do this, the energy you once used to manage your external environment begins to return to you—allowing you the energy and space you require to meet yourself and focus on your needs, desires, and values again. Hallelujah!

WAIT. Are we saying that on the other side of the container you will be an energized relationship wizard? YES. Yes, we are. We go from chasing others to heal our wounds to becoming the type of person who creates relationships where wounds are healed.

This is the beautiful work of liberating yourself from patterns and healing what our relationships and life often prevent us from feeling. You are worthy of everything your heart desires. Unlike what your culture (ahem, Disney) taught you, your value is not in someone choosing or saving you. Your value is your birthright. It is innate. It is. And you are. You are valuable and worthy, full stop. You must choose to press pause and acknowledge that value, so you can stop chasing it in others.

EXERCISE
Creating Your Cocoon

Before you begin to map out your healing cocoon and the specifics of your container, we invite you to drop into your heart and name your intention for doing this work.

Grab a piece of paper and draw a giant circle on it. At the top, write your intention for doing this work. Then, below, write your start-date and end-date (*we recommend a minimum of three months*).

Within the circle write down everything that is a "yes" for you. These yeses will be the ways in which you **nourish** and support yourself in honoring your intention.

SOME EXAMPLES OF YESES:

- Sisterhood/brotherhood circle
- Asking for support
- Saying "no"
- Honoring your nervous system's capacity
- Dancing/movement practices
- Eating nourishing foods, staying hydrated
- Spending time in nature
- Creating a practice of solitude and stillness
- Ceremony and ritual (cacao, tea, grounding, etc.)
- Reading, singing!
- Writing, painting, drawing
- Honoring your body
- Pleasure

Outside of the container write down everything that is a "no" for you. These are the things that will distract and push you further away from living in alignment with the work you are being called to do. These are the things that de-anchor you, disconnect you from you, and drain your energy/life force.

SOME EXAMPLES OF NOS:

- Numbing with substances
- People-pleasing and caretaking (at the expense of self)
- Scrolling on social media and distractions
- Dating, dating apps, sex, flirting, seeking (if you want to enter intentional celibacy)
- Saying yes out of obligation/expectation
- Abusive/toxic environments
- Sourcing validation from others or from social media

In the right corner of your paper (outside the circle) make a list of your "maybes"—these are the things you are exploring and discerning whether they are supportive for you currently.

SOME EXAMPLES OF POTENTIAL MAYBES INCLUDE:

- Alcohol and substances (examining your relationship with them)
- Dating and dating apps
- Sacred sexuality (intimacy)
- Asking for support (financial, etc.)
- Deepening relationships with family members

When you are tuning into your yeses, nos, and maybes, it's important to check in with the motivation underneath the decision. *Is this coming from a space of connection (taking me deeper into connection with self), or is this a way to disconnect and default into familiar patterns? Which part of me is making this choice? The integrated adult or the fearful inner kid?*

This is a space to be fully human—to mess up—and to learn along the way. We will all bump up against the edges of the containers we created. That's the point. To get curious where the edges are and to meet the parts of us that are terrified to move into a different way of being in this world. It's in these intentional containers where you get to meet the parts of you that are ready to be seen, witnessed, and held.

7

The Body Is the Bridge

Most of us feel at odds with our bodies. We judge them for how they look, deny or numb the signals and sensations they bring forward, harm them through toxic behaviors, and do our best to try to control and dominate them into submission. If we used these same words to describe any relationship dynamic, we would easily, without skipping a beat, say that this relationship is dysfunctional. And, like any dysfunctional relationship, our advice to anyone would be simple: something needs to shift ASAP.

What is your relationship with your body like? Is it nourishing and kind, or punitive, controlling, and shame-based? Do you listen to your body's innate intelligence and feedback, or do you ignore it?

The process of befriending the body and inhabiting it fully is layered, and for many, a complex and painful one. It certainly was for us, and even with the immense amount of grief and pain that accompanied us at moments along the way, this return back to the body is and *always* will be worth it. Restoring trust in the body, coming alive to felt sensations again, and *remembering* the inherent wisdom and divine nature of the body can be described in one word: *life-changing*. Before we begin this journey home to the most important relationship we have—that with our bodies/selves/

souls—we want to explore how this relationship became so distorted and fractured in the first place.

The body itself has been objectified, sexualized, violated, racialized, subjugated, commodified, colonized, and exploited for a very long time in many regions on this planet. The degree of impact each of us experiences from these traumatic imprints depends on the body we inhabit, what we (and our ancestors) have experienced, and the environment we find ourselves in today. The reason we treat our bodies in harmful ways is because this is the only way we know how to cope with the activation and pain they carry. In addition, we treat our bodies in self-harming ways because self-domination (controlling how we show up and what we bring forward) is how we learned to survive in this world. If taking up space or sharing your emotions was punishable or dangerous, you'll do what you need to do to stay small and silent. If being valuable and desirable means losing an extra ten pounds, you'll do what you need to do to slim down.

These traumatic imprints and the culture(s) we live in have done and continue to do a tremendous job at severing us from our bodies—our roots—which in turn disconnects us from ourselves, our natural human rights, and our test ground for truth.

One of the trickiest parts about naming and healing these intergenerational imprints and the trauma adaptations that come with them is the fact that we were born into them. They are the *invisible* limits we inherited and the subconscious survival instructions we live by—until we recontextualize what has been decontextualized over time. This layer of trauma didn't happen to us, but it *still* travels with us, determining what we subconsciously believe is possible and safe and what isn't. Many of the blocks we experience—mentally, emotionally, somatically, professionally, and relationally—have to do with the trauma our ancestors experienced and the trauma adaptations that have been transferred to us through our DNA. To break through these invisible limits (internalized parameters) and break free from these inherited trauma adaptations, we're going to zoom out and explore how intergenerational trauma, in addition to individual and collective trauma, keeps our bodies and minds frozen in the past. We call this "the great thaw" because that's exactly what we'll be doing:

thawing our systems from survival states and stories that have kept our ancestors—and now us—stuck, depressed, and anxious.

The Great Thaw

Activated and afraid, a group of lab mice ran away and found themselves frozen with terror when the *heavenly* smell of cherry blossoms was piped into their cage. Objectively, cherry blossoms are not a threat to mice. But for these mice, simply smelling cherry blossoms triggered a survival response. This confused the mice. In their little minds they were wondering, "Why are we so anxious and afraid when we smell cherry blossoms? They smell so good! And yet, all we want to do is run." These mice, like many of us when we run into invisible walls in our lives and relationships, are missing the full picture. It wasn't until they traveled back in time and two generations up their ancestral lines that they began to gain more context as to where this fear originated.

Their grandparents, when introduced to the smell of cherry blossoms, were simultaneously zapped with mild electrical shocks—causing a stress and fear response that became associated with the smell of cherry blossoms. To protect themselves from the impending shocks, their bodies went on high alert whenever the scent of cherry blossoms entered the air. Cherry blossoms equaled pain. These mice weren't "broken" because they were afraid of a smell; they were conditioned to have a stress response in order to protect them from danger. They were *taught* to fear cherry blossoms, just like many of us have been taught to fear—through the trauma of oppression—our own power, authentic expression, sexuality, sensuality, magic, and brilliance.

From this study, the researchers determined that these mice developed epigenetic markers that transmitted a traumatic experience across generations—changing the way their offspring behaved, related to, and reacted in the presence of cherry blossoms, despite never having had their own negative experience. This is survival. This can serve us; however, it can also mysteriously hold us back from self-expression, love, connection, access to emotions, trust, and so on. This research, along with other studies in neuroscience, continues to show us that what's happening within our bodies—our nervous systems—is dependent not only on what we ourselves experience in this lifetime but also on what we *silently* carry in the form of survival instructions and trauma adaptations from the previous generations.

What cherry blossoms were you taught to fear? Speaking your truth, stepping into your power, becoming too successful, setting boundaries, opening your heart, trusting others? What comes up for you? Whatever your cherry blossom is, when we have something we've been unconsciously taught to fear and avoid (as so many of us do) we unknowingly sabotage ourselves as a form of self-protection . . . and then blame and beat ourselves up for why we won't *just do that thing that seems* so *simple*. We stay within the lines because, like the mice, we don't trust what's on the other side.

And while the reasons are valid, living in a perpetual state of distress— dodging the cherry blossoms—takes a major toll on our bodies, hearts, and minds. To move out of freeze mode and thaw, we need to come home to our bodies, glance up the family tree, and restore an embodied sense of safety. It's time to step outside the lines and limits we've been handed and claim what is rightfully ours.

It starts with the body.

There's a reason we've been redirecting you back to your body and nervous system again and again and again: *your body is the bridge to your essence, embodied sense of safety, and wholeness.*

As author and healer Resmaa Menakem writes in his book *My Grandmother's Hands*, "The body, not the thinking brain, is where we experience most of our pain, pleasure, and joy, and where we process most of what happens to us. It is also where we do most of our healing, including our emotional and psychological healing." As we make the descent into the body and open ourselves to sensation again—the language of the body—we slowly encounter the preverbal, personal, ancestral, and intergenerational imprints that have disconnected us from our body, soul, and the parts of us that love play and creativity. Hidden underneath these intergenerational and historical imprints, survival identities, and stories lives your original design and divine innocence—the part of you that can never be taken from you, because it *is* you. No matter how far away this truth feels at times, it's here patiently waiting for you to remember. The great thaw is a process of return and remembrance.

The body is always communicating to us through sensations and symptoms. When we learn to listen and get curious about what our body is whispering (or yelling) at us, we cross the bridge back to our body and the wisdom it holds to guide our lives. Maybe you, like us, have experienced sleeplessness when a decision needs to be made, or a stomachache when you're about to have a big vulnerable conversation. When we bring caring attention to the body and the unprocessed pain it has been carrying, we begin to thaw and reopen our system to life, joy, grief, anger, and love again. This happens as we expand our somatic capacity and thus feel safe enough to feel what we're feeling. As we metabolize the pain, we begin to slowly rediscover the beauty of having and being in a body.

Okay, but if being fully embodied is an enriching and magical experience, then why is it so challenging to return to the body and thaw?

Great question.

Just like the mice, we're afraid. And we don't necessarily even know *why* we're afraid, or even that we *are* afraid.

We resist the idea of journeying down into the body—thawing it from head to toe and connecting with every atom—because it's uncomfortable to sit with the embodied grief, rage, shame, fear, trauma, and everything else we (and our previous generations) haven't had the capacity to metabolize.

But it's a beautiful process as well, and hopefully with some time, loving support, and intention, we can learn to love the smell of cherry blossoms again.

The Descent

On this journey to reconnect with our bodies, we're going to take a top-down approach and make our way from the mind to our throat to our feeling heart, through our powerful solar plexus, down to our lower back, pelvis, womb, and testes, and eventually to our root, the base of our spine and the foundation of our physical selves.

Although this journey is mapped out in a linear fashion—from head to root—healing and coming home to the body is far from linear. The body and all its beautiful cells are inseparable and interconnected. In other words, as we heal in one area, we support the healing of every other area.

The reason we're beginning with the mind/brain system is because in the West, most of us live in survival mode, experiencing life from the neck up. It's been safer to live in the mind than in the body. This is especially true when we're in codependent or dysfunctional relationships and our system is either orienting around others or disassociating from ourselves altogether. When we are disconnected from the body and living in our analytical minds, it's hard to hear, trust, and discern the wisdom the body carries via our instincts, emotions, and intuition.

This neck-up orientation leaves us disconnected from not only our throats, hearts, solar plexus, creative center, and roots but also from our truth, creative agency, power, and sense of safety. With care and attention and moving at the right pace (not too fast or too slow), we'll move down and in. Remember, *there is no right or wrong pace, there is only your pace.*

To support you in your thawing process, we will share a variety of tools for each part of the body called "How to Thaw" that have aided our clients to reopen, restore, and reconnect to their bodies. We've already sprinkled many of the tools we mention in this chapter throughout the previous pages: we're thinking of the practice of attunement (emphatic listening and caring for your body), adequate resourcing, and mindfulness. These tools are here to support you to build capacity in your nervous system, creating the space you need to be in the present moment while holding the past and allowing yourself to heal. These tools increase your ability to pause, come back to the body, differentiate the past from the present, and discern what the best path is for you in *this* moment.

To deepen your reflection, we've also included the natural human right associated with each part of your body. It's called "Remember and Restore." For example, the natural human right of your heart is the right to love and be loved. These natural human rights are just that, *natural*, meaning there are no conditions to these rights. You don't have to "earn" them or do something "right" to have them. These are the rights you were born with as a human being. These rights just are. As we thaw our systems, we remember these rights and attune the nervous system to living aligned with our natural rights. Our birthrights.

The Mind

In the West, the body has been split from the mind with logic, mindset, and rationale—the things that perceivably live in our heads—being valued and placed above the body and its wisdom. This split and pseudo-hierarchy has created a division so pervasive that many of us believe that the answers we seek solely live in our minds. That liberation lives in transcending the body, and the healing we crave is found in mindset work. And while mindset work (mindfulness and belief work) is an important component of healing, it's what's happening in our bodies—underneath the brain—that determines which stories play in our minds. *When we are in survival mode, the rational mind goes offline.* So, while we might think we are making a rational choice in these instances, we are far from it. Integration happens—and conscious choice is found—when we come back home to our bodies and restore the mind/body connection.

Our stories don't just live in our heads, they also live in our bodies. Cognitive understanding is not enough. We must learn to *feel* again.

In fact, the *state* of our autonomic nervous system is indicative of our mental landscape. *What happens in the body changes what happens in the brain.* Research demonstrates that 80 percent of the information we receive moves from the body to the brain, while only 20 percent of information moves from the brain to the body.

In other words, the ANS state we are in—whether it be ventral vagal (safe), sympathetic (mobilized), or dorsal vagal (immobilized)—determines the stories we tell ourselves. First, we experience something in the body outside of our conscious awareness, and second, the mind makes sense and meaning from the body's experiences.

Let's take a simple interaction to illustrate this. You go to bed with your partner and you're feeling excited to connect after a long day. Your partner jumps into bed and immediately turns to their phone and begins scrolling social media. You haven't communicated your desire to connect because you think/feel that they should also desire this. A couple of minutes goes by and you're now stewing silently ten inches away. You notice your desire to pick a fight—throw psychic daggers, kick your feet, sigh heavily, or leave the room altogether. Your mind jumps in to validate this mobilized (fight/flee) response, telling you: *He doesn't care about me; all he cares about is his phone; he never makes time for me.* Ten minutes later you think to yourself, *There's no use,* so you turn your back, pull your energy and love away, and give the cold shoulder. Your system has now moved into freeze mode and the mind explains this shift by telling you: *Nothing will ever change. This is just how it is. It's not worth a conversation, he won't hear me anyways. Let it go.*

All of this, with zero words uttered.

Over time, the states we chronically live in, and the stories we tell ourselves to validate these states, begin to present as anxiety (sympathetic response) and/or depression (immobilization response). The tricky part about this is your mind will do everything to keep you in the state you are in to keep you safe and within the lines of what is known. It's safer to turn a cold shoulder and collapse into apathy then it is to bring our voice forward and express our desires.

As depth psychologist James Hillman said, "You cannot heal what you cannot separate from."

This devotion to creating space between the state and story you're telling yourself is a process of differentiating *what is happening (and what is available) right now* with *what happened back then.* This space is created by cultivating the pause, sitting in the space the pause provides, getting curious about the story, and grounding back into the body and present moment.

To circle back to our example with the bedtime phone escapades, it's easy to let the story roll on about why our partner is on their phone and to disconnect from our true desires. We can let this dynamic play out over and over . . . or we can stop, hit the pause button and take a couple of deep breaths, and turn toward our partner and say something like, "Hey, can I share something with you? I'm feeling far from you, and I would love to create some intentional time to connect with you when we get into bed. How does this feel for you?" When we interrupt the pattern, we say yes to solutions and possibility.

As we expand our capacity to regulate and resource in nourishing ways, we create the space and safety our body needs to get curious about the thoughts and stories we hold ... and eventually shift out of them by creating new neural pathways that affirm goodness, worthiness, and agency. This is the transformative power of remembering the mind/body connection. Until we bring what is in the unconscious up and out into the conscious mind, we remain trapped in the stories and limitations of the past. The more at-tuned and aware we become, the less charge these stories hold. Instead of controlling us, they begin to inform us.

How to Thaw: Tracking and attuning to your nervous system states throughout the day helps you notice when you're moving into a state of dysregulation and activation, allowing you to tend to your body. This is the first step, noticing the state you're in or the thoughts you're having. From here, we invite you to name the thought: "I'm noticing the thought that ..." We name it to tame it and to create the space we need to witness/observe the story without becoming it.

As you do this, check in on the sensations in your body. What state are you in? What do you need, and how can you support your system in moving toward regulation? Notice what happens to the story as you shift back into regulation. Does it soften and lose its grasp?

Remember and Restore: As we begin to open our minds and complete stuck survival responses, we remember and restore our natural *right to see and be seen*. When we're no longer frozen in the past, we begin to see life, self, and others more clearly. What do you wish people could see in you? What do you wish to see in yourself? In others?

The Throat

It's often been said that the throat is the bridge between the mind and the heart. It is through our voice that we invite others into the world of our emotions, beliefs, and inner experience. When we feel safe and accepted in our fullness, our throat opens and we communicate with more ease. When we don't feel safe, our throat closes, our "no" is frozen, and we struggle to communicate with authority, or at all.

For some, this pendulum may swing and instead of shutting down to find safety, we create a wall of words around us. We create this wall of words through our verbosity to control the depth of conversation and the level of intimacy available in our connections. Underneath both strategies, whether to dial the volume up (*wall of words*) or dial the volume down (*invisibility*), is a fear of what might happen if we are *truly* seen.

In codependent dynamics, our voice orients around what we think others want to hear to ensure connection and safety. This keeps us disconnected from our authentic expression and the depth of intimacy we crave.

Several of our clients struggle to share their voices and reveal what they are really thinking and feeling with their partners. In some cases, throats would literally close or get sore.

At the core of our clients' closed throats is a fear of what might happen to their relationships once they openly share their authentic expression. *Will they leave me? Will I be misunderstood? Will they judge and reject me? Will I be gaslit? Will my partner treat me how a neglectful caregiver did?*

The truth is, you don't know what will happen when you begin to open that beautiful voice of yours and share what's really going on below the surface. What we do know is this: *everything in life is enriched when we lead with honesty, transparency, vulnerability, and our authentic voice.*

How to Thaw: Where do we begin building this muscle of authentic self-expression? A great place to start is by strengthening your emotional literacy. Being able to name your emotions and your emotional needs is a crucial building block to authentic self-expression. When we can name what's happening within, we can bring it to others with more clarity and kindness.

Practice sharing your feelings, story, and experiences with safe people who can hold you and honor you in your vulnerability. These interactions with safe people model a new way of healthy relating, restoring the belief that your voice matters, and that people can hear you, hold you, and do care about you.

Remember and Restore: It's a beautiful thing when we remember our *right to speak, be heard, and listen.* There is nothing more powerful than feeling our voice shaking but continuing to speak. This is what happens when we show up to our life and relationships committed to the hard conversations regardless of the outcome. The restoration of your right to speak, be heard, and listen in return reaffirms that what you have to say matters and is enough.

The Heart

Returning to our feeling hearts can be a tender process. We might resist opening our hearts for fear that they will be hurt again. We get it; living on the planet today with an open, deeply feeling heart is not always the easiest path to walk. And still, to feel the energy of love move through us makes it worth it.

Our rupture and closing ceremony cracked open our hearts in a way we've never experienced. The tears flowed and flowed, and our hearts quite literally ached. But we didn't run from the grief or the pain. We held it, contained it, and tended to it as if it were sacred—because it is. This metabolized grief cleansed and opened our hearts, inviting us to see the world, each other, and ourselves through a lens of innocence again. But how did we open and thaw? It was less of a how, and more of a surrender.

How to Thaw: We thaw the heart by peeling back the layers of emotional armor that have been protecting (and blocking) us from feeling and receiving love to our fullest capacity.

There are many modalities to support our hearts in being held. Some of our favorites include a breathwork ceremony, cacao ceremony, tea ceremony, and bodywork. These ceremonies and contained spaces are so powerful for healing because they create a contained cocoon of safety. The safer we feel in an environment, space, and/or relationship, the more access we have to feeling/processing what desires to be held, felt, and seen. Grief—our holy tears—is the medicine that peels back the layers, enlivens us, and recenters us. (We'll be going all in on grief in chapter 9!)

Remember and Restore: As we grieve, we increase our capacity to love and be loved. We restore our *right to love and be loved.* And holy moly, what a gift this restoration is to the planet. One, in our eyes, that could transform and heal humanity.

The Solar Plexus

As we move down into our solar plexus, aka our gut, we're invited to explore our relationship to power, our sense of agency, and our ability to take up space. When we find ourselves in dysfunctional environments and codependent dynamics, our ability to access this power, self-confidence, and sense of agency is diminished. If we had access to our power and sense of agency, why would we choose to stay in these types of dynamics? *We wouldn't.*

When we ask our clients about their relationship to power, many of them express that they don't feel like they have a strong connection to their power, gut, or intuition. So, what's blocking them from experiencing their power and stepping into it? One of the biggest blocks to our power is shame and the beliefs of self-disgust and self-hatred that stem from this shame. As author Robert Bly simply states, "Where shame is, power is not."

To showcase the impact of shame, notice what happens to your solar plexus, body, and energy when you read these words: "You suck." "What's wrong with you?" "No one will ever love you." Maybe you noticed your body collapse or your breath become shallow. Or maybe you noticed anger pop up and a desire to move away or defend yourself from these toxic messages. If so, hooray! This connection to your anger is healthy, loving, and protective—a clean anger—and what we're after in this thawing process.

How to Thaw: As we externalize what has been internalized and hand shame back, we begin to gain access to our clean anger and sacred rage. A powerful tool that can support you in this thawing process is your imagination. When you connect to your anger, tune in—what does it want to do and/or say? How does it want to move? Give yourself permission—in your mind's eye—to let your anger move authentically and, if accessible, let your body join in and act it out. As we reconnect to our anger and feel safe enough to feel it, we feel empowered to implement healthy boundaries. Our energy and power returns as we begin to trust that we can protect ourselves and have our own backs. Ask yourself: *Where can I reclaim my power and take up space in my life?*

Remember and Restore: When our gut is strong and our intuition—our inner sun—is shining bright, we feel alive, centered, and empowered. We remember our *right to be in our power* without needing to prove ourselves or earn our right to take up space.

The Sacral

The sacral region of the body, found in the lower back, is home to emotions, creative expression, joyful sensuality, and procreative energies. When the energy is flowing in our sacral area, we're able to feel our emotions, dance with passion and pleasure, honor our "yes" and "no," create without conditions, and experience the beauty of being alive. However, when our energy is blocked here, as you can imagine, the opposite is true—we experience a *lack* of joy, creativity, sense of aliveness, and passion in our lives. In our bodies this imbalance presents as lower back pain, fertility issues, challenges in the genital area, and/or a lack of sexual desire.

What tends to block the flow here is a lack of permission to feel, a lack of self-consent, a lack of internal and external boundaries, and an internalized judgment around our emotions, creativity, sexuality, pleasure, and joy. We might think, *Who am I to feel joy?* or *No one cares about what I have to offer or create,* or *My emotions and feelings are too much,* or *Being sensual and in tune with my body is a sin,* or *It doesn't matter what I want, it matters what they want.* These internalized messages split us off from our feelings, our desires, and our right to respond in ways that are self-honoring.

How to Thaw: To heal this split, we practice giving ourselves the permission we've previously sought outside of ourselves. We create for the sake of creating. We begin dancing because we can dance. We create space to feel when we need to. We say "no" when it's a "no" and "yes" when it's a "yes" (this is a big one when we're breaking free from codependent dynamics).

Another way to support opening this part of the body is a loving-touch practice. The invitation is simple: slow down and intentionally and lovingly put lotion on your body after a bath or shower. Notice what comes up for you when you slow down and tend to your body. How do your body and mind respond when you touch your skin with love and care?

Remember and Restore: As we restore our natural *right to feel*, we begin opening our creative and sensual centers, reconnecting us with the energy of life, creation, and joy again.

The Root

The root, located at the base of our spine, is where our sense of safety, security, and belonging lives. When we are anchored in our root and experience this stable center, we aren't easily pulled by things that are nonthreatening, like a relational challenge, receiving feedback, differing views, or a conversation. The more grounded and secure we are in ourselves, the easier it is to hold our nervous system steady without getting pulled into someone else's activation.

This is the opposite experience of a codependent dynamic, where we always feel like we're having to walk on eggshells and orient around another's emotions to feel safe. This external orientation, as we've discussed, occurs when we are severed from the body.

When we are severed from our root and standing on a rocky inner foundation, we spin in a scarcity wound, feeling like there's never enough, or *I'm not enough*. This scarcity wound feeds the belief that we are separate, worthless, and alone. It feels unsafe to be ourselves and to trust life. This chronic dysregulation expresses physically as an inability to sit still, fatigue, weight swings, chronic illness, and digestive problems. When our roots aren't firmly planted, it's hard for our bodies to access rest and digest mode. It's harder for us to land, open, and be fully here.

How to Thaw: Reconnecting to our root is quite literally finding our feet on the ground and planting them firmly. When our nervous system can access and easily come home to ventral vagal—regulation—our bodies soften and come back into the present moment.

One of the biggest components to thawing our system is remembering the abundance of nourishment and love we have available to us outside of our human relationships. To do this, step outside, breathe in some fresh air, firmly find your feet on the ground, and with deep gratitude ask the Earth to hold you and support you in these ways. As we come home to our connection with all things big and small, we're no longer searching for safety or nourishment outside of ourselves; instead, we remember that we are not separate from life, that we do matter, and that we are here for a purpose. It is in this power and reconnection to self and others that we find our centers. This felt experience of self-belonging opens the door for true belonging.

Remember and Restore: Reconnecting to our root restores our innate *right to be.* As humans this is our base right. You came to this planet on purpose, and you are not a mistake. You weren't born from sin, and you don't have to earn your right to be you and be all that you came here to be. In fact, the reason you're here is exactly that: to be *you* and be all that you can be. When we feel anchored and secure in our center, we're able to move into the depths of intimacy we crave—with ourselves, others, and the world.

This descent is a journey home—to the body, to our hearts, and to our roots. As we thaw, heal, and reconnect to the wisdom of our bodies we restore a sense of coherency. What does it mean to live coherently? Coherency is when all parts of us are aligned, in congruence, and moving in an intentional, life-affirming direction. Not a bunch of disembodied, disconnected parts, but a holistic being where we feel safe and secure.

This felt sense of safety emerges when there is alignment with what we know as truth, and what our bodies feel as truth.

True integration is the congruency between the mind and the body—head, throat, heart, solar plexus, sacral area, and root. When we are congruent, we're able to say: "All of me is here, and aligned with my choices, decisions, and actions." We finally get to play our unique role in the web of life and bring our medicine, our gifts, our voices, and our hearts to the world in a way that only we can. We finally get to enter into a relationship as a whole, sovereign being where one (whole human) plus one (another whole human) equals three (a third energy and entity). When we maintain our wholeness in relationship(s), we give birth to a third energy—where the sum is greater than its parts—a space where two embodied souls can cocreate and contribute their unique gift to the world in a way that only they can. How sweet it is to remember and restore our sacred role in this collective dance.

EXERCISE
Check-In

Set a reminder (literally—whether it's on your phone or on your written to-do list) to check in with your body, emotions, nervous system. Do it three times a day for two weeks. Ask yourself: *How can I support myself right now? What do I need to come back to center? Which part of me is desiring attention, care?* When you notice your system move into activation, place one hand on your heart and another on your solar plexus and repeat: "I'm here. I've got you. I'm not going anywhere. I will breathe with you until we are one."

8

Boundaries as Doorways

Not to sound dramatic, but boundaries are *everything* when it comes to how we make our way through the world. They have the power to transform our relationships, our selves, and our lives. While the *Oxford English Dictionary* defines a boundary as "a line that marks the limits of an area; a *dividing* line," in the context of relationship, we like to think of boundaries as semipermeable cell membranes—determining what is and what is not allowed to enter a certain space and, ultimately, what happens in that space. Boundaries are not just about keeping out what we don't want but also about bringing more of what we *do* want in. *Boundaries aren't walls, they are doorways to deeper levels of love and intimacy.*

Boundaries, like most things in life, aren't static. They shift depending on who we are relating to moment to moment, what's happening in our lives, and what we're perceiving about ourselves in the process. Our boundaries and our limits are ever changing and evolving alongside us, constantly adapting based on the information we receive from our relationships and environment: *Is this safe? Does this feel good? Is this mine? Is this nourishing and healthy?* As relationship educator Kelsey Grant says, "Boundaries are the high quality information we share with another so they know how to love us best." We love this definition because it invites you to jump back into the driver's seat of your life, tune into your body, and practice discernment: *What do I want? How do I wish to be spoken to? Loved? Touched? Treated?*

Boundaries, in addition to determining what is and what is not welcome in a particular space, help us determine what is our responsibility and what is their responsibility in any dynamic. Essentially, boundaries determine *where you end and someone else begins.* Boundaries give birth to an authentic and autonomous "I." When we know what's ours and what isn't, we can stand grounded in our own beliefs, emotions, values and needs with more ease. When our boundaries are flimsy and porous, we risk being influenced and overridden by the thoughts, emotions, and energy of others. For recovering codependents, this journey back to self (your thoughts, your needs, your desires, your emotions, your energy) is big sacred work.

The boundless beauty of boundaries? *You* get to say what's a "yes" and what's a "no" for *you* in *all* aspects of *your* life—emotionally, energetically, spiritually, relationally, physically, and sexually:

+ **Emotional boundaries** are about being in charge of our self-expression and how we share our feelings. We get to decide the level of openness surrounding our emotions, as well as when we'd like to share. Emotional boundaries separate *our feelings* from *their feelings.* They determine the kind of behavior we *invite, accept, and reject from others.*

+ **Energetic boundaries** determine what is energetically ours and not ours, where we direct our energy, and the energy we take on and absorb from others. When our boundaries are healthy, we feel contained and clear in our own thoughts, emotions, beliefs. Our energy rises and we have more life force to direct toward the things that bring us alive! We're no longer influenced and overpowered by the energy, thoughts, and emotions of others.

+ **Spiritual boundaries** determine your beliefs about the world and your spiritual experience in this world (e.g., not allowing fear/guilt to be used as a tool of oppression). Spiritual boundaries are protecting and preserving what I believe versus what you believe.

+ **Relational boundaries** determine how you relate to certain people in your life—what is acceptable and what isn't acceptable according to the type of relationship you have—and the shared agreements within those roles (e.g., how you interact with your boss is different from how you interact with your partner).

+ **Physical boundaries** determine things like the physical space between us and others and how much physical contact is okay under different circumstances and in different contexts.

+ **Sexual boundaries** determine your preferences in the bedroom (or wherever you get down). These boundaries determine what you are okay with and what you are not okay with sexually, and how you like to be touched versus how they like to be touched versus how you would like to touch them.

+ **Material boundaries** determine how we and others interact with our material/physical items. These items can be tangible (e.g., toothbrush, razor, car, office/desk items, clothes, makeup, etc.) or private (e.g., journal, intimate items, etc.). Your material boundaries indicate your level of comfort around others touching or going through your items.

+ **Financial boundaries** determine how you share, disclose, save, spend, and give money to others. This includes the access others have to your financials, agreements made around gifts and loans, and asking for money.

When our boundaries are *healthy* they protect and preserve our wholeness and our energy—whether it's in the bedroom or the boardroom. When our boundaries are intact it makes it easeful (second nature) for you to direct your life force toward people and choices that bring you alive and away from environments and dynamics that deplete and siphon your energy. *A person with healthy boundaries knows what's in their lane, what's in someone else's lane, and what is shared.* They know their "nos" and honor their "yeses" with confidence, kindness, and clarity. Doesn't that sound dreamy?

Alas, many of us weren't modeled healthy boundaries. Instead, we were modeled something in between porous boundaries and rigid boundaries. Someone embodying porous boundaries gives more away than is healthy or sustainable for them and takes on far more than is theirs. Every door to their house is open, even when this isn't serving or nourishing them. Will all the overgivers, people-pleasers, and martyrs please stand up? Those with porous boundaries will likely find themselves in nonreciprocal relationships, always putting in way more than they are receiving in return. Enter: cycles of burnout and heaps of resentment.

Those embodying porous boundaries don't have a good sense of their own limits (because their limits likely were minimized or neglected at one point in their life) leading to them being overridden by others and themselves. This looks like overcommitting, overworking, and overgiving. If you have porous boundaries, you feel disconnected from your ability to say "no" and protect yourself. We see you, freeze mode. At the end of the day, those with porous boundaries are afraid to draw limits around their time, energy, money, body, and within their relationships because they fear this choice will lead to disconnection or abandonment. Because of this, they struggle to stay connected to themselves (their needs and desires) and be in a relationship. Enter resentment. This internal mixtape sounds like, *If I say no, they won't like me anymore. I'm not allowed to change my mind, I made a commitment. Why do I always get the short end of the stick? Why do I always lose myself in relationship?* or *Putting myself first is selfish and self-centered.*

On the other side of the spectrum are those with rigid boundaries. They are really good at walling themselves off and avoiding any situation where vulnerability is required or invited. Those with rigid boundaries don't trust others to honor or meet their needs, so they opt for the route of rigid self-reliance. Sometimes those with rigid boundaries unconsciously keep people out by setting high "standards" that are really just walls. We're looking at you, Ms./Mr. Independent. Underneath this strategy is a desire to be in control at all times.

Those with rigid boundaries close all the doors to their house, not allowing in any input/thoughts/emotions that might disturb their equilibrium. This also keeps connection, love, and intimacy from entering. For those embodying rigid boundaries, trusting others and themselves when it comes to setting boundaries, opening and receiving feels like *a lot*. This mixtape sounds like, *I don't trust them with my heart, or my body; When I get in relationships, people become too needy; People get so emotional when I let them close. Blegh!; I don't trust myself in intimacy;* or *I don't want to be messed with; They are using me; They are going to manipulate me and betray me;* or *I will not tolerate this, and I will not compromise here.*

After reading through these descriptions, which boundary system are you embodying: healthy, porous, rigid, or somewhere in between? Now that you have a better sense of the current status of your boundary blueprint, let's keep this thread of self-awareness going and shift gears. We're going to focus on moving out of rigid or porous boundaries and into healthy and secure boundaries.

Reconnecting to *clean anger*—your embodied "no"—is going to lead the way.

The Power of Your Embodied No

Underneath every dysfunctional relationship lives a dysfunctional boundary blueprint. And underneath this dysfunctional blueprint is a disconnect from clean, self-protective, and embodied anger. When we don't have access to our clean anger, and haven't been modeled a *healthy* boundary blueprint, we find ourselves oscillating between feeling defenseless and enmeshed (taking on what's not ours) to feeling emotionally cut off and walled off (guarded and isolated). When we find ourselves embodying rigid or porous boundaries, we are living without a loving, protective, and healthy inner-gatekeeper.

This was the case for Julia. Terrified of losing herself in her next relationship like she had in her last one, she signed up to work with me (Mark). She was eager to get to the bottom of this pattern. In one of our initial sessions, I asked Julia what I ask every client who struggles with setting boundaries and honoring their limits: "What is your relationship to anger like?"

After sitting with the question for a couple of moments, she looked at me and said, "I don't really *get* angry."

Ding, ding, ding! This is a common response from those embodying porous boundaries. Without a healthy connection to anger—the energy/emotion that fortifies our inner gatekeeper—we continue to let things slide, blow by our warning signs, and tolerate dynamics that diminish our worth, self-trust, and sense of safety. The more we override our anger (consciously or unconsciously), the more anxious we become.

Without a healthy, intact inner gatekeeper, there is no such thing as liberated love. We need boundaries to feel safe, and we need to feel safe to open into love.

Julia isn't alone in her disconnect from clean anger. In fact, most of our clients, when asked about their relationship with anger, say something along the lines of, "I don't get angry," "I'm hot-headed," or "My anger scares me because I attack and get reactive when I'm triggered." Just to clear the air here, anger isn't the problem; it's what we *do* with it that determines if it's problematic or not. Which brings us to a much-needed distinction: the difference between clean anger and aggression.

Anger is the core emotion that protects and safeguards our boundaries. When embodied and clean, it is protective. Aggression on the other hand is what emerges when we are avoiding or disconnected from our anger. *Anger is constructive; aggression is destructive.* Instead of protecting and safeguarding, the energy of anger becomes distorted and morphs into aggression. Aggression is a way we source a feeling of significance. "*You will hear me!*" We get big, we get scary, we try to control. It shames, blames, and penetrates the personal boundaries of others.

Another shade of aggression shows up in passive aggression, where snide remarks, criticism, and a lack of personal accountability reign. Aggression, in all its forms, is the avoidance of the *real* problem at hand. Instead, these avoidance strategies reinforce familiar dynamics using manipulation and force that prevent the movement into clean anger and healthy sovereignty.

So, why do we split off from our clean anger?

We are born connected to all of our core emotions, *including* anger. If you've ever been around a newborn baby, you know the signal cry that is accessed with zero inhibition when they are in pain, need something, or don't like what's happening. Anger, when intact, emerges to protect us when a boundary is being violated and/or a need is not being met. Anger informs our system that something is "off," that we need something, or something needs to change *pronto*.

If it wasn't safe to access or assert anger and frustration in early childhood, we likely split off from them. In early childhood, staying connected to our caregivers is more important than staying connected to our anger. So instead of this energy being used to gatekeep our external environment— determining what is allowed and what isn't—it turned inward and now gatekeeps our internal environment by controlling what we share and bring forward. Anger when turned in on itself morphs into self-hatred, self-blame, and shame, keeping us small and in check so we don't rock the boat and disrupt our core attachments.

The same blind spots (shame, dependency, guilt, survival) that prevent us from recognizing and embodying the truth also prevent us from asserting ourselves and drawing lines around our body, time, energy, and resources.

After Julia understood the importance of anger and boundaries, she asked what most in her position would ask: "Okay, *how* do I reconnect to my fire and activate my inner gatekeeper?" The answer is simple: it starts with self-consent. As Rachael Maddox writes in her book *ReBloom*, "Deeper than consent with another is consent with yourself. Self-consent is the foundation of sovereignty."

Sovereignty, here we come!

Giving Yourself the Green Light

Self-consent—the process of honoring your limits and your boundaries— sounds simple, doesn't it? Well, it is, in theory, but to a body and nervous system that has been trained for decades (possibly centuries via inherited patterns) to bypass, override, and minimize its fire/power/truth/"no" . . . it's not so simple. If our boundaries were disregarded, neglected, and exploited throughout our lives, coming home to them can be a tender and scary process. *Who am I to say no? My needs don't matter. This is all I deserve. They won't hear me anyway. I don't trust myself. I don't know what is good and what isn't. I'd rather tolerate this than have nothing.*

The process of becoming intimate with your limits begins with asking yourself regularly and intentionally: *Is this a yes or a no for me?*

If you're used to overextending yourself and overriding your capacity, we recommend you hit the pause button often to create the necessary space to tune into your body and hear what it's *actually* saying. This is the medicine of self-attunement and unconditional positive self-regard. This is what creating a container is all about. It allows you to discover your edges, your desires, and what and who you want and don't want in your space.

In action this sounds like, "Thanks for the invite, let me get back to you," or "Can we hit the pause button? I need a minute to check in with myself before moving forward." If you're not familiar with honoring yourself or you're afraid to disappoint someone else, this step might kick up some anxiety. Below the anxiety that may show up, ask yourself, *What am I afraid will happen?* The anxiety might sound something like: *Will they dislike me, hurt me, or leave me if I say no, if I ask to move slower, or if I honor my needs?*

Reminder: *emotionally mature adults can handle disappointment and honor someone else's limits.*

One thing that I (Kylie) have found helpful is pursuing support from experts in fields related to the work I do. One of those experts was Nicole, my somatic experiencing practitioner (a professional who uses a body-oriented therapeutic model that helps heal trauma). The disconnect between what my true limit was and what I was allowing into my space was made evident in an exercise where we sat across the room from each other and I was invited to determine the desirable distance between us by asking Nicole to move closer or farther away.

With each ask to move closer or farther away, I was invited to check in with my body. *Was she too close? Just right? Too far?* After asking her to move closer a few times in a row, my hands started to turn inward, and my system started to freeze. Afraid to hurt her feelings, I continued to override my limits and let her come closer. One step. Two steps. *She's safe, I like her! I don't want to offend her.* It wasn't until she pointed out to me the shifts she had observed in my body that I even became conscious of the disconnect. *Wow,* I thought, *this programming runs deep.*

The goal of self-consent work isn't to judge ourselves but to lovingly restore a connection with the body by honoring our limits regardless of how we or others feel about them. This takes practice, especially when we've never asked ourselves questions like: *What do I need? What feels good for me? Do I like this? Is this too much?* We like to invite our clients to start with these questions: *What does a "yes" feel like in my body? What does a "no" feel like in my body? What does a "maybe" feel like in my body? How can I slow down this process and give myself the space I need to locate the most nourishing answer?*

As we begin to orient our lives around our true yeses and our sacred nos, we will likely run into external and internal resistance. Change shakes the system. Remember, you're shifting out of patterns and roles that have been embedded in your nervous system and your family's collective nervous system for a long time.

But don't worry! Shaking the system is the medicine we all need in order to break free from the roles and agreements that keep us small, complicit, and disconnected from our most authentic selves.

So, let's get to shaking. With care, of course.

Shaking the System

When we've existed in relationships where there have been few to no boundaries, shifting to becoming a human with healthy boundaries can be quite disruptive to our relationships. This might seem counterintuitive because, ultimately, boundaries invite more love, communication, authenticity, and safety to the relationship. But for those not initiating the change, these shifts might be seen as a potential threat to the relationship. This is especially true if the former dynamic operated on rigid roles and compliance instead of consent. Agreements rooted in compliance are about keeping the system together, possibly at any cost, including the cost of your own capacity and your partner's capacity, as well as psychological and emotional safety. And, of course, in the more extreme cases, our physical safety.

When you begin to change the rules of engagement, define a more autonomous, empowered self, and threaten the status quo of an important relationship, you will likely be met with what Harriet Lerner, psychologist and author of *The Dance of Anger*, appropriately calls "a countermove." Those who are threatened by the changes you're making will enact countermoves as an attempt to shift the dynamic back into a familiar place, you back into the "old" you, and the relationship back into relationship 1.0. Their behavior doesn't mean they don't love or care about you (although it may feel like that). They enact these countermoves to reduce the anxiety they feel about your shifts and the invitation for growth that comes with it.

Lerner gives eye-opening examples of what a countermove might look like when we start to shake the systems around us, writing:

> *Countermoves can take any number of forms. You may be accused of disloyalty ("Do you know how much you hurt your father by visiting Uncle Charlie?") or selfish disregard for others. ("You can't say that to Mom. It will kill her to know the truth!") You may be accused of being misguided, crazy, or just plain wrong. ("I know you can't really mean that.") The other person may threaten to withdraw or even terminate the relationship ("We can't be close if you feel that way"). Or they may sulk, argue, fight, gossip about you, or do whatever they do when they get anxious and threatened. Your kids will test you over and over to see if you "really meant it" when you tighten the structure.**

Some of you might be shaking your head as you read this list of countermoves, thinking, *Yep, I've definitely experienced that before,* or *I've definitely*

---

* Harriet Lerner, "Coping With Countermoves," *Psychology Today*, December 20, 2010, https://www .psychologytoday.com/us/blog/the-dance-connection/201012/coping-countermoves.

done that to someone before. Change invites internal and external resistance. It's a part of the process. The best way to work with this resistance is to anticipate it and resource in ways that allow you to sit with the discomfort so that you can stay in your own lane and continue to move in a direction of greater coherence and authenticity.

After Mark and I broke up, I knew that if I wanted to individuate out of old roles, shift my story, and break free from codependency I would need to implement some boundaries with my family. I was concerned and afraid of being swayed by their comments and desires for my life. In other words, I didn't feel anchored or secure enough in myself yet to receive this input, so I placed a boundary with them that stated, "Currently, I am working on deepening my own self-trust, and aligning with what I want for myself, my purpose, and my life. I am taking the space I need to process this chapter of my life and come back home to myself. At this time (or unless explicitly asked by me), I am not open to receiving advice, feedback, or hearing opinions on my relationship(s), life, and choices. Should this happen, I will politely request you to stop, and I will remove myself from the conversation." After placing this boundary with my family system, my anxiety shot through the roof. The story on repeat in my head was: *They're going to be mad at me. I'm going to lose them forever. They won't accept this version of me. I'm going to die without their support.*

When we don't trust ourselves or others with our boundaries quite yet, we might swing from embodying porous boundaries to embodying rigid boundaries. When we're strengthening our self-trust muscle, this pendulum swing can be a necessary part of the process. In other words, sometimes we need to build some walls before we decide where the doors are going to go. Over time, as we cultivate trust in our ability to assert ourselves and deal with the anxiety and/or countermoves that might show up on the other side, our system can soften and move into deeper levels of security and confidence. The medicine/healing isn't in the response we receive but in the actions we take.

In my case, this boundary was met with love and respect from my family, but this certainly isn't always the case.

It definitely wasn't the case for Velvette's husband. Velvette shared her experience with me (Mark) right after I'd given a presentation on boundaries at a conference. She said that she and her husband had been together for more than fifteen years, had two kids together, and that recently he'd started to pursue things he loves. He had shared with her that it was important that he spend more time doing things that he really enjoyed. She expressed resistance to this and told him she felt it was selfish of him to prioritize himself now.

"Has he invited you to join him in his interests?" I asked.

"Yes, he has. But I don't *like* mountain biking," she replied.

"Well, what do *you* like to do?"

"I like to do lots of things, but I don't have time to do them."

What Velvette experienced comes up a lot when couples begin to move from codependency to liberated love. When one partner makes the move toward sovereignty and an individuated self by establishing boundaries, it is only natural that a relationship that thrived on self-erasure would begin to feel unstable. Instead of celebrating that our partner has found a passion or stepped toward something they love, we try to get them to remain the way they've always been. To go back into our old patterns so that we can calm the anxiety that growth and expansion can bring up. Just like Velvette, we often use martyrdom and shame instead of connecting to the excitement that we can have a self *and* a relationship.

It seems odd that we often don't recognize that what's best for each individual's growth and aliveness is *also* what is best for the relationship. Instead, we become afraid of each other's power. We become afraid of each of us coming alive because then it means we have to sit with the grief that we haven't felt fully alive for [insert number] years. Trust us: *the more you step into yourself, the more room the relationship will have to learn to hold both of you.* Instead of a painful amalgamation of two boundaryless and codependent people, the relationship becomes a separate entity composed of two fully formed, autonomous individuals. An entity that liberates your power instead of controlling or containing it.

When you are more open, more impassioned, more in your purpose, more in your heart, the relationship can be all of those things too.

We get afraid of a partner's power when we think developing independence will pull us away from each other. And in response to that fear, we cling tighter to our smallness. We hook in deeper and become the unconscious reason neither of us will allow the other to soar. To love in a way that is liberated celebrates the expression of the individual *separate* from the relationship, and separate even from needing to "stay together." This doesn't mean we can't want to grow and stay together. And it doesn't mean that it is not possible. But it *does* mean that we have to loosen our tight grip on trying to direct our relationship rather than ourselves. It also means that as soon as we make staying together more important than living in a way that makes both of us come alive, we are living in fear. Our relationship then becomes a prison of self-abandonment. Resentment builds and stirs until the choice to leave becomes the only choice.

Velvette had a choice: to get curious about what her husband's pursuit of his passions brought up for her and what they could do together to create a future that felt liberating and exciting for both of them, or hold on tight to the familiar, to what was.

Opening the Doorway

Setting boundaries and sharing what we want and need can be exciting, terrifying, fun, and anxiety-inducing. We often hear from people after they've learned about boundaries in one of our retreats, workshops, talks, or courses that they now understand boundaries, but they just can't seem to put them into action. They *want* to share them. They *know* who they want to share them with. And yet, they just can't get a sound out of their mouths. Been there, done that.

You have to remember that if you are bringing boundaries into your life, you might be the first person in your family lineage to do that in years! Decades! Millennia! So, be gentle with yourself. You're doing the work of your ancestors (no small task, right?). The wonderful thing is you'll be able to pass on beautiful, healthy boundaries to everyone in your life moving forward.

Having a communication framework in your back pocket is essential—a process that will allow you to pause, take a moment, identify what you're feeling, connect to that feeling, and then put into motion what you need to move forward in a more connected and protected way in your relationship to yourself and others.

This framework is from Dr. Alexandra Solomon's brilliant book *Loving Bravely*. It's called Name, Connect, Choose. The Name, Connect, Choose process helps us get clear on what's ours, what isn't, and what's shared when navigating the terrain of setting boundaries.

1. **Name the pattern:** What boundary (or boundaries) are being violated? What is yours? What isn't yours? Name what is happening in the situation. State the facts. Claim the truth of your experience. (E.g., My mom gave her unsolicited opinion about my life.)

2. **Connect with your feelings:** How did I feel before, and how do I feel now? (E.g., I feel angry. I feel sad. I feel judged. I feel misunderstood.)

3. **Choose something else:** Explore what your boundaries currently are like with this person. Use the feelings you're experiencing to inform where you need a boundary and what that boundary may look or sound like. Consider requesting a change in how you and that person relate, or decide that you will commit to a different boundary going forward. (E.g., In order to continue having this conversation with you I need you to stop criticizing me.)

Always remember: You have the right to your boundaries. You have the right to your needs and desires and deal-breakers. You have the right to feel safe in your body and your relationships. And it is YOUR JOB to take responsibility for how you want to love and relate.

When we honor our own boundaries, we invite and honor the boundaries of those we're in relationship with. Most of us don't often know how to be in a relationship *and* hold on to ourselves—we either lose ourselves for connection or hold on to ourselves at the cost of connection. This balance of being able to be connected both to self and to others is a practice. It requires that we reconnect to the truth of our bodies and our intuition. When we bring in boundaries we are saying, "This is how I'd like to be loved. This is what I need to blossom in our connection. What do you need?" The more permission we have to honor "nos" and limits in relationship, the more liberated we will feel. Knowing that you and your preferences belong as is opens the doorway to real intimacy, true belonging and embodied freedom.

Walls keep people out. Boundaries teach them where the door is.

This is love. And this is how we liberate it.

EXERCISE
Finding Your Sacred No and Your Holy Yes

Boundaries aren't just about getting in touch with our "no" but also about honoring and embracing our "yes." Here are some journaling prompts to get you started on the path to fully seizing your yes:

- *Where in your life do you struggle the most to maintain and put boundaries in place?*
- *What are some of the internal stories, ideas, or beliefs that stop you from honoring or maintaining your boundaries? Where in your life has this behavior been modeled?*
- *In what ways do you feel guilty about putting yourself first? And what would be possible in your life if you made the choice to finally put yourself first?*
- *What blocks you from sharing information and being vulnerable with others in your life?*
- *What is the fear associated with withholding?*
- *When was the first time you recall compromising your voice or truth in a relationship? Are you doing it now?*
- *What kinds of relationships do you feel silent or inauthentic in?*
- *What circumstances in the past have caused you to withhold your truth?*

- *What core beliefs do you have that have kept these old patterns of communication in play?*
- *If you didn't hold back, what would you say? What would you do? Who would you become?*
- *Can you think of a positive impact on yourself, etc., if you were to begin setting boundaries? Can you think of any negative ones?*

· 9 ·

Walking with Grief

I t's hard to outrun grief. Even when we think we've come a long way from the source of pain, grief comes knocking on our door reminding us of what has yet to be fully felt. It may enter our lives through the death of a loved one, the loss of a job, an unexpected health diagnosis, or a divorce or breakup. Whichever door grief enters through, it demands to be felt. It demands that we stop and sit with the sadness in our hearts and bones.

Many of us are told to keep things "up top." In other words, put a smile on your face and stay in the land of logic. "There's no room for showing feelings here so stick to the superficial." Which means only talking about things that hold little, if any, emotional weight—like what's happening in some celebrity's life, the weather, last night's sports highlight, or what so-and-so is doing down the street. Everything else—grief, rage, pain, joy, sensuality, and excitement—is off the table. The best place for our wild, raw selves is in the shadows. Out of sight.

This choice to keep our emotions repressed is affirmed by the dominant cultural narrative(s) as well. When we're in pain, we constantly receive messages and pressure from others to "get over it," "stop being weak," or "take this drug." We're told that these are negative or low-vibration emotions. *Good vibes only, please.* So, we take the pharmaceutical aid (we're not shaming that support if it's needed), push our feelings down, and do our best to get on with life. We continue to follow the norm and opt for the path of denial, repression, and avoidance. We act like everything is great when it's not, jump into another relationship to try to forget the last one, or try our best to anesthetize our feelings by drinking, eating bonbons, doing drugs, shopping, having sex, or working well beyond nine to five. We get it—these coping mechanisms do the trick when we're in need of short-term relief.

Eventually, though, grief catches up to us and pulls us down into its dark waters where we have no choice but to face and feel what we've been running from. In some spiritual circles, this moment or season of life is called the "dark night of the soul" (a term that comes from a poem by St. John of the Cross), and it is the time where we can no longer run from the darkness, sorrow, and parts of ourselves that we've exiled.

What if we told you that you didn't have to wait for the knock at the door, and instead you could choose to open the door and welcome grief? What if, just as our Earth-connected ancestors did and have been doing for eons, we created a ritual space and loving container to be with loss and be worked on by grief's sacred hands?

This is exactly what Theresa did.

Theresa was chronically single and constantly dissatisfied with her dating life. In our (Mark's) first session she said, "I keep attracting men who are emotionally unavailable." We spent the session exploring the basis of where that pattern came from (surprise, surprise, it was from an emotionally unavailable parent) and then created a path to change that pattern by finding a sense of self outside of it via a relational reset. She bravely dedicated six weeks to deactivate her dating apps, turn off social media, stop hitting up the singles bars, and *heal*. She was ready to put an end to the escapism. Ready to stop the projection. Ready to allow the gravity of grief and the wisdom of "no escape" to do its work. Ready to walk with grief, hand-in-hand, instead of run from it.

For Theresa, this descent into grief was catalyzed by her conscious choice to step away from dating and the possibility of being in a relationship altogether. What Theresa quickly realized after stepping into her healing cocoon was how much mental and emotional energy she had been unconsciously spending on seeking a partner and finding "the one." She was so caught up with the chase that when things finally slowed down and she stepped out of her familiar patterns, she was met with an intense amount of grief, a deep fear of being alone, and a profound feeling of emptiness.

A couple of weeks into the reset, she shared, "I'm afraid I'll never stop crying if I start." She was afraid to dip her toe into this well of grief, and therefore continued to settle for crumbs in her relationships. The irony? This only reaffirmed her core wound of feeling "too much," "broken," and "unworthy of love." Inside her healing cocoon, and through our work together, she felt safe and contained to open the door to this unacknowledged grief and so much more. She grieved for her younger self, her adolescence, and all the parts of her that had felt unheard and unseen for so long. She grieved for her unavailable father who had also been raised by an unavailable father (*that* pattern likely went on for generations). She grieved the wasted years and the hurt she unintentionally caused others.

The reset and dedication to feel it all—anything and everything—gave her space to love herself, reconnect to her creative energy and passions, find nourishment in sisterhood, restore her relationship with her own body, and locate her true values and soul's purpose. But first, she grieved what was in the way.

When we open the door to our grief, we open the door to liberated love.

The Five Gates of Grief

What gets most in the way of deep intimacy and love? *Unprocessed* pain.

When we consciously meet our grief, we choose to walk a path of love. We choose to let life and loss crack us open instead of letting them close us off further. We choose to be fully in our bodies and in our hearts. *Learning to walk with grief is choosing to live with an open heart.* This is sacred and courageous work.

In his book *The Wild Edge of Sorrow*, psychotherapist and soul activist Francis Weller beautifully describes the five gates, or doorways, in which grief and pain enter our lives. While we might be more familiar with one or two of these gates, every single one of us carries loss and grief at each gate.

In our experience, and in working with our clients, the more familiar we become with these gates, the easier it is to pinpoint our grief and metabolize our pain. If we want to go deeper in love, this is the work we must do. Doing grief-work allows us to be with, witness, and integrate the pain that sits between us and the love and life we desire. Are you ready to walk with an open heart? Beautiful! Let's dive into some grief-work and discover Weller's five gates.

Gate One: Everything We Love, We Will Lose

The grief that accompanies us at this gate arrives when we're met with one of life's hardest truths: the reality of *impermanence*. At the heart of this grief is the truth that we will eventually lose everything we love. Even as we say that, we feel the tenderness that lives in this recognition and are reminded of these wise words from Judah Halevi: "A holy thing, to love what death can touch." It is a holy thing, indeed.

We all know the grief that sits at this gate well. Some of us, too well. It is through loss, death, illness, and heartbreak that this grief arrives at our doorstep. When we let it enter, this grief cracks us open as we feel into the depths of sorrow around the loss of someone we love, a beloved pet, our health, or a career. Oftentimes, outrage will accompany our tears at this gate as we feel the anger toward another for leaving, life for being unfair, or God/the Universe for putting this challenge on our path. This too belongs.

Losing someone or something we love is hard. It's even harder when we don't have the permission, empathic witnessing, and support we need to be with the loss, the grief, the outrage. Without these components, we tuck it away and opt for protection and avoidance. We layer on emotional armor, keep a safe distance from potential loss, and stick to the shallow end of the pool. To quell the grief at this gate we attempt to control life, limiting the depth of intimacy and love we will allow in. We hear echoes of our own wounding, *If love always leaves, why should I let it in?*

Let us answer that for you. Not letting love in leads to an unfulfilling, guarded, and dull life. *The truth is, the deeper we love, the more we will grieve. To love is to accept eventual loss. To open is to say yes to that loss.*

As we sit with the grief at this gate, we're invited to soften the armor around our hearts and invite in the bittersweet medicine of impermanence. We're invited to hold loss and love, grief and gratitude, tears and trust simultaneously. I (Kylie) remember a brief exchange I had with a man in Italy who was fresh out of a six-year relationship. When I asked him about his relationship, he said, "We were together for six years, and they were the best six years yet." This loving response shocked me. He was able to hold gratitude, trust, and love alongside his grief. He was embodying what an ending can look like when we let it be a "good death." When we trust our path and another's path wholeheartedly. This is mature love. This is liberated love.

Gate Two: The Places That Have Not Known Love

The grief that accumulates at this gate occurs in the places untouched by love. These are the parts of us that have been cast aside, exiled, and neglected; the parts that have lived outside the circle of warmth and welcome. The parts that have been shamed away. As Weller writes, "What we perceive as defective about ourselves, we also experience as a loss. The proper response to any loss is grief, but we cannot grieve for something that we feel is outside the circle of worth." To access this grief, we must externalize the shame-based identities and self-disgust we've internalized and the belief that it's *our* fault that we didn't receive the love we needed and longed for. It's not your fault. It never was.

So many of our clients have been so afraid of grief for such a long time that when we cast a wider circle of welcome and invite these exiled parts out of the shadows by validating their pain and experience, they become overwhelmed by the immensity of grief they feel. They begin to access a deep sorrow that stems from not being seen or cared for. And just as we share with them, we'll share with you: *both your anger and your sadness are welcome and necessary companions on this journey home to wholeness.* You have every right to your anger and your sadness; it's what you do with these emotions that determines if they become medicine or poison, healing or harmful. Remaining in our adult selves while accessing and opening to our grief is what we're after here. We'll share some ways that support us to stay anchored in our adult self at the end of the chapter—which brings us to another facet of grief that awaits us at this gate.

This is the grief we feel when we begin to see how our survival strategies have hurt others and those we love.

This was a big one for Tammy. As her system thawed, and her capacity to sit with discomfort expanded, Tammy was finally able to take an honest look at her life. In one of her sessions she wisely said, "It's one thing to feel my own grief, and it's another to see how my survival strategies have caused others pain and kept me from the very things I desire." It can be easy at this point to spin out in regret, shame, and blame, but as we've learned, punishing ourselves for not knowing that we have access to a different path is not the answer. *When we reject the pain that comes with awareness, we reject the inherent wisdom that lives in that awareness.* As Maya Angelou so wisely said, "Do the best you can until you know better. Then when you know better, do better."

What Tammy needed—what we *all* need—at this junction of the journey is a massive dose of grace, compassion, and forgiveness. And, when necessary, honest and vulnerable amends. *Where can I take ownership for my side of the street and offer a heartfelt apology? Where can I forgive myself for not knowing what I do now?*

As we open ourselves to this grace, we are restored. A beautiful thing about this opening is the ripple effect it brings into our lives. If we can receive grace, we're more likely to give it. As we do this, the circle of welcome expands and healing amplifies in all directions.

Gate Three: The Sorrows of the World

The depth of grief that sits at this gate didn't enter my (Kylie's) consciousness until one evening during a cacao ceremony. I was in Whistler, British

Columbia, a special and sacred place that is abundant in trees, alpine lakes, and snow-covered mountains. During the evening ceremony, I found myself being pulled by the beauty of an expanse of pine trees that swayed in the window against a darkening, moody sky. As I moved deeper into connection with these trees, a sudden wave of grief washed over me and moved me to tears. In that moment, I could feel the trees' sadness. I could hear the cries of the Earth. Her pain entered my heart, and I wept. This encounter forever altered and opened me. It reminded me, once again, that we are not separate from the Earth. We are one with the Earth.

Author and activist Chellis Glendinning names this feeling "earth-grief," writing, "To open our hearts to the sad history of humanity and the devastated state of the Earth is the next step in our reclamation of our bodies, the body of our human community, and the body of the Earth." There is so much for us to grieve at this gate—the loss of forests, wetlands, hundreds of species—and the continued desecration of the Earth for the sake of profit. So many of us—and more every season that's filled with wildfires and floods, droughts and rising sea levels—feel it. Whether we're conscious of it or not is the question.

Underneath these losses lives our original rupture, our disconnect and severance from the natural world. A pseudo-separation that has placed humans outside and above the whole circle of life. Because of this separation we've lost the parts of us that come alive and feel anchored when we honor the land, work with the elements, sing with the birds, connect with the stones, and dance with the stars. This loss of engagement with the living, animate world around us is responsible for the growing feeling of emptiness and loneliness we collectively feel.

What if the feeling of emptiness you experience wasn't about you? What a relief, right?!

When we approach the grief that awaits us at this gate, we choose to restore our connection to the living world and return to our sacred responsibilities as human beings: to protect and honor all living beings. As we embody the reality that we are interconnected and a part of the circle of life, we heal the original disconnect—the one with the natural world—

that inhibits every other connection in our life. To reaffirm Glendinning's words, this is the next step in the reclamation of our bodies, the body of our human community, and the body of the Earth.

Gate Four: What We Expected and Did Not Receive

It might be tricky to name the losses that sit at this gate because it's hard to identify something we never had to begin with. Even though we can't name them, our bones and souls feel that something fundamental is missing. What could it be? We expected many things when we arrived on the Earth. We expected a warm welcome, adequate touch, ceremony, elder support, loving reflection, and a village rooted in the land and myth. Many, if not all of us, barely got a crumb of these things. Weller writes, "Of course, we were disappointed with our parents. We expected forty pairs of eyes greeting us in the morning, and all we got was one or two pairs looking back at us ... We needed to have many hands holding us and offering us the attention that one beleaguered human being could not possibly offer consistently. It is to our deep grief that the village did not appear." *Oof*, we feel that to the core.

The grief at this gate nearly swallowed me (Kylie) whole during the first trimester of my pregnancy. At first, I struggled to name and place the dense feelings of sadness I was experiencing. *What is happening here? This is what I want, so why do I feel like I'm sinking? Am I depressed?* The picture didn't start to crystallize for me until my mentor shared these words with me in one of our sessions: "When we lived in village, pregnant women were supported, held, witnessed, and cared for as sacred." With tears streaming down my face and dishes stacked in the sink, I exhaled. Finally, I could see beneath and beyond the clouds. She affirmed my grief and normalized my needs, reiterating that this is a time to receive. This conversation was the giant permission slip I needed to ask for support in ways I've never allowed myself to. It was vulnerable as heck *and* it was necessary if I didn't want to slip deeper into the well of sorrow. Without the ability to name these losses, we default to thinking the sorrow and emptiness we feel are a personal failure, or we blame those closest to us for not being able to meet or understand us in ways we deeply crave. Being able to name the losses that sit at this gate allows us to tend the sorrow, and eventually act in ways that support us in creating the very things our hearts long for.

This was exactly what Ashley wanted to explore in our (Mark's) work together. In our first session she shared, "I feel like I am here to do more than just earn a living." *Say it louder for all those in the back!*

Ashley, like all of us, longed to share her unique gifts with the world. She longed to be seen for who she truly was, which was way more than her title at work and the many roles she played in her life. Slowly, we worked on peeling back the layers, inviting Ashley to reconnect to her inner-spark—discovering what activities, people, topics, and environments brought her to life. She followed this flame all the way home, and so can you.

This is the beautiful thing about meeting the grief that awaits us at this gate. We're invited to step into our calling and our true purpose for being here. The choice to ask this question and devote your energy to finding the answer realigns your life in profound and magical ways, bringing you closer to the people who celebrate you, who desire your gifts, and who will actually see you. When we cultivate these soul connections in our lives, they begin to set a new standard for what we accept and tolerate from others. When we know who we are and why we are here, we stand more firmly in our center. Walking hand in hand with our grief and longing guides us back to what matters most: our soul and essence.

Gate Five: Ancestral Grief

At this gate we are invited to go beyond our personal timeline and venture into the history and experience of our ancestors. This is called intergenerational/ancestral healing work, and as you can imagine, it goes *deep*. This gate holds an invitation to tend to the sorrow and pain our ancestors didn't have the capacity or space to tend to, along with the coping mechanisms they used to survive and manage this pain (and the impact these coping mechanisms had on our families and communities). Why do we do this work? To break the generational cycles that keep us looping in survival states. As the saying goes, "What we don't heal repeats."

When I (Kylie) shared this concept—how patterns and stories travel down our lineage and repeat themselves until they are healed—with my client Larissa, her whole nervous system relaxed. She resonated with this expanded lens of inquiry, so we followed the resonance and traveled up her family tree.

Larissa was working with a deep fear of taking up space, honoring her feminine nature, and advocating for her needs. *Is this mine? How old does this feel?* After reflecting and looking up her matrilineal line, she started to see a pattern—the women (as far back as her memory could go) in her lineage were cut off, guarded, judgmental, and repressed. They weren't the type to advocate for their needs or dance with wild abandon. I invited her to live into the questions: What had happened to the women in her lineage? And what would happen if she broke the cycle and returned to her wild feminine nature?

Her answers were simple: It wasn't safe for the women in her family to take up space and connect to their sensual nature. It was seen as dirty, and "sinful." She feared that if she were to break the cycle, she would trigger the unacknowledged grief of her mother from having been oppressed and cut off from these parts, and potentially lose the relationship with her altogether. Break the cycle or remain complicit—this was the choice Larissa had to make. It's the choice you have to make too.

Another component of grief we face when we cross this threshold is the potential loss of our cultural and indigenous roots; the ancient, old ways that nourished and sustained us for thousands of years. When we're not connected to tradition, to a life-nourishing myth, to song, ritual, and the land beneath our feet, we feel homeless, and lost. *Who are we? Why are we here?* When our ancestors were forced to leave behind their myths, songs, rituals, land, and language, they encountered a massive severance from who they were. Although the original rupture and severance took place hundreds, potentially thousands of years ago, the sorrows our ancestors experienced (and the loss we still feel from this severance) still live in our bodies today. Many of us feel this void in our bones. We feel culturally orphaned—constantly seeking for things we can't name, or practices from other cultures to try to fill the void. It's time we turn back and recover the threads of our ancestors and indigenous soul.

Doing grief-work expands and ripens the conversation we get to have with ourselves, the living world, and with others. It points us to the *true repair* our hearts and souls need. Now that we know what awaits us at each of these gates, let's explore the pathway to renewal and repair.

Approaching Grief

How we approach *anything* in life—a conversation, an ending, our own grief—determines the quality of the engagement and what emerges on the other side.

We all have seen this in action with our loved ones. If we approach someone with blame and shame—"You always do this . . ." or "You never do . . ."—what happens? Their walls go up, and they either defend themselves (of course) or collapse into a shame spiral. This same principle applies when we approach our internal world. If we approach our grief and emotional terrain with criticism—"What's wrong with you? Why are you so broken?"—we don't make it very far. If we desire change, we can't approach these tender spots with the same energy that led to the original rupture in the first place.

It's time to take a different approach. An approach of reverence . . .

Creating the intentional space and solitude to be with grief is one of the most loving and reverential things we can do. This can be created in many ways. Some of our favorite ways to be with our emotions are through journaling, sitting in a tea ceremony, having a morning coffee, going for a walk outside, or putting on a playlist and letting our body move in *any* way it desires. All of these practices are just that—*practice* in meeting our edges, containing them, and moving through them.

One of the most reverential ways to approach grief is through ritual.

Francis Weller defines ritual simply, yet profoundly: "Ritual is any gesture done with emotion and intention by an individual or a group that attempts to connect the individual or the community with transpersonal energies for the purposes of healing and transformation."

This reminds us of a powerful ritual we cocreated at the end of our own relational resets. We knew that in order for us to step forward and explore a possible relationship 2.0 we would *both* need to release what happened in relationship 1.0 and get clear on what we were committed to changing and cocreating moving forward. We decided to hold a threshold ceremony for who we were in our relationship 1.0—to grieve the previous versions of ourselves and welcome in the next version of ourselves. Our mutual sacred pauses resulted in two *wholly changed* people, but even positive losses are invitations for processing pain.

We both learned a lot about ourselves and our previous dynamic during our time apart. It's why at the end of the sacred pause, and before stepping back into a committed relationship, we decided to create an intentional space to release, clear, repair, apologize, take responsibility for, and make new commitments and agreements to each other. To honor the threshold between what was (relationship 1.0) and what could be (relationship 2.0), we physically crossed a threshold. We started by taking the time to write out what we were ready to release—the old patterns, the old versions, the ways we used to be—and burned these in a fire. We shared with each other what we were ready to release, what we needed to clear, and what we needed to apologize for. After this purification process, we both, one by one, crossed our homemade threshold of plants, flowers, and candles and stepped forward into the possibility of what could be. On the other side, feeling lighter and alive, we sat with each other and shared our commitments to ourselves, to each other, and to the relationship. It was the fresh start we needed—one we all need at certain times in our lives, after we emerge from a time of loss, growth, change, or transformation.

One beautiful thing about ritual space and intentional pockets of solitude is they give our emotions a bottom. They create a container strong enough to hold, witness, and work with the wild terrain of grief. Within this contained space, the repressed and denied aspects of who we are can rise to the surface to be witnessed, seen, and heard, so we can stop hiding and start living. What we've seen time and time again in our work is the power of grief-work to recenter us, enliven us, and increase our capacity to love and be loved.

Working with our grief is the essential gateway to intimacy with the world around us, between us, and within us.

EXERCISE
A Simple Grief Ritual

Listen, if slowing down, connecting to the earth, and performing rituals is new and foreign to you, and feels a bit "woo-woo," good. It means you're going to your edge. Know that ritual and ceremony are as old as humans are. It is us who have forgotten. Ready to get weird? (And by "weird" we mean actually getting back to your roots.)

Once you are clear on your intention, we invite you to grab a journal and pen and any personal items you wish to offer to the earth or have with you during your ritual. Once you have these, locate a place in nature where you feel at home, relaxed, and supported. This could be by a river, in your backyard, near your favorite tree, or any place that allows for presence and solitude. When the time is right, head to this place. Once you have arrived, set up your space, get comfortable, and connect with the earth by placing your hands on the ground. In your heart and mind, or in any way you feel called, ask the earth for her care, guidance, and support in your healing process. Once this feels complete, grab your journal and free-write for ten minutes (or however long you feel called). *I am ready to release . . . I am sorry . . . I forgive . . . I wish . . .* Once you feel complete, dig a small hole in the ground (if possible) and place this paper alongside anything else you wish to release at this time. Release what needs to be released into this hole, allowing the earth to hold and transmute your tears, your pain, your grief. Once you feel complete, cover the hole, and give gratitude to the earth for holding you and supporting you.

Remember, there are no rules for creating rituals. Whether you find yourself in partnership or single, explore what you're ready to leave behind and what you want to create moving forward.

1. *Get clear on your intention.* For example: I am grieving/honoring an ending, a loss, a death, a story, a previous version of self, a chapter of my life, etc.
2. *Determine who, where, when.* For example: Do you want others to be present at this ritual or do you want to be solo? Where do you feel called to hold this ritual (at home, in nature, a meaningful place)? When would you like to hold this ritual?
3. *Curate objects, items.* For example: Are there any objects or sacred items you want to bring into the ritual space to anchor in your intention (candles, journal, personal items), to illuminate a connection or memory (pictures, jewelry, etc.), or for added support (water, fire, earth, stones, etc.)?
4. *Make it happen.* Keep it simple and trust your knowing.

PART 3

Relationship 2.0

10

Reopening Your Heart

You can't rush transformation.

In fact, we like to say, the slower you go, the faster you heal.

The caterpillar knows this truth all too well. If a caterpillar or butterfly tries to emerge from the cocoon too soon, its wings won't fully form and the alchemical process that was underway will be suspended. The same is true for us if we rush the healing process and override the call to stay in the cocoon. Luckily, for butterflies, nature knows and trusts the sacred ingredient of time.

It's—ahem—time we learn to do the same.

Before we jump back into the dating pool, have the conversation about reuniting with a previous partner, or discuss the next step in our current partnership, it's a wise move to give ourselves some transitional time to integrate the journey we just embarked on. Creating this transitional period between your healing cocoon and your next relational adventure is important for many reasons. First, it allows you the breathing room you need to check in with yourself and honestly ask: *Do I feel ready to leave this container of transformation and self-reflection? How much time do I need or desire to explore this new version of myself before moving forward?* And second, the integration period is just as important, if not more important, than the time we spend within a healing container.

Why is integration so important? Integration supports us in meeting, reflecting, and processing what emerged for us on the journey. It creates the space to witness and lovingly welcome these parts home. It's the time where we let a more aware, alive, and open version of ourselves—with all its new energy—settle in our bodies and bones. If we skip this part and jump back into the normalcy and familiarity of our day-to-day lives, there's the possibility that we miss the medicine available in the homecoming, the space where we welcome more of who we are home.

Here are some questions we love to hold and reflect on during an integration period:

+ What have I learned and discovered about myself?
+ What am I ready to call in?
+ Who am I now?
+ What do I need to stay awake and connected to these deeper knowings and values?
+ What matters to me *now*?

As a butterfly emerges from its cocoon, she doesn't rush to fly away— she sits there patiently, hanging upside down to complete the emergence process. The wings are folded and crinkled, and the butterfly must begin the process of expanding and drying her wings before flight is even possible. She reorients to the world *slowly*. This is the energy we're inviting you into—to take your time and reorient to the world with fresh eyes and deeper roots.

Unlike a caterpillar's journey into a radiant butterfly, those closest to us won't be able to literally see the changes we've undergone. They can't see the depths we've traveled, the wounds we've alchemized, and the fears we've liberated ourselves from. But just because the change isn't visible to those around us doesn't mean they won't feel or experience it . . . or have something to say about it. "Woah, what happened to you?" "You're not like how you used to be . . ." "You've really changed . . ." This is the whole point—to be changed, to remember, to embody a wider sense of self.

For some, these changes will be celebrated, and for others, they will be minimized or disregarded entirely. We're not gonna lie, it's challenging when others can't release us from the grip of our old identities and the stories that come with them. Instead of growing and releasing, they hold us to these old identities—sometimes making it challenging to move forward and create new dynamics within these relationships. *Those who say others can't change haven't changed themselves.* When this happens, it's best to stay in your lane and let others think what they wish. Just because you haven't changed in *their* story doesn't mean you have to stay in it with them. This is the test that healing codependency brings: Can you stay in your center and orient to these historic relationships? This is the butterfly effect of healing.

Surrounding ourselves with souls who see us, accept us, and give us permission (and grace) to grow is deep medicine. It's important medicine on the journey of reopening our hearts.

When we reunited, we were not the same two people who existed in relationship 1.0. To be honest, if we *were* the same people, we wouldn't have decided to get back together. We were entering into what we appropriately call "relationship 2.0," as two changed beings devoted to creating a relationship based in love, truth, and reverence. It was an entirely new dance, one that we needed to feel into and explore together. To do this, we created a dating container.

Dating Containers

If you can't tell by now, we're a tad obsessed with creating intentional time-bound containers. We're obsessed with them because they *work*. A dating container, similar to the container you created in chapter 6, invites in the clarity and structure you need to stay anchored in your values, intentions, and desires when dating, and helps facilitate your newly liberated self by sharpening your intuition, flexing your boundaries, and living and loving with discernment. So often we see people succumb to some arbitrary dating rules and timelines that have been determined by someone else. We all know those headlines for articles and videos: "How to Get a Man to Text You Back!" and "Five Things You Should NEVER Do on a First Date!"

These, friends, are *games*—oriented around winning someone and often losing yourself, inviting behaviors that are not *embodied*. What we're teaching you makes it so you don't have to play games at all; you become the referee. *You* get to determine what's a goal and what's a foul. When you know you have your own back, you won't give an eff about games. You won't care because you're not dating to "get" somebody; you're dating to find somebody who's a match for the gloriousness of who you are. *This is what it looks like to date while liberated.*

But we get it. Catchy headlines are effective. So, in an effort to *really* grab your attention, we've come up with our own:

Five Things You Should NEVER Do on a First Date:

1. Don't hide what you want. Declare it! Afraid it will scare this person away? Well, if what you want scares them away . . . BYE.
2. Don't talk about your ex (and if you do, certainly don't talk badly about them). One day this person might be an ex, and how you speak about those who've shaped your relational journey says more about *you* than about your exes.
3. Don't pretend you're needless, or "go with the flow," blah, blah, blah. Because those are just ways of pretending you don't take up space and you're low maintenance. Have needs. Take up space. Be real.
4. Don't look at your damn phone! Put it in your pocket and let it vibrate your privates instead of ruining your connection. People want to know they're more important than your social media feed.
5. Don't tolerate disrespect. It's a first date—you owe them nothing. If their behavior is out of line, if they get drunk or are rude, it's a hard pass.

6. Bonus! (Because who doesn't want another one?!) Don't dismiss them because they don't fit your "type." Observe your judgments and your edges. Explore how you relate to being open to being flexible in your type. Especially if you've been unsuccessful going for the same type . . .

When we created our dating container, our shared intention was simple: determine the highest, most aligned path for our relationship. We set our start date and decided to enter a dating cocoon for three months. The questions we held close to our hearts over those three months were: *What is in highest alignment for us, and for our relationship? What is the best form for our relationship (friendship, romantic, business)? Is this relationship bringing more love into the world?* In addition to sitting with these questions, we got clear on what was going to be a "yes" in this space, and what was going to be a "no." For example, some of our yeses were:

+ Exclusivity—We were both clear that dating other people would be off the table during our dating container.
+ Separate spaces—For us, having separate spaces allowed us the space we needed to honor our hearts and tend to our nervous systems.
+ Leading with truth—We knew that if we wanted to create a new dynamic that we needed to lead with truth *no matter what.*
+ Check in often—We wanted to explore how the container felt in a proactive way. What things were coming up? What needed to be healed and heard? The container facilitated this coming forward because of the previous yeses.

And some of the nos of our dating container were:

+ No penetrative sex—Hormones are a real thing. When we engage (too soon) sexually we cloud our judgment, and potentially avoid the conversations that lead to more intimacy, love, and truth in our relationships. We returned to the magic of loving touch, and first, second, and third base.

+ No financial support—This eliminated any financial hooks and previous codependent dynamics we had around money.

Imagine the difference between "I know what I want and what's a yes/no for me" versus "I'll take what I can get" and "I'm afraid I'll be alone forever if I don't do *X, Y, Z*." As relationship educator Kendra Cunov writes, "The energetic blueprint we begin a relationship with becomes the foundation for your entire relationship." It's time to shift out of fear and into love and trust. To an emotionally mature adult, there is nothing sexier than someone who knows what they want and is clear about their intentions and desires, and won't collapse to keep connection.

Whether you decide to see new people or are exploring a reunion with a previous partner, we highly recommend creating a dating container. In the exercise at the end of this chapter we provide you with a roadmap to design a dating container that aligns with you and your relationship desires, but before we jump ahead, let's dive into what it looks like to date from a place of wholeness and explore some of the common red and green flags to keep an eye on when reopening your heart.

Dating from Wholeness

When many of us think about dating, we feel deflated. We say it's exhausting, frustrating, and instead of changing how we orient toward dating, we avoid it or pursue it with our inauthentic selves. Dating should be a vehicle for empowerment. Instead of feeling "heavy," dating can be a light and fun exploration of your edges and skills, allowing you to see the power of *choice*. Empowered dating happens when you are clear on who you are and what matters to you.

It is the act of observing and filtering the dating pool so that we can find someone who is aligned, and in turn, get into alignment ourselves. As the saying goes, "If you want to find the one, be the one."

Most of us wait for someone to choose us. We're hoping that we're finally enough and that someone will see just how amazing we are. Imagine if you dated knowing that you *are* amazing? Well, then *you're* no longer chasing; you're choosing. You're filtering. You're discerning, keeping watch for deal-breakers, red flags, and green flags.

Deal-Breakers

You know when you go to the carnival and there is a height requirement to go on certain rides? I (Mark) remember those all too well. I still wince at the memory of walking up to what was usually a little finger marking the height requirement and it being nowhere near my head. Alas, no ride for me. And while that experience of rejection sucked, the height requirement served an important purpose: for safety reasons, this ride was not for me.

Dating is not so dissimilar (some of us even have height requirements, although that won't be the thing that matters in the end). We need to have standards. Standards that we hold. Standards that are nonnegotiable. Standards that protect and preserve your safety and ensure that you don't let someone into your life who is ambivalent about you, or is disrespectful, destructive, or abusive, or who brings pain and suffering into your life. This seems obvious, doesn't it? And yet so many of us find ourselves in experiences with people like this time and time and time again.

It's time to raise the effin' bar. It's time to draw a line in the sand. It's time to establish some nonnegotiables that, when not met, mean a boundary gets set, and a choice gets made. And once you do this in your dating life, it will trickle into every aspect of your life. You will no longer tolerate dynamics and environments that make you feel unworthy and unloved.

Part of honoring your dating/relationship intentions is getting very clear about your deal-breakers. These are things that you are *not* willing to negotiate on. They are the standard. The bar. The "price of admission."

Some common areas where deal-breakers come up include:

+ What type of relationship you want to create
+ To have a child/children or not to
+ When you want to have a child/children
+ What religion or beliefs you want your partner to have and to share
+ How to spend your shared time
+ Drug, alcohol, and tobacco use
+ If you want to get married or not
+ When to get married

It is important that you communicate your deal-breakers at the beginning of the relationship, when you have the least at stake and you can filter out the partners you don't want. If you don't want to date a smoker but then you say, after meeting one, "Well, I guess I can date a smoker," then you're dishonoring yourself to be in a relationship. In that way, you make being in a relationship more important than your values and needs. You have to stay committed to what you want. You have to choose to take responsibility for your life and the relationships you want to create. You have to decide that you're going to step up and be the person that is required to get the kind of life and love you desire.

The thing is, *if we don't honor our own deal-breakers, we often won't honor other people's.* When we create standards, we create a sense of groundedness, safety, and mutual respect for what someone else may be looking for too.

Red Flags

To become a master dater, you've got to spot red flags like a sixth sense. Red flags are a big indicator of some underlying issues and work that still needs to be done by the other person—and we need to stop the "But I've got to give them a chance!"

How about you give yourself a chance? A chance to stop dating "potential" and to step into your own?

Here are some common red flags:

- They are unkind to strangers.
- They have inconsistent communication.
- They drop "L-bombs" right away.
- They try to rush into taking you away on a trip very early on or spend too much money on you.
- They buy lavish gifts, especially after they mess up or let you down, rather than take responsibility for whatever happened.
- They are unkind to you.
- They have a very hot/very cold switch.
- They don't ask you any questions.
- They don't reschedule after a cancellation.
- They never change or they change only for a moment.
- They aren't open to feedback/growth.
- They get defensive when you express a boundary.
- They make you feel like everything is your fault.
- They belittle you, and/or don't celebrate your success and power.
- They overshare on the first date or talk trash about exes.
- They're overly protective of you and you have to defend innocent behavior.
- They are obsessed with dating hacks. (Articles like "Send 12 Texts That Win His Heart" or "How to Be a Pickup Artist" or "Why Men Love Bitches" that give us the illusion of self-worth.)
- Your body/intuition is like *Hell no*, or it just feels like there's *something* off. This one requires an abundance mindset because it asks us, *Can I trust myself and the Universe to continue to direct me toward alignment and my partner enough to let go of this connection?* Hell yes.

There are certainly more red flags out there, and although you may not see them at first, with practice and a connection to your body's wisdom you will get better at spotting them ahead of time. You can save yourself time, frustration, and painful breakups by noting these red flags when you first start dating.

Green Flags

Green means "go." These are signs of a healthy person, someone who works on themselves to heal and be a better partner.

Some common green flags:

- They are kind to strangers.
- They have a good relationship with their family (and/or good boundaries with them!).
- They are good at communicating their thoughts and feelings.
- They act and speak respectfully to you.
- They ask you questions and are interested in getting to know you.
- They reschedule after a cancellation.
- They want/seek similar things to those you do.
- They're willing to meet you halfway.
- They take responsibility for their mistakes.
- They celebrate your success, power, and growth. They are happy for you.
- They want to take it slow with you and don't pressure you to have sex.
- They honor your "me time" and respect your sacred space.
- They don't try to avoid meeting your family and friends.

There are plenty of other green flags out there; the common themes are that the person respects you, honors you, isn't afraid of a true relationship, and is confident in who they are as an individual. Someone like this is ready to step into a relationship.

EXERCISE
Seeing in Color

Think about each of your past relationships one person at a time, and consider the challenges you experienced. Try to remember when you first met and your first interactions. Did you miss any **red flags**? List them. No matter how long the relationship lasted, what was the earliest red flag you remember? Where did your intuition give you a nudge or warning? Did it try to tell you more than once? By acknowledging these signs and feelings, you will be able to recognize them when they come up again and take appropriate action to avoid heartbreak. Past forks in the road become moments of wisdom in the future when you recognize a pattern and change course.

Now, make a list of **green flags** that you desire to see from a future partner. Expand your thoughts on each one, answering why it matters. It could be a simple one-sentence why, or you can go into depth (even if it's based on something that was missing in a past relationship). Anything goes here!

Centering Your Desires and Needs

Creating a dating container and getting clear on your values, nonnegotiables, red flags, and green flags makes it easier to stay focused on your desires and needs. We like to think of it as the "prep work" one does up front that makes the rest of the journey go smoother. As always, it's better to be prepared than not be prepared.

As someone who has historically struggled to stay centered and in my own desires and needs in a relationship, it was made evident to me (Kylie) how important this level of clarity and commitment to self was for me on my flight back to Vancouver to see Mark for the first time since the completion of my own "no-man" container. I was equal parts nervous and excited. However, the closer I got to landing, the less excited and the more anxious I became. *What if I fall back into an old pattern? What if I'm not ready? Can I trust myself to stay connected to myself and my values no matter what?* These are common questions and fears. Noticing the anxious energy in my system rise, I decided to hit the pause button and take a couple of deep breaths. A practice I find useful when I notice my nervous system moving into activation is visualizing all of my energy coming back into the container of me and the present moment. I then bring this energy down into my feet where I imagine roots growing from the bottoms, re-anchoring me into the core of the Earth. To soothe my anxious parts, I say: *I am here, I've got you, I'm not going anywhere. I will breathe with you until we are one.* After this grounding practice, and with more access to my center, I pulled out my phone and made a list. I needed to remind myself of my desires and needs. Here's what I wrote:

Relationship Desires:

+ Creating ritual together and making life sacred
+ Centering nature/community/giving back
+ Moving slow and cherishing each other's bodies
+ Honoring each other's soul's purpose and mission
+ Cultivating a right relationship with Mother Earth
+ Releasing the attachment to technology and prioritizing true connection
+ Cocreating and individually creating what brings us alive
+ Ensuring our relationship is in service to love, unity
+ Practicing energetic and spiritual hygiene

My Needs:

+ Solitude/soul time
+ Slow pleasure/slow sex/loving touch
+ My intuition honored
+ My capacity honored
+ To lead (at times)
+ Daily movement
+ Honest conversation
+ Growth

+ Play/dance
+ To be acknowledged for my work and imparted wisdom
+ Presence/dedicated couple time
+ Land stewardship
+ Reclaiming the ancient ways of ceremony

The act of writing this list along with my conviction to these desires and needs settled my system and anchored me back into ME. When the plane landed and I walked through the airport's exit to greet Mark, I felt clear and centered. I was ready to date him. Having a list like the one above that you keep in the Notes app on your phone or posted on your mirror is an anchor we can't recommend enough. Heck, post it anywhere and everywhere if you ask us! Another *major* support when you're entering the dating arena is practicing the art of right distance and right pace.

Finding the right distance in a relationship is the distance (not too close, not too far) that feels supportive and nourishing for both individuals. The Sun and the Earth are pros when it comes to right distance; if they were a tiny bit closer, life as we know it would burn up, and if they were a bit farther apart, life would freeze over. Pretty wild, right? The same applies in our relationships as well. If it's hard to stay in our center and our nervous system is running hot (activated 24/7), it could indicate that we might be too close feeling lost or consumed by the relationship. On the flip side, if we don't feel nourished or warmed from the connection, we might be too far. Finding the right distance is a constant dance, and a conversation when we're in the dating process. *Are you too close? Too far?*

Finding the right pace in relationship means finding the speed (not too fast, not too slow) that feels supportive and nourishing to both individuals. Practicing this real-time within our relationships is an art form: there is no such thing as a one-pace-fits-all approach. The distance and pace will shift depending on the relationship we are in, the capacity in our nervous system, and the capacity within the shared nervous system. To illustrate how the art of finding a right pace and right distance shows up in our relationships and dating lives, let's weave in the attachment styles we discussed in chapter 3.

Anxious attachment: For those with an activated anxious attachment, a faster pace and a closer distance is desirable. These souls tend to "fall fast and hard." If you find yourself here, when dating, notice your tendency or desire to speed things up as a way to seek certainty and safety. Do you tend to collapse into commitment too quickly? If you are the anxiously attached one in a relationship, your invitation is to anticipate the needs of your nervous system, adequately resource, and learn to sit with a slower pace and manageable distance. When you notice your nervous system move into activation when dating, check in: *What do I need right now to feel safe? What does the younger part of me need to hear right now? What do I know to be true? Is there a conversation I need to have?*

Anxious attachment causes us to leave ourselves and our center. It makes us prioritize the connection to the other over the connection to ourselves. When we're dating, we need to remind ourselves that we are still figuring out if they're a great fit. We need to lean toward the edge of not going *all in* the moment we feel a tingle in our loins. This ability to remind ourselves that we're assessing the relationship and the fit allows us to be discerning. At first, our system can feel dysregulated because not abandoning ourselves is foreign. Staying true to ourselves is new! Not allowing the space or uncertainty to make us over-pursue is a different way of being. But, we promise you, if you can stay in the new way of being a *little* longer you'll begin to source the safety and security you formerly looked for in others from yourself.

Avoidant attachment: On the exact opposite side of the spectrum from the anxiously attached we find those with an activated avoidant attachment, for whom a slower pace and more distance is the preference of choice. Those who exhibit avoidance are afraid to lose themselves in dating. They're afraid of being hurt again. So, they pursue and relate in a way that allows them to control the depth of intimacy. They might be more drawn to "friends with benefits" and will often sabotage as things get too close and/ or if someone begins to really see and love them. The unprocessed pain (that we're processing!) leads avoidants to unconsciously fear touching it.

If you are typically the avoidant one in relationships, your invitation is to share what's present for you when the pace increases or the desire for closeness emerges—letting the person know that you're here and present, but might need to move at a slower pace in order to get closer. But you're not going anywhere. You just need a bit to breathe and process. Bringing the fear of engulfment to the connection will invite the person you're relating with to reflect on how it makes them feel and how they relate to space as well. By communicating your experience, you're inviting the other person to explore theirs. *This*, friends, is how *secure* attachment is created. As someone prone to avoidance you're invited to lean in when doable . . . slowly increasing your capacity for closeness. When you notice your system move into activation with this closeness, check in: *What do I need right now to feel safe? What story is coming up for me regarding closeness, intimacy? What is the right pace for me right now? What am I committed to?*

Now here's an interesting truth: often anxious and avoidant people fall in love. Why on earth would we do that to ourselves?! Here's why: we confirm each other's view of the world. For anxious people it's that when people get to know us, they distance, abandon, or reject us. For avoidants it's that when people get close, they get needy. They become a lot. They demand more than we're able or willing to give. This type of connection confirms our story. So, instead of reliving it, let's write a new one, shall we?

Disorganized attachment: Those with an activated disorganized attachment swing between both poles—wanting to move closer when the distance is too far and wanting to move farther away when the distance is too close. This might look like being really excited about a person and pursuing them, and then going from hot to cold once they choose us back. "I love you, I love you, I love you" to "Oh lord. This feels like a lot. I don't want this." The reason it is so easy to unconsciously switch from one to the other is that we don't have to become secure, so we switch between insecure attachment styles.

When you notice your system move into activation when dating, check in: *What do I need right now to feel safe? What made me so excited about this person at first? What qualities do they have that I'm drawn to? As my desire for distance came in, what was it that triggered it?*

Secure attachment: Those who are securely attached feel *good* when things are moving forward at a pace that isn't pressured or prolonged. In dating, the securely attached feel comfortable in the dance of closeness and independence.

I (Mark) like to joke that when I exhibit all the attachment styles I'm just trying to keep things interesting for Kylie. Trying to mix it up so my moves are unpredictable. To keep the mystery alive, ya know? I say all of that to bring some levity to what is so *human*. Moving between attachment styles and even seemingly having many of them can be frustrating because we don't know why we can't just relate to people "normally." But remember, "normal" is a lie. We are diverse and complex creatures. We want closeness and autonomy, but we don't tend to trust it. Dating allows us to rebuild that trust. When our attachment system kicks in, it is sensing *something is up*. It is our work as adults to get to the root of that, not shame it.

Even though it may not always feel like it, dating is an opportunity to explore our limitations, and to consciously and intentionally open our hearts again. But not just to anybody—to people who are worthy of it. The only way we can wholeheartedly know that is by staying in discernment and having our own backs. No matter the relationship, the relationship with yourself always comes first. If you have to leave you for anyone, that is not a match. Full stop.

Love should invite us to be more of who we are, not less.

Dating is about creating that space—not just for you but for the person you're going on dates with. You stepping into *your* voice, your desires, and what is true for *you* is what brings sacredness to the dating practice. If they can't hold that or are not aligned or on board to being intentional, then they're not a fit.

No more changing yourself to accommodate the limitations of others. If you do that, the other person's limitations become yours. Instead, invite the limitlessness of the love you bring to the table to expand how *they* show up, as you do the same.

We said it at the start, and we'll say it again: you can't rush transformation. Reopening our hearts takes time, patience, care, safety, and trust. Expanding the edges of intimacy is a never-ending, joyous adventure that we have the privilege to embark upon.

Become an Energized Relationship Wizard

Listen, up until this point we've been relatively gentle with our invitation to you to claim the love and life that is rightfully yours. As you reopen your heart, we can't in good conscience let you move forward without pointing out how wildly serious this actually is.

Here's the ugly truth: if you have work you know you need to do and changes you know you need to make, you *must* do it. By not choosing to step toward your wholeness and the cocreation of magical love, you are not in integrity with what is possible for you. Yes, this may be hard to hear, but it's absolutely *critical* that you sit with this so that you can feel into the pain you are knowingly (re)creating—because *if you can accept a lesser version of yourself in love, you can be certain you're doing this in other areas of your life.*

Now, you might think, *It's fine. I'll just keep going how I've been going and things will be fine.* F*ck fine. Reach for the stars. Embrace miracles. Bloom to the max. You didn't come to this planet to waste your life and love with half your heart. Your soul is dying for you to give birth to your potential. So, why not now?!

You have the knowledge. You've got the tools. You *finally* know what you want. You know how to get it. You are a bona fide relationship wizard; a friggin' Jedi of the heart! You're not here to live a *normal* life. You came here to grow. To love. To be open. To engage with all that life is presenting you so that in this incarnation, you can become everything that is being asked of you. To wield your wand and use your lightsaber.

As you move into what is next for you, stop looking for what is familiar and normal. Stop tolerating mediocrity from yourself and others. Stop buying into the bullshit beliefs and templates of relationships and how they *should* be. Stop choosing others over yourself.

When you look back upon your life, what will have mattered most? That you didn't rock the boat? That you gained the approval of everyone around you? That you had the longest marriage or relationship of anyone you know (but were miserable the whole time)? That you kept your heart closed off? That you never experienced heartbreak again?

Or that you loved all out? That you chose truth over comfort? That you became everything you could be? That you opened your heart up to the possibilities of liberated love?

You already *know* the answer. But will you *live* the answer?

EXERCISE
Your Dating Container

It is time to put it all on paper. No matter your relationship status, a dating container will support you in getting clear on your dating intention, what you are saying yes to, and what you are saying no to. In the middle of a blank piece of paper, draw a circle large enough to be able to write in.

To create your container, begin by getting clear on your start date and end date. For example, *For the next three months I am going to date (single), then, for the following three months we are going to date again and determine what the highest, most aligned form of our relationship is (reunion or partnered).* Once you have determined your start and end dates, write them anywhere on your paper outside the circle. Okay, now it's time to zone in on your dating intention.

On the top of your paper or somewhere outside of your circle, write down your dating intention. For example, "My intention for dating is long-term/marriage/to create a family; casual connection; polyamorous relationship; monogamous relationship."

Inside your circle write down everything that is a "yes" for you.

Outside your circle write down everything that is a "no" (deal-breaker) for you.

11

Trust the Triggers

Every single one of us enters into a new relationship with a unique story, set of wounds, tender places, and triggers. It's how we hold and reveal these internal dimensions, both individually and within our relationships, that determines if we move toward healing or retract into protection. It is within our dance with another that we are invited— over and over again—to meet these tender spaces, stories, triggers, and patterns with care and presence.

When our clients are doing the necessary healing work, we often hear them say things like, "I thought I had healed . . . and then I got triggered! I feel like a failure and that I'm starting over." The truth is that triggers don't simply disappear when we heal. What changes is how we *respond* to the trigger, how we hold the information, and how we share that information. The more embodied we become, the higher the bar of integrity we are asked to hold. In other words, as we come home to our body and trust the somatic wisdom it holds, we are invited to stand in deeper integrity with our whole self. *It is in our ability to honor our somatic triggers, intuitive hits, and instincts that we pave the pathway to liberated love.* Which brings us to a potent and powerful moment that happened for us within our three-month dating container as we were coming back together.

From the outside looking in, it was a simple exchange. Mark offered to pay for my (Kylie's) plane ticket to Vancouver for a visit. Generous, right? Yeah, I thought so too. Moments after accepting Mark's offer to purchase my ticket, I noticed my body and nervous system move into activation.

Something was *off*.

Confused and upset with my somatic response, this energy quickly morphed into a shame spiral. I thought, *What is WRONG with me?! Why can't I receive this offering?* I sat with this energy—this story—for a couple of hours, asking myself, *What is happening here? Why can't I open and receive this? What am I missing?*

Eventually, I shared my experience with Mark, to which he replied, "What if, instead of looking at your response as if there's something wrong with it, we looked at it from the perspective that there's something incredibly right with it? I trust your somatic wisdom and what's coming up for you here. So, instead of seeing your response as a problem, what if we explored from the perspective that it's intelligent?" Immediately after receiving these words, my whole system softened, and I started crying. This was the first time that my inner experience and intuition had been validated, honored, and trusted in a relationship. We both knew, deep down, that something was being illuminated for us.

Mark, being the receptive and caring man that he is, continued, "Yeah, to be honest, something about my offer felt off too. It didn't come from an unconditional space. The moment you agreed to me paying for the flight, I felt the little Gollum in me say, *If she accepts you paying for the flight, now you've got her.* BLEGH. I didn't like that. But I shrugged it off. Now I see that that is what you were picking up."

Becoming conscious of these subtle codependent hooks becomes the stepping stone path we all must walk to an embodied freedom unlike we've ever known or experienced.

Love is liberated one honest conversation at a time.

Codependent Hooks

So, you might be asking yourself, what exactly is a codependent hook? A codependent hook is an attempt to hook into another's energy in order to mitigate the chances of being rejected or abandoned. When we are the object of being hooked in these ways, we unconsciously give our power away. When we are the one trying to hook another, it's an unconscious attempt to exert power and control over them. It is the attempt to create a *perceived* hierarchy in a relationship to try to reinstate familiar, codependent patterns.

These codependent hooks aren't malicious in nature. They are the ways we learned to source safety and security in our earliest years and within our previous relationships. As we become aware of these codependent hooks, bring them forward in our relationships, and unhook from them, we free everyone (us and them) from outdated and unfulfilling relational dynamics.

Let's explore some of the most common codependent hooks together so we can begin to spot them on the path to liberation.

While it's top of mind, let's start with the financial hook.

A **financial hook** occurs when someone pays for things and/or provides material items without communicating any conditions or expectations. We know a financial hook exists in an exchange when we receive money or material items and feel obligated to do things we wouldn't do in other circumstances. It's a hook (attempt to control) when it's conditional. It's a clean and clear energetic exchange when it comes from a space of unconditionality and generosity. This hook sounds like: "I will give you this, but I *expect* this in return. I gave you that, so now you *must* do this. I did this for you so now you *owe* me."

Of course, there will be times when a healthy financial/material exchange happens in a relationship. It is when we make the implicit explicit that we liberate ourselves from any unconscious hook that might be present. *Where do I feel obligated? What is my intention in giving this?*

An **emotional hook** occurs when someone uses shame and manipulation tactics to destabilize another's self-esteem and knock them off of their center. An emotional hook can come in many forms, from exploiting one's tender spots to gaslighting, blackmailing, love-bombing, objectifying, withholding, martyring, judging, and/or using a moral high ground to create a pseudo-hierarchy and power dynamic within a relationship. All of these strategies could also be placed into one box and labeled "emotionally abusive." Although they aren't always intentional, they are (un)consciously manipulative and originate from the desire to maintain control (and perceived safety) of one's environment and relationships.

Let's take a common emotional hook like gaslighting and see how it operates. Gaslighting occurs when someone denies another's reality ("You're making that up"), calls into question their memory ("That isn't what happened"), pretends not to understand ("I have no idea what you're talking about"), diverts the conversation away from the real issue and toward the person's thoughts ("I can't believe you think this"), and negates/minimizes one's experience or needs ("You're making a big deal out of nothing")—which eventually leads someone into questioning the validity of their own thoughts, experience, and reality (*Maybe this is all in my head and I'm overreacting*).

An emotional hook may sound like: "I will die without you. If you leave me, I will _____ [insert something harmful]." "You are crazy. I'm going to tell X what you did if you don't _____." "You're too X [chubby, skinny, muscly, emotional, needy]." "You are pathetic. You'll never find someone else." "I need you to meet this need or else." "You'll never do better than me."

A **sexual hook** occurs when one uses sex and/or intimacy to hook another in a hormonal and energetic way. This can occur by agreeing to be friends with benefits when what we really want is a relationship. We might use sex and arousal as a way to soothe our own dissonance or disconnection in a relationship, or the feeling of our own self-abandonment and not feeling fully chosen by the other person. One example in dating and relationships is if one person senses the other pull away or fears the loss of the relationship, they might heat things up in the bedroom as a way to reestablish safety and connection. In some extreme cases, the fear of losing someone might push one into getting pregnant to ensure the connection lasts.

A **spiritual hook** occurs when one uses spiritual cards like "You're my twin-flame" or "You're my soul mate" that interfere and override our genuine feelings and desires. In addition to the spiritual cards are the contracts, vows, and marital agreements that are rooted in obligation, fear, and older versions of ourselves. This may sound like: "You'll go to hell if you leave," or "You made a promise," or "Until death do us part."

A majority of the time these subtle dynamics—being hooked and hooking others—play out unconsciously. We don't even know we're doing it because we've always been doing it! This is the trick of codependency.

In intimate relationships it shows up in repeated patterns, loss of attraction, or continuously finding ourselves in the same conversations and the same frustrating circumstances. In dating, it shows up in being drawn to the same people, or being unable to allow anyone close because we don't trust people and fear intimacy. However, as we begin to wake up to the ways we've been historically hooked into and have attempted to hook into others to source safety via control, we become what we call "unhook-able," aka "un-eff-with-able."

Our wounds are where these codependent hooks attempt to take hold. When our inner ground is polluted with shame, and/or we lack a strong sense of self, we are more easily hooked. As we heal, tend to our bodies, and pay attention to our needs, it becomes easier to somatically register and sense the difference between a hook and a clean and clear energetic exchange. This work is energetic Jedi work, and it begins with trusting your body's wisdom, tuning into the energetic dynamics, and learning the language of energy. Our bodies will inform us when something is off, and then it's our job to discern what's ours and what isn't and move into a direction that honors both the messenger (body) and the message (intuition, instinct).

The Paradox of Safety

The safer our relationship is, the more our triggers will come to the surface to be healed. Why? Because in the process of creating a loving, open, and compassionate space, the things we have held back, the vulnerabilities we've avoided, are now safe enough to touch and be processed. Liberated love liberates us from our limitations.

This reminds us of a pivotal moment that occurred within our three-month dating container. Mark and I (Kylie) went to our favorite café to grab some goodies when I sensed that something was off between him and the woman running the till. I didn't know what was happening, so I discussed with Mark what I was sensing, sharing, "Hey, is there or was there a connection between you and her? She seems caught off-guard, shy, and anxious . . ." I had connected with this woman multiple times before and knew that this was not her usual demeanor. Mark replied and said, "Nothing happened. There's nothing there for me. This must be your insecurity."

There was an insecurity popping up and an invitation for both of us to heal and create more safety in our relationship. But this insecurity wasn't just about me. And having it made about me felt dismissive and that my experience, and my feelings, were being gaslit.

Initially, Mark's response made me question myself and what I was experiencing. I thought, *Maybe I am overreacting. Maybe this is all mine.* That night as I restlessly lay in bed, I thought to myself, *This is one of those moments where you either honor your body or collapse and split off from your body.*

Emotionally exhausted from the day—*oof*, triggers can do that—I decided to sleep on it. That night while I was sleeping my dreams popped in with a message and a visual. This time, I morphed into a fire-breathing dragon who was fiercely standing her ground and protecting her well-being. *Poor Mark.* When I woke up, I felt the fire running through my blood and it was clear. *I'm not going to deny what's coming up for me.* Afraid that this conflict could be the end of our relationship but also knowing I couldn't go back to denying my reality and my intuition, I decided to bring it forward again.

Mark apologized for how he had responded in the moment and, unlike in the café, turned toward my fire and my feelings with curiosity, equally desiring to get to the root of the situation and the trigger. In essence, something about their interaction felt like a door was being left open for him to source attention, intimacy, and connection from her. By talking about it rather than ignoring it or letting it fester, this trigger and situation illuminated that there was actually a deeper need for more safety and containment in our relationship. It wasn't about the woman in the café—it was everything it was bringing up for us to hold and work with together.

There are three components we wish to highlight from this exchange:

fierce love, embodiment, and curiosity. The three components are what make us unhookable. For one of us (Kylie) it was practicing fierce love with her body and within the relationship. For the other (Mark) it was practicing curiosity and the desire to learn from the wisdom and intuitive feelings that were coming up. *What comes up for one is medicine for both.* Fierce love is the flame that invites one to see their blind spots. It is also the dragon fire that initiates others to take responsibility for their actions, well-being, and energy. Fierce love walks away when something isn't working, healthy, or aligned. *Fierce love is the remedy we all need to move beyond our shadows, survival tactics, and small stories.* It says, "I love you enough to have the hard conversation." It says, "I love you and myself enough to not play this game or feed into this dynamic." It says, "I love you and me enough to stand for truth, honesty, and reverence." It says, "I love you and me enough to call you and us into deeper levels of integrity." Fierce love embodied is the movement toward emotional maturity—practicing self-accountability, right relationship, and repair—when triggers surface . . . because they will.

Rupture and Repair

Ruptures occur when there is a disruption in our connection with another. A rupture can happen when we're in conflict, navigating a disagreement, and/or experiencing harm from another. Not only are ruptures inevitable, but they are also to be expected. How well we repair after a rupture determines the health, safety, and depth of the relationship.

After the rupture with Mark in the café, I (Kylie) could've put my head in the sand and just moved on as I often had in relationship 1.0. But, as we all know, just because something is out of sight doesn't mean that it doesn't linger and take up space between you and another. Everything unsaid gets said, but rather than verbally, it is through the way we treat one another. The more undealt with and unaddressed stuff that lives in the space between you and another, the less safety and intimacy you will experience in that relationship. If you've made it this far, you, like us, aren't interested in that type of dance anymore.

Which is why we practice and preach the concept of having a low negativity threshold in all of our relationships. When we have a low negativity threshold, we don't allow negativity to exist for long periods of time or for it to build up in our relationships before addressing it. "Sweep it under the carpet" is not how we roll.

To swing back to the café story, the rupture was brought forward the day of and the day after the experience . . . not six months later. *What we don't address keeps addressing us, whether we like it or not.* When we live and love at this level of emotional maturity and self-integrity, it requires that we become skilled at looking in the mirror, owning our side of the street, and taking accountability for what is ours (and nothing more).

When we have the relational skills to repair, it becomes easier to maintain a low negativity threshold in our relationships. For many of us, the process of repair was not modeled well, if at all. One of the main reasons for this is shame. When the internal ground we stand on is polluted with shame, it is challenging to take ownership and apologize. To prevent the collapse of self or an unwanted confrontation with shame, we deny, project, and blame instead. This is why most ruptures never get resolved. This is why most ruptures lead to even more disconnection, instead of deeper connections. When you reflect on your ability to repair, what comes up? How did your primary caregivers model repair? What prevents you from repairing with others?

Listen, we get it, it's much easier to protect an old identity and story than it is to lean into repair, eat a piece of humble pie, and trust that something else is available to us on the other side. Being the first to practice and model repair in a relationship—whether it's a fresh or a lifelong relationship—takes courage. It takes courage to be vulnerable and say, "Hey, when you said that yesterday it really hurt my feelings." It takes courage to say, "Hey, I'm sorry for what I said to you yesterday, that wasn't kind or okay, and I'm committed to doing better." Or "I wasn't kind in that moment, and I should've taken a step back."

According to renowned couples therapist and marriage researcher John Gottman, the differentiating factor between the "masters" and the "disasters" in relationship is that there is a shared relationship agreement that says,

"Baby, when you hurt, the world stops and I listen and try to understand and empathize. I'm not going to leave you in pain. I'm there for you." Consistent repair puts deposits in the emotional bank account. It fosters trust and safety.

True repair is more than saying "I'm sorry"; it's about acknowledging what happened, taking responsibility for our role, and acknowledging the impact we had on another. It is also about hearing our partner's version of what happened and getting curious about how we contributed and cocreated the dynamic. It's also about being proactive, setting necessary boundaries, and creating a plan to reestablish connection, safety, and care in the relationship moving forward. Talk about adulting, right?!

Liberated love begins to enter our domain when we make repair and reconnection more important than the ego and being right. To come full circle on the rupture and repair cycle, Mark repaired by saying, "I can see how that dynamic triggered you, and how my response made you feel disregarded. I'm sorry I didn't approach that alongside you with more curiosity. I honor your intuition and am committed to learning what is here for me, and for us. I love you."

Choosing to repair is choosing to let love in again. It's choosing to see the humanity in another and offer grace when we trip and mess up. When we let love lead over shame, retaliation, and punishment, we both win. Relationships become rock solid when we cultivate a culture where we come back again and again and take turns being the first to say, "I'm sorry. I shouldn't have said that. I am committed to being better. You matter to me. It hurts to see you suffer. I love you."

The Good Triggers

Now that we've explored the triggers that lead to repair, we're going to explore the other side of the coin: the good experiences that may also trigger us. Yup, good experiences can be triggering to our systems as well. Good experiences, such as vulnerability, being intimate, sharing a need, going after what we desire, and being seen, can activate our nervous system. If we're not used to being seen, or being vulnerable in our relationships, these experiences might, at first, feel overwhelming to us. It's normal for our system to code "closeness" as unsafe, so as we open up again we have to be mindful that although we've walked this relational path before, this time we're packing some new skills so we can change where the story goes! No more autopilot . . . hooray!

For example, when we are healing from previously dysfunctional connections, begin dating, and finally find ourselves in connection with good, reliable people, it can prove very destabilizing. It can trigger us in a good way. We might find ourselves wanting to distance from them, telling ourselves stories that they're unattractive, or that they have no edge. We are often used to chemistry being miscoded as unreliability and uncertainty. To be triggered by trustworthiness is to begin to heal and trust ourselves and others. Another small example of how this might show up is an inability to receive a compliment, so we deflect, minimize, or criticize ourselves to deal with the discomfort and dissonance we feel.

When our system becomes overwhelmed by the good, or we don't yet trust it, we will unconsciously focus on the negative, keeping us stuck in our sadness and our wounds. Spiritual teacher, medical intuitive, and author Caroline Myss aptly calls our attention to this attachment to the wound that she calls "woundology" and describes it as the place we live "when we define ourselves by our wounds." So often we get stuck in the eye of the wound—not because we wish to deny ourselves goodness, but because we fear what happens on the other side if we do. *We fear what might happen because of what did happen in the past.* It's a vulnerable journey to open, release, trust, and receive what we never have.

Let's take this a step further and shine a light on the brighter side of our wounds. The gold that lives in the muck for us all.

The path to our liberation is in the wisdom that dwells in the wound. Until we consciously turn toward relationships and connection, our wounds are something that we build relationship patterns around protecting and preserving. Our relationships suffer when we live from the center of our wounds, not our integrity—when we try to avoid touching them rather than cultivating the wisdom that dwells within them. What if, instead, we garner the wisdom that lives in our historical pains, and in turn learn the skills, words, and actions that are required to be *empowered* by the pain rather than avoidant of it? Then, and only then, can we step into mature and thriving relationships where we see our past being in service and in honor of the future we want to create.

We offer this perspective on wounds to loosen the grip with which we hold on to the past, so that we can slowly, and with great care, open ourselves up to the goodness, wonder, and beauty that await us on the other side. When we enter this unknown space in our relationships, it's natural for fear to rise. Instead of pushing it away and bolting, we invite you to bring it forward.

This may sound like, "Wow, I've never opened up this much, or taken this step with anyone . . . and it scares me. And while I want to run, push you away, or find something wrong, I'm choosing to stay and stand in this goodness." At times, you might need to hear some reassurance to soften the mental mixtape of fear that can often get kicked up as we move beyond the familiar. This might sound like, "Hey, I could use some reassurance right now . . . can you remind me that everything is okay, that you're here, and that you love me?"

As we bring what's in the way up and out, our hearts continue to heal and open. This is where love begins to lead, again.

Let Love Lead

On the journey to liberated love, we'll be asked over and over to increase our tolerance for good things and decrease our tolerance for the not so good. Opening and expanding into these deeper levels of intimacy with another—*through the good and painful experiences alike*—is the practice of letting love lead.

The journey to liberated love is a call to stand in integrity. This call becomes easier to embody when we trust and know that everything that is emerging in our relationship(s) is emerging for a reason. Author and psychologist Dr. Alexandra Solomon calls this the golden equation in relationship: your stuff plus my stuff equals our stuff. What's emerging for one person is emerging for both of you. Trust that.

Your triggers are a gift. When turned toward with curiosity and a desire to heal and grow, they become the catalyst that brings the relationship to the next level.

EXERCISE
Opening to the Good

When you become triggered by someone else's words or behaviors, how do you respond? Are you prone to fighting or fleeing? Do you resort to criticism, defensiveness, contempt (e.g., rolling of the eyes), or stonewalling (e.g., shutting down, ghosting, leaving the room)?

When you were young, what did you witness from your primary caregivers and other adults in your life? How did they handle ruptures and repairs? Did you witness apologies? Did you take responsibility and apologize in experiences you had with them?

How do you handle ruptures and repairs with others today?

How did your primary caregivers manage and express their own (and others') feelings of upset, irritation, or anger? How do you? How did they manage and express their own (and others') feelings of joy and excitement? How do you?

FILL IN THE BLANK:

My biggest block/fear to allowing joy, goodness, and intimacy into my life is _____.

I'm afraid if I allow it into my experience, what will happen is _____.

I am ready to open and receive _____.

· 12 ·

Restoring Sacred Sexuality

When I (Mark) started working with Emerson and her partner, Eric, Emerson had reached out because she and Eric had reached a point of extreme frustration and couldn't find their way through it. She shared with me that everything in their relationship was great! They had great communication. He was a great guy. She loved him. He loved her. They listened to each other. They encouraged each other's growth. Everything was great . . . *except*, she said, that they just didn't have a sexual charge when they were intimate. They were both at their wits' end because here they were, with everything else feeling nailed (*not nailed?!*), and yet there was a lack of desire and arousal.

Gosh, who else can relate to this? Our relationship may be free from significant conflict, we seem to have lots of safety and great communication, yet we just don't want to do the humpty-hump with them.

I asked Emerson and Eric if there had ever been chemistry between them. They both answered with a resounding and emphatic, "*Yes!* We used to have great sex. We had a fiery connection!"

Ah, so something *changed*. I dove deeper.

"When you two are intimate, and let's say Eric is in the midst of pleasuring you, Emerson, do you share what you like and don't like? Do you give him feedback in real time, or even after?" I asked, anxiously awaiting her response.

"Um, hmmmm," she replied a bit sheepishly, "I mean, not really. I just let him do his thing. Sometimes it works for me, sometimes it doesn't."

"Gosh, you could have a custom-made cunnilingus machine if you shared what works for you! Instead, he's down there with his tongue about to fall off trying to do everything he can!" I joked, to loosen them up and lighten the tension.

They both laughed and we came back to the question that was about to bring it all to light: "Why don't you share what works or doesn't work for you? What are you afraid of that prevents you from sharing what brings you pleasure?" I asked.

"Because I'm afraid to hurt Eric's feelings."

There it was. The hidden seed of codependency that was lurking far below their seemingly incredibly healthy relationship.

Codependency kills desire in long-term relationships.

You know the "honeymoon phase"? That special time in a relationship at the very beginning? The part where you're willing to do anything (and we mean *anything*) to see your new love and be with them? You're on your best behavior. You hide your triggers. You're not reactive. You use public washrooms to poop so they operate under the illusion that you somehow don't go number two.

There are plenty of reasons for honeymoon behavior. Mostly, we are captured by novelty and the incredible neurohormonal cocktail that is flooding through our bodies. We've got dopamine, oxytocin, noradrenaline, vasopressin, testosterone, and oh, so much more.

We ravage each other. Our appetites are insatiable. But we get so caught up in the drug that is the other that we forget about ourselves.

The honeymoon phase in some ways not only plants the seeds for codependency but also anesthetizes us to it as well.

In Esther Perel's book *Mating in Captivity*, she shares:

The grand illusion of committed love is that we think our partners are ours. In truth, their separateness is unassailable, and their mystery is for-

ever ungraspable. As soon as we can begin to acknowledge this, sustained desire becomes a real possibility.

The bottom line is: We don't want to be intimate with someone whom we blame (unconsciously or consciously) for losing ourselves. We don't desire someone who has lost themselves either.

When we hide our voices and our needs and our wants, like Emerson did, we are not fully expressed. When we're not fully expressed, we won't desire our partner because we don't feel psychologically safe to be ourselves. Do you see how sneaky it can be?

From here I explored with Emerson and Eric where else truth was being held back to protect each other's feelings. Where else were they not telling the *full* truth?

The fascinating thing about intimacy is that often (almost always) the challenges that come up in the bedroom are really challenges that have not been confronted in the relationship. This can look like a lack of desire, but it can also look like the need to create conflict and chaos to fuel desire.

Either way, there are patterns that need to be healed. And once we heal these patterns, we clear a path to sacred sexuality and divine intimacy.

Sex is not an isolated event that happens inside a vacuum. As we saw with Eric and Emerson, *what shows up in our sexual experiences is a magnification of everything else that is or isn't happening within our relationships.* We know this intellectually, of course, but when it comes to peeling back the layers and looking at what's going on underneath our sexual desire (or lack thereof), we'd rather not. Why is this? Welp, because underneath the sheets is all of the nonsexual stuff—like our unresolved wounds, lack of resonance/alignment, somatic blocks, spiritual lessons, and the unmet nonsexual needs—that we'd rather not touch.

In addition to all the *other stuff* we'd rather not look at is the fact that sex and sexuality carry a lot of cultural baggage. Sex, and what's going on in the bedroom, can be a touchy, vulnerable, and taboo subject for many. When we begin to explore the messages that we've been sent around sex and sexuality, the discomfort we feel begins to make a lot of sense. Here are a few of the responses we received from our community when we asked them to share the main messages they were sent around sex and sexuality:

Sex is . . .
sinful, where a man leads and a woman submits, disgusting, dirty, un-
clean, performative, for marriage only, shameful, private, all about a
man's pleasure, all about pleasing the woman, where the woman's or-
gasm is the focus, where the man's orgasm is the focus, how women source
power, how men source worth, a woman's primary value, "off-limits."

What were the implicit and explicit messages you were sent around sex, intimacy, and sexuality?

Needless to say, there's a whole boatload of internalized messages that we must navigate to restore the sacred in sex. And yet, if we're courageous enough to explore what's under the covers, we can discover and bring sex/ sexuality back to its rightful place—to a place where reverence, intimacy, ecstasy, and connection flourish.

To embody this new sexual pattern—where reverence reigns—we'll explore how sex and sexuality present themselves in both codependent dynamics and relationships rooted in liberated love. To begin, let's take a peek at what's going on in codependent dynamics.

Sex at Every Stage

Codependent Sex

One of the main places codependency shows up is in the bedroom. Some of the ways it shows up are when we override our own limits to placate a partner ("This will keep them happy for a little bit") and use sex as a tool to source security ("I will give you this in exchange for this"). In these dynamics, we also use sex as a way to discharge anxiety in relationship and distract ourselves from our pain. Underneath all of these strategies? We're trying to get the right things (our needs) met in the wrong places (the bedroom).

Some of the needs we try to source through sex—in addition to security and safety—include the need for love, affection, approval, and connection. When we do this, we are eroticizing our wounds.

Sounds sexy, right? Let's dive a little deeper and look at some of the ways sex and sexual energy are held when we find ourselves in codependent dynamics.

Eroticizing our wounds. When we eroticize our wounds, it means our wounds are driving arousal. Wild, right?! How this looks is that we are often choosing to engage in sex from a desire that is mainly rooted in childhood. We're looking for sex to give us something we needed, didn't get, and still desire. For some this is a need for approval, for others it's a need for love and affection. And while these needs are beautiful and important, when this energy is present in the bedroom sex becomes less about intimacy and connection and more about soothing a need that desperately wants to be met. When we have unmet nonsexual needs that are attached to sex, it can feel like there isn't a lot of space in the bedroom for real intimacy to exist—and how could there be, when the desire feels like it's coming from a wounded ("I need this now") energy?

Lack of sexual containment. This is when we have shaky (uncontained) sexual energy and porous sexual boundaries. Meaning, our sexual energy is flowing in other directions outside our relationship, which creates a lack of safety and limits the depth of intimacy in our romantic relationships. Some of the ways this may show up include building inappropriate emotionally intimate relationships with others, flirting and using sexual energy to magnetize others to you, energizing sexual fantasy with others (in the bedroom and outside the bedroom), and/or pornography use. These strategies show up for a myriad of reasons, but some of the main reasons are to create distance in our relationship, to source attention and connection from someone else, and to discharge anxiety and create distance from uncomfortable emotions.

Relying on sex to make us feel better. When we try to rely on sex to make us feel better—to soothe an activated nervous system—we're mistaking the high we get when we reconnect (after being disconnected) for love and passion. Sex, when kept hostage in this activation/soothing cycle, becomes a temporary and pseudo source of relief instead of a place of deep connection and intimacy.

Over-importance on orgasm: When we're overfocused on the end game—orgasm—instead of connection and intimacy, we lose the whole plot. And in our eyes, the pressure to make orgasm the point is what keeps orgasm off the radar for many. When liberated from the pressure to O, sex becomes a place where play, curiosity, and intimacy can come back to the forefront, and in our experience, new levels of embodied pleasure can unfold.

Remember the desire that initially fueled Emerson and Eric's sex life and that, over time, fizzled out? The heat we experience in a codependent dynamic is the heat of enmeshment (a collapse of our boundaries), which is wildly different than the sustained heat we experience when we choose to expand our boundaries to create a loving, respectful, and erotic space between two separate selves. This expansion is what we're after—where all of who your partner is and all of you who you are is welcome and honored.

Liberated Lovemaking

When sex is liberated from any obligation to make us feel better (or another feel better), a more profound and sacred sexual experience begins to emerge—one we call liberated lovemaking (sorry, we had to). Liberated lovemaking happens when a foundation of safety, trust, and love *already* exists between two embodied, self-honoring humans. By doing the work to come home to you, your body, your needs, and your desires, you have been creating the foundation for liberated love to flow in the bedroom. Here are some of the pillars that enrich our sexual experience and deepen intimacy:

Embodied connection: Our bodies can sense when someone is fully here with us and when they aren't. When we are in our bodies, we are present, here, alive, attuned, and engaged in the moment and with another. This depth of presence and embodied connection is required if we wish to open and surrender into new levels of connection.

Emotional safety: We feel safe to share what's coming up for us in and out of the bedroom. This felt sense of safety arises when we know our limits and feel safe to bring forward and receive information within the shared space of intimacy. This is the experience of being fully naked, accepted, and welcomed in a space.

Held as sacred: Both you and your partner hold sex and intimacy as sacred. You honor each other's bodies and each other's needs, and lead with curiosity, collaboration, and compassion. This sounds like, "What do you need? How can I support you? What are you interested in experiencing?"

Not attached to outcome: In liberated lovemaking, orgasm isn't the sole purpose and end goal in mind. Instead, the focus is on connection via touch, eye-gazing, embodied presence, opening, and exploring everything else that exists in an intimate space.

Take charge of your sexual energy: This pillar is key for liberated lovemaking. The containment of your sexual energy allows for a deepening of safety in the relationship. When you notice an attraction to another (which is natural) you redirect that energy back into your partnership instead of opening your energy to another and entertaining the charge and attraction.

After reading through this list, you might be thinking, *This all sounds good in theory . . . but how do you shift what's been normalized in the bedroom? How do we begin to cocreate this foundation and bring the sacred back to sex?* While we will share the pathway that we walked and continue to walk, the pathway to liberated lovemaking will look different for everyone. While there isn't one path or a cookie-cutter answer, there is a much wiser and more well-equipped guide that we all have available to us on this journey: your one and only body.

Honoring the Body

Like many women that I've worked with, sex was a place where I (Kylie) took a back seat in any relationship. Sex wasn't about shared pleasure; it was about pleasing the man and doing what needed to be done in order to keep the man (and my source of safety).

For a long time, it didn't matter what I wanted or what my womb or body were up for. Overriding the body and disassociating takes its toll. It's important to note that this wasn't something that happened *to me*, meaning I wasn't forced or exploited by another—this orientation to male pleasure and self-erasure, for me, was the norm because it was generations old and culturally validated. In fact, the first time Mark asked me, "What do you like? What feels good for you?" in the bedroom, my whole body froze. I thought, *Why is he talking to me? We don't talk during sex* . . . Underneath the freeze lived a deeper truth: I had no idea what felt good, or what I liked. My desires, along with an understanding of my body, were hidden, untouched, and, quite frankly, *terrifying* to touch.

And this, my friends, is where the unraveling of patriarchal conditioning begins. Where we first come home to our own bodies, heal the violations (from self and other), and restore our integrity with our sexual organs. To do this, we're going to circle back to the wonderful land of self-consent. This time, we're going to bring it into the bedroom (with ourselves and with another). This looks like exploring your limits (*Does this feel good? Do I like this?*) and tracking your nervous system (*Am I fully here? Is this leading to greater connection or disconnection?*). When we honor ourselves in these ways, our bodies begin to thaw, and what was once numb becomes awakened and invigorated.

On this journey from numbness to sensitization, from doing what we've always done to trying something new, we may be invited (or forced) to hit the pause button and enter a period of conscious celibacy. As we discussed in chapter 6, when we take an intentional pause from any behavior or dynamic, we create the distance and space we need to disrupt unconscious patterns and heal. So often the sexual and emotional energy that would've been discharged through previous sexual dynamics, when paused, forces us to heal and enter new levels of intimacy within our relationships.

Author and Jungian therapist Marion Woodman brilliantly shined a light on this in one of her talks on transformation, saying:

The body's symptoms must be acknowledged as a thermostat in a *relationship* [our emphasis]. *The conscious body will attempt to force* *the relationship onto a new level of spiritual intimacy which can then be* *embodied at a very different level of sexuality . . . which may bring about* *a period of natural celibacy.*

This was the case for our relationship.

When Mark and I entered into relationship 2.0, I was one month into a period of conscious celibacy. I was committed to walking this path of celibacy for seven months to allow my womb to heal. What we didn't realize at the time was just how catalyzing this intentional pause would be for our combined healing process.

The emotional and sexual energy that once sought security, connection, and release through sex was off the table. We were no longer looking for sex to make us feel safe, connected, or loved. Instead, we were being invited to have the conversations that invited a new level of safety and intimacy to emerge.

For me (Mark), it tested my dependence on sex for connection and also allowed me to become very clear with what needs and wants I had and how those could be met alongside Kylie's. It made intimacy not center around penetrative sex, but rather play and creativity. The period of healing was also important for developing both of our voices in order to express what we wanted, needed, desired, and enjoyed in the sacred space of sex. And that curiosity led the way.

So many of the messages we are taught growing up must be given conscious space to be healed in the sacred container of connection. Our vulnerabilities come forth when we are naked, both figuratively and literally, and our insecurities have an opportunity to be loved rather than avoided and shamed.

While we walked this path consciously, sometimes we are forced onto it. When we go against our own bodies and dismiss our instinct (for whatever reason), the body will step in and manifest symptoms we won't be able to ignore. We've seen this happen a lot in our client work and have witnessed this pathway to growth many times. And while it's not the most easeful path to walk, the body's wisdom is not shallow, and it will demand we shift something—like becoming celibate—until we deal with the *real* problem, *a misalignment, a call to deeper integrity, a new level of sexual intimacy,* in our lives. The body invites us to have the conversations we're afraid to have . . . so that we can, as Marion Woodman says, step into a new level of spiritual, physical intimacy.

Look, we get it. Choosing celibacy might sound extreme to you. But, in our experience, it can be a vital way to reset and heal at any stage of relationship. Why is this? When we take a pause from doing what we've always done, we free up our sexual energy from previous pathways so that we can examine deeper issues that might exist in a relationship (like insecurity, unmet nonsexual needs), heal from previous violations (by self or others), and intentionally clear out any sexual energy from previous partners. Essentially, choosing to be celibate for a specific amount of time shakes things up so that something more aligned and nourishing can emerge.

Together We Heal

Sexual challenges are relational challenges. In order to heal our patterns we have to step out of them so that we can observe them and feel what is coming up for us in the space between. This is what *choosing* celibacy does. For me (Mark), the idea of choosing celibacy felt trite at first. I wanted to come back together from our sacred pause and get right into that ravishing come-back-together kind of sex.

When Kylie proposed taking it slow and not having penetrative sex I was like, "Nah. That doesn't work for me." And then I sat with it. I asked myself, *Why? What is my resistance?* And whether you're single or in a relationship reading this, you may be asking the same. When I explored what was coming up I found that I had a fear that if we weren't having sex then things weren't okay—that I *needed* penetrative (gosh, that word is weird to use!) sex in order to feel connected and safe, and that things were back to "normal."

I was resistant to celibacy because I had sourced so much from intimacy and arousal. I was resistant because I didn't know how to enter (pun intended!) a relationship slowly. I didn't know fully how to be with the pace that discernment allows. I didn't know how to sit with the fears that it might not work, or that Kylie wasn't going to be a good match now, or that I didn't know if she was really going to choose the relationship fully this time. All these fears I had I was hoping to medicate with sex. But by choosing celibacy and choosing to be very intentional and mindful of how we navigated the coming back together, I stayed in my body and my heart and communicated my fears, and it led to powerful conversations of connection. We also got to have a lot of fun, like a couple of teenagers who weren't ready to go "all the way"!

So, if you're reluctant, explore that. If you're resistant, be with that. Ask yourself what you may be afraid of? What have you used sex to source?

Liberated love is about the restoration of the sacred in every area of your relationships, and in turn, your life. To be liberated in one area we must be liberated in all areas. To bring our voice, our integrity, our power, our wants, our needs, and to worship and be worshipped in the sacred space of sex and intimacy is a profound experience. We want that for you. And we know that, through fully embodying and living in choice (*Does this work for me? Is this a good fit for me? Do I like this?*), we are practicing self-consent and are building self-worth and self-trust.

When we're connected to our bodies, limits, and desires and experience a felt sense of safety—a space of total acceptance—with another, we get to experience the physical manifestation of liberated love. This is the raw, surrendered space where we drop the masks and armor and allow someone in. *True intimacy is when we feel safe enough to tell the truth and let someone see us in our totality.* In liberated love, sex and physical intimacy become the cherry on top of an already decadent, rich, and fulfilling connection. In liberated love, we remember the healing power of our procreative sexual energies and honor sex as a ritual. A place we go to cocreate and energize goodness, healing, and love.

EXERCISE
Sacred Sex

Below are some journal/conversation prompts to help you explore what sacred sexuality might look like and to provide a path for how you might cocreate that with your partner:

- *When you hear the term "sacred sexuality," what comes up for you? What would a sacred sexual experience feel/look like for you?*
- *What are your needs and expectations when it comes to sexual connectivity?*
- *What is your deepest desire in the bedroom?*
- *What is your biggest block in the bedroom?*
- *What can you do—solo or with a partner—to work through this block?*

13

It Takes a Village

*I*t takes a village to live and love well. This is exactly what doctors and scientists discovered when they arrived in Roseto, Pennsylvania, a small town that was home to hundreds of Italian immigrants who had ventured across the sea seeking a brighter future.

The Rosetans had not only brought their desire for a more beautiful life with them to America, they also brought with them their cultural values. It was these values—community, family, kindness, spirituality, and egalitarianism—that turned this isolated, rocky hillside of Pennsylvania into a warm, socially rich, and vibrant community. And when the risk of heart disease was on the rise in the 1950s, the Rosetans remained, somehow, shielded.

Stumped and mystified by these health outcomes, head researcher Dr. Wolf and his team went on a search to find out why the people in this village were *healthier* than their peers who lived in other places. They explored diet, environment, genetics, exercise—all the typical markers of health—but after reaching dead end after dead end, they expanded the magnifying glass beyond the individual and zoomed out to the culture. It was here, through a wider lens, that the mystery was solved. It wasn't their diet or genes that kept them healthy; it was their tight-knit social structure and the health of their relationships that kept the community thriving.

This is the magic of *interdependence*—and if the Rosetans can't convince you, the longest-running study on human happiness, the Harvard Study of Adult Development, found that the key to health and happiness is having good relationships and community.*

Interdependence is the life-nourishing magic that happens when we live in a relational ecosystem of *mutual* dependence—of authentic individuals coming together in community. It is the bone-deep knowledge that *I can depend on you, and you can depend on me.* It's how we, much like the Rosetans, moved through life together on Earth for eons. When we know we can count on others to really be there when we need them, we feel safe to be ourselves and walk our authentic path.

As author and expert in the field of attachment theory and trauma resolution Diane Poole Heller reminds us, "Interdependence means that we can take care of ourselves with the help of others, and others can achieve an interconnected autonomy with our involvement and support. To truly explore ourselves, we need one another, to be together deeply, we need to take care of ourselves." In other words, the balance between healthy dependence and autonomy makes way for interdependence—where dependency is reciprocal, nourishing, and generative. This balance allows for an interconnected sovereignty to emerge instead of codependence.

For some, this journey to interdependence is the movement toward opening up, being vulnerable, and asking for and receiving support from others. For others, this journey to interdependence is cultivating the capacity to be with themselves, pull back projections, and come back to center. Many of us oscillate between the extreme expressions of these: on one side we have hyper/hypo-independence, and on the other side we have codependence.

---

* Robert Waldinger and Marc Schulz, "What the Longest Study on Human Happiness Found Is the Key to a Good Life," *The Atlantic*, January 29, 2023, https://www.theatlantic.com/ideas/archive/2023/01/harvard-happiness-study-relationships/672753/.

Hyper-independence sounds like, "I don't need anyone, I can do it all on my own."

Hypo-independence sounds like, "I don't need anyone, and I can't do it on my own."

If either of these sounds like your story, it's likely because it hasn't been safe in your experience to rely on another, or you don't believe you deserve support. Maybe you saw a caregiver who struggled emotionally and you never wanted to be like them. You may have experienced a lack of consistency and neglect in early childhood, making the turn toward self-reliance the safest option for you. Maybe you've internalized the cultural narratives that needing support makes you "weak" or "vulnerable," and that you *should* be able to do it all on your own. For those who believe you don't need anyone, we get it. It's a terrifying and vulnerable experience to acknowledge that sometimes you are *not* okay and that you *do* need support—but we also want to remind you that it is okay, understandable, and healthy to not be okay 100 percent of the time, and it is okay to ask for support. Okay?!

Codependence sounds like, "I need you; I can't do anything on my own," or "I need you; and I can do it all for both of us."

If this is your story, it's because for you to feel safe, you have needed other people close. This state of helplessness, of not feeling confident and competent in yourself, has an intricate root system. At the center is a chronic state of dysregulation—a feeling of not being okay. To cope with these feelings, you become who you need to be to keep people close. As we explored earlier in the book, sometimes this looks like embodying helplessness in a dynamic, and at other times this looks like embodying the role of the caretaker (who does everything) to ensure people stay close and dependent.

The problem with both hyper/hypo-independence and codependence is that no one's true needs (being seen, heard, loved) are being met. For starters, no one can meet all of their needs on their own. It's impossible, although the main cultural narratives (once you have X you will be happy and whole) would advise us otherwise. And on the other side, one person could never adequately meet all of our needs—especially when their trying to do so comes at the expense of their own well-being.

In fact, for our needs to be met well and for our souls to be nourished, we need not only a network of healthy human connections but also to remember the relationships we have with the Earth, unseen allies, animals, the elements, and beyond. The more avenues we have to get our needs met, the more resilient and secure we feel. The more valuable and wanted we feel in our communities and relationships, the more connected and meaningful we feel.

To give you an example of the magic of interdependence, let's say you've had a hard day and could really use a hug and a caring touch. If you only have one person in your life who can meet this need, you're going to be pretty reliant on and at the whim of this one person. When this is the case, requests can quickly morph into demands ("I *need* this from you"). Now, let's say you've cultivated a vast web of connections and feel confident in asking many people in your life for some extra love. You may turn to your circle of friends and ask if anyone has some time to connect and give you some extra hugs or love. You might head down the street to get reflexology or call your bodyworker. You might cuddle up with your pet and watch a movie or head to a yoga class with your favorite instructor. You might ask your partner to hold your hand on the way to dinner or for a long hug when you both get home. You might go outside, lie on the grass, and allow the earth to hold you. Do you notice the difference in your system when you sit with these two options—having one person who can meet your need for touch versus having multiple people, places, beings who can hold you well? The second of these is what interdependence feels like. It feels like flexibility and resourcefulness. It's this flexibility that softens our nervous system and opens the door for true choice to emerge.

The beautiful thing about opening ourselves up in these ways—to humans, animals, the earth, and beyond—is that we begin to heal a collective receptivity wound (the wound that says it isn't safe to receive) that has blocked us (or limited us) from the experience of gratitude, connection, reverence, and sacred reciprocity. When we can receive *fully*, we can give from a generative place. When we receive unconditionally, we honor, have gratitude for, and protect the very relationships that sustain and nurture us. When we receive, we allow love to flow in and back out in ways that are nourishing and life-giving. We allow love to liberate us and everything around us.

Here are some of the receptivity blocks we've witnessed and walked through, both personally and professionally, on the journey back home to interdependence:

+ Unconscious hooks of obligation and expectation: *If I give you X, you need to do Y.*
+ Fear of punishment: *If I take this [support/gift/affection], they might take it away and punish me by removing it later.*
+ Vulnerability: *If I ask for support, I will be seen as weak and vulnerable.*
+ Worthiness wound: *I don't deserve this, who am I to receive this?*
+ Intergenerational imprints: *It isn't safe to receive, and my desires are not welcome here.*
+ Fear of rejection: *What if they reject me? Think I'm too much? Dismiss/minimize my needs?*
+ Lack of trust: *I don't trust others to show up. I don't trust myself to accept someone's "no."*

We come by these receptivity blocks wisely. When growing up in cultures that operate on dominance, contempt, paternalism, urgency, exploitation, extraction, competition, and manipulation—rigid self-reliance or an overt dependence on external systems have become the two pathways available to us for survival. The degradation of village, family, and communal frameworks has made way for a world where "the state and the market are the mother and father of the individual," as Yuval Noah Harari writes in his book *Sapiens.* The degradation of village, to us, is costing us our health, our planet, and our relationships. It's this separation from one another, the Earth, and the whole circle of life that is leading us into endless cycles of burnout, anxiety, and depression.

What we're doing isn't and hasn't been working.

If we desire to live and love well, we need to take a page out of the manual of the Rosetans, who had neighborhood gatherings, all the children from the community playing together, friends and family to laugh, celebrate and cry with. Where we know the farmers, butcher, baker, and our neighbors. Where we hold each other's children, and each other. For liberated love to flourish we must cultivate communities that are well-resourced, healthy, and anchored in life-affirming values. We need to restore the village and our connection to the Earth, soul, and spirit.

Restoring Village

When we talk about restoring village, we're not only talking about healing our relationships, we're also talking about analyzing the cultural myth—the story—we've all been living out and agreeing to. The story that determines how we view, relate to, and treat ourselves, others, and life. One that determines what we as a species value and how we survive and find belonging here.

The story? Progress is good. Self-reliance is everything. Life is about ascension, growth, and always moving toward what feels easy, light, agreeable. "Good vibes only," as the T-shirts say.

But we all know that real and truthful relationships are not easy and light all the time. Alas, the vibes are not always good. We know that family and community can be gritty—filled with differentiating thoughts, feelings, beliefs, opinions, and desires. Life is filled with pain, grief, and challenges. *Living a life that checks all the boxes is not a sign of success but rather one of assimilation.* This isn't to say that everything we learn or everything culture values isn't important, or that those who live the story they're taught are wrong—it's that much of the story we've been taught almost always comes at the expense of the relationship we have with ourselves and the ones we have with others. This story has us focused on belonging to a system that is unwell rather than seeking relationships filled with truth and depth that sustain and enrich our lives. This is what happens when we live in a story that is rooted in separation, disconnection, and scarcity—and it's a story we are shifting together as we answer the call to heal and reconnect.

To begin the process of restoration—of creating a new story—we're going to begin with a healthy dose of self-reflection. Ask yourself: *How am I showing up today? How am I treating others? How do I show up when I am operating in survival mode? How do I silence myself to maintain connection in community? How has this caused others and me pain? What story am I energizing (one of scarcity or one of abundance)?* Naming how we've shown up, and how we've treated others and ourselves when we were operating from survival mode, is a tender and necessary process.

When I (Kylie) began this journey of self-reflection—of exploring how I treated myself and others when I was operating from survival mode—I found myself in a deep pit of emotion. It's hard looking down the timeline of your life and seeing how you've hurt others and yourself. I felt shame and disgust (*I can't believe I did that*), grief (*I am so sad that was the only option I saw available*), anger (*I wish I knew then what I know now*), and relief (*Thank the heavens I have more options and choices available to me now*).

What allows us to do this work? Holding ourselves in a compassionate space of both/and. This sounds like: *I am sad and ashamed I showed up that way AND I have compassion for the part of me that was scared and in pain.* When we can hold ourselves here, it becomes easier to hold others in the same way. When we walk with self-accountability and healthy boundaries, we can heal the wounds that keep us disconnected from the connections we need to thrive.

Some of the communal wounds we are being invited to name, process, and heal as we do this work together in community are: betrayal, competition, exclusion, violence/harm, bullying, exploitation, and shame/judgment. It's likely that we've all found ourselves on both sides—the one experiencing or the one inflicting these wounds—at different times in our lives. While neither side feels *good* to be on, the new invitation that has arrived at your doorstep is to stop tolerating and stop engaging with these types of behaviors.

Once we know better, we can do better.

One example of where we see this wounding is in communities that shame those who step out of line with the imposed "moral" views of a religion or community.

I (Mark) had a client named Steve who grew up as a Jehovah's Witness. He was raised in a small town and had not been exposed to much life outside it. At nineteen years old, much like his family did before him, he got married. He didn't know any different. He was doing what he was taught. At twenty-five years old he moved to a city and got exposed to different ways of living and thinking. It shattered the narrow framework of what he had been taught life had to be. He was excited about all the possibilities! He wanted to pursue his dreams and follow his heart . . . and his wife did not. She felt like he was abandoning their religion, and she was terrified he would grow away from her, so she desperately tried to control him by using shame and threats that the community would abandon him if he left her.

But Steve's awareness of the life he craved could not be turned off. Eventually he got divorced, moved to an even bigger city, and left his old life and religion behind. In making those choices, he was disowned by his parents. They were ashamed of him for getting divorced and expressed that their love was available on the condition he repent and come back to being a Jehovah's Witness and ask for Jehovah's forgiveness.

When families and communities are unhealthy, they exile people based on their choices or mistakes, or for taking different paths. When people go through changes or difficult times, their community should be the soft place they can land. Healthy communities seek to learn from the adventures, trials, and tribulations of their members. We're not saying that everyone should always tolerate anything and everything but instead should hold standards and boundaries, model repair, and become communities that raise a high bar of integrity and embody unconditional love.

We get so excited when we think about what's possible for humanity (and the planet) when we heal these communal wounds. We've seen and experienced so much healing in communal spaces—where for the first time a man feels safe to shed his tears with other men, or a woman feels safe to break down and rage after having to keep it all together with other women. It's one thing to feel safe in ourselves, and it's a whole other experience to feel safe in our relationships and communities. When this happens, our birthright, interdependence, is restored.

Some of the ways we can shift the story, heal these wounds, and treat one another is through: celebration (*instead of tearing someone down*), collaboration (*instead of competing*), vulnerability (*instead of shaming/judging*), integrity (*instead of betrayal*), honesty (*instead of exclusion*), fierce love (*instead of violence*), and gratitude (*instead of exploitation*).

Every time we choose to lead in these ways, we energize a *new* story. A story where someone else's well-being enhances yours instead of coming at the cost of yours. A story that orients around the truth that we are all interconnected. A story that honors the heart and soul of another. When we energize and embody this story, a new set of values, much like the values of the Rosetans, begins to take hold—values like reciprocity, gratitude, family, community, sacred responsibility, right relationships, sovereignty, and kindness.

Now as much as we'd love to see these cultural values take root overnight, we know that sustainable shifts happen slowly, one individual, one conversation, and one moment of awareness at a time.

We call these individuals, the ones devoted to creating a new story through right action, pillars of remembrance.

Pillar of Remembrance

As we heal, individually and relationally, we become a pillar of well-being, healing, and regulation in our communities. As the saying goes, we become the change we wish to see in the world.

You might know someone in your life like this—a person who leads with grace, compassion, and honesty, a soul who feels easy to be around, who is engaged with life, owns their side of the street, and walks their unique path. These souls are equally as magnetic as they are triggering at times, right? And that's just it—when someone walks into our life embodying health, authenticity, and well-being, it triggers us awake (in a good way). It invites the parts of us that are ready to be healed and the parts of us that yearn to be deeply seen to come out of hiding. Why is this? Our bodies' and psyches' natural inclination is toward healing and wholeness. When we find safe people and loving communities, our armor and masks can soften. We can, ourselves, become pillars of healing within our families, communities, and workplaces.

This is the ripple effect of healing that we're after.

As we heal, we no longer tolerate dysfunction and dynamics that are toxic. Instead, we become an entry point for a new dynamic to emerge. We say, "I'm not interested in energizing this story, but I am interested in moving toward *this* one. Do you want to join me?"

When Rebecca contacted me (Mark), she was having challenges with her mother. Her mom was incredibly toxic, emotionally abusive, and had been a very painful person in Rebecca's life. "But it's my mom," she would say, "I can't cut her off. That's not unconditionally loving!" We explored her childhood and what she had been through. Countless stories of verbal abuse and incessant manipulation. She would try to express herself to her mother only to find herself feeling four years old whenever her mom would erupt with a slurry of harsh words, calling her "fat" and "stupid," and telling her she would never amount to anything. Rebecca explained how her whole family pivoted around the abuse. Everyone was afraid of Mom. And everyone was dealing with different mental and emotional health challenges.

When there is a truth or reality that a system doesn't want to confront, the system learns to orient around it. As we discussed at the very beginning of this book (chapter 1), we all take on masks to keep the system going, only to find ourselves as adults exhausted, anxious, depressed, and/or addicted, wondering why we just can't seem to get our head above water, set some boundaries, and just enjoy our lives. Toxic families and communities require lots of psychic energy to keep afloat. We put our life force into just surviving in toxic systems, instead of into our own expansion. We are al-most always born into these systems, so we don't know that there's another way. But our hearts do. Our souls do. The symptoms of self-abandonment make themselves known, but when ignoring them has become normalized in our families, it is "abnormal" to answer the call. To answer the call that shakes the system.

Rebecca was answering that call. She was following the nudges of her soul that were saying, *We have to change this NOW*. When Rebecca and I went deeper, she recognized the patterns. It was an exchange with her mother, combined with her new awareness, that allowed her to feel with her whole being the amount of pain she had suppressed and the amount of abuse she had tolerated. She had had enough.

Rebecca set boundaries, eventually cutting off her mother. Those bound-aries were responded to with more toxicity. Rebecca reacted by getting a restraining order against her mother. She fully rejected the story she was told about who she was, who she should be, and what she should tolerate. As she stepped into her power, her family system imploded—the kind of implosion that sets fire to the dark patterns and invites all of those willing to orient around kindness, respect, love, and intolerance for abuse. Her father left her mother shortly after. Her brother ceased contact with her mother too. Everyone was liberated through Rebecca's courage. Phew . . . Exhale . . . right?!

From a newfound self-trust and power, Rebecca continued to build the family and community she always sensed was possible. She is now in a loving relationship, has a beautiful daughter and an incredible relationship with her father and brother, and knows that she has her own back.

And her mother was invited into a new way to live as well—one of ex-pansion, liberation, and love. Mom was asked that big, inviting, liberating question, "Do you want a great relationship?" It was up to Mom to answer the call.

Rebecca became the pioneer of a new way for all of those who have the honor of being in a relationship with her. Her village was liberated through her willingness to call out abuse and stand in the truth, her values, and her worth. Bows to Rebecca.

The Golden Net

When we are surrounded by well-resourced and loving humans, we are cultivating what we call *a golden net*. We're talking a rich mixture of sisterhood, brotherhood, soul family, blood family, fur family, earth kin, and beyond. A net we can fall into if we need it. A net we can rely on for support. A net of nourishment, belonging, connection, and fierce love. But it's more than all of that. When we are anchored and supported by this golden net we can surrender more fully into love. As Sigmund Freud wisely said, "How bold one gets when one is sure of being loved."

When you know you are wanted, loved, and appreciated, you don't stay in places (for long) that aren't that. This is the gift of the golden net. When you know and have the felt experience of feeling loved, safe, and cherished, you give this gift to others and invite the world (and everyone you are in relationship with) to join you in holding this bar of love. You become a home for belonging, instead of seeking it.

Now, you might be thinking, *This sounds great in theory, but how do I create that for myself?* This golden net might feel like a far-off dream—*we hear you*—and we want to remind you that the process of cocreating the golden net takes time. It doesn't appear overnight. It might take years or decades to build it, and that is natural. Good, solid, and sustainable things take time. Just like a romantic relationship, healthy friendships happen one hard conversation, rupture, and repair at a time. Yup, we are triggered in friendships too!

Every step you take that brings you closer to you—to your authentic expression and embodiment—brings you closer to the people who are here to weave this golden net with you and alongside you. To support you in finding "your people," we have included an appendix at the back of the book. Read it. Expand it. Act on it.

Your people are waiting for you.

EXERCISE
Cocreating a Village

Creating a new story and a new community starts with self-reflection.
Ask yourself:

- *What are my values?*
- *What do I care about?*
- *What guides me?*
- *What is the world I want to live in?*
- *Who do I want to be in this world?*
- *What am I committed to?*
- *How do I wish to contribute?*

14

The Greater Reconnection

Our souls are nudging us to reconnect—reconnect to ourselves, the ones we love, and the world around us.

In fact, it is your soul's desire for evolution and expression—a desire rooted in returning to oneness and wholeness—that is bumping up against your survival programming and the old relational templates that are no longer serving you. This rub between our self-protective neurobiological circuits and our soul's true longing is creating a benevolent friction that is knocking on humanity's door with a message:

It's time to wake up. It's time to reconnect.

In this friction lives an invitation to remove, transmute, or transform all the barriers that separate you from you, you from love, and you from the world. It is a call to restore your essence, your body, your soul, and the world you live in and walk upon.

We see this journey of reconnection as synonymous with incarnation, where more of you comes back into your body and back into the world; whereas disconnection is synonymous with soul loss, where more of you goes offline, armors up, and disassociates. This is the choice point: to check out or to check back in.

In these moments, ask yourself:

1. Is this dynamic, environment, or relationship taking me farther away from myself or bringing me closer?
2. Is this dynamic, environment, or relationship bringing more ease, joy, and love into my life?
3. Is this dynamic, environment, or relationship in service to love?

We trust that the sacred tension—the friction—between *what was* (protection) and *what longs to be* (possibility) will continue to push us into the places we've been running from so that we may thaw the parts of us that have been frozen in the past, and land more fully here, fully present, fully engaged. Eventually, hopefully, it will bring us to choose *reconnection* over disconnection, *possibility* over rigidity, *love* over fear.

Yes, love. Our deep desire for love is why there is no greater catalyst to working with this tension and healing than our relationships. Whether it's romantic, familial, platonic, or otherwise, it is the relationship, and everything that comes with it, that pushes us into the places we'd rather not go.

When Mark and I (Kylie) ended relationship 1.0, I remember vividly making a commitment to myself amid the heartbreak. My commitment to myself was: *I will do, look at, heal, and shift whatever I need to do in order to remove the blocks I have to love.*

For me (Mark) this commitment was, *I am all in on creating the love I desire. I am committed to live in the integrity of my heart. To show up fully to life and love and all that it demands of me.* It is this fire, and devotion to love—to possibility—that creates the heat necessary to birth a new template of love.

We took a sacred pause, we worked on ourselves deeply and individually, and we returned as our whole selves, ready to create a new story.

Every step you take to reconnect brings you closer to embodying and birthing a new paradigm of love in your life. We know this because we've lived it. This experience of love is your birthright, and it is available to you, your next-door neighbor, and any soul who desires it. No matter where you are relationally—on the heels of a divorce, married, single, dating—this journey can be for you if you choose it.

What happens when we go all in on love and say "yes" to this journey?

We meet other souls who are ready for a new depth of love alongside us. We invite those in our lives to join us. Everyone is welcome if they wish to choose it, too.

When two divinely led, embodied souls come together, they give birth to a new relational template—a new story—one we have been referring to throughout this book as liberated love.

A template that:

1. Honors the divine connection and authentic path of every soul. *Instead of controlling, trying to change someone, or relating with contempt.*

2. Leads with truth. *No more minimizing, hiding, dishonesty.*

3. Orients from kindness and compassion. *No more shaming or punishment.*

4. Lives in the integrity of our hearts. *Leans into vulnerability over and over again.*

5. Is in service of our individual growth. *The relationship serves as a space to bring both of us more alive. It is where our gifts are ripened, and our individual fire is stoked.*

6. Is rooted in collaboration, where both beings in a relationship are honored and have space to lead. *No more submission (e.g., men lead, women submit).*

7. Honors free will, agency, and choice. *You are free to go as you wish. No more hooks, outsourcing, or codependency.*

8. Respects differences of thoughts, feelings, and opinions, and honors that these differences foster deeper intimacy, safety and the creation of something new. *Instead of enmeshment, collapse of self, and avoiding conflict.*

9. Maintains wholeness while moving into intimacy. *Instead of shrinking yourself or needing another to complete you and choose you.*

10. Is grounded in reverence and positive regard. *Instead of pedestaling or infantilizing another. "In you, I see an aspect of the divine. In me, you see an aspect of the divine. Through you I find the divine."*

4. Is anchored in purpose. *Choosing life-giving relationships over life-draining ones. "Our union is here to contribute something unique and good to the world."*

5. Is anchored in fierce love. *No more placating ego and unhealthy behaviors.*

As we work to embody this new template of love in our relationships, we will be continually invited to liberate ourselves from the stories, limitations, and templates that have blocked love's flow for a long damn time. This is courageous heart work. To liberate ourselves from the ancestral, cultural, and historical constraints that have kept us bound to a small story ("This is who you need to be, and this is what is possible for your life, relationships, and love") is love in action.

The beautiful thing about this journey?

There is no end point. No destination in mind. Instead, we get to live into the mystery that is love, and life on this planet. The story of who we are and what is possible continues to expand and deepen as we surrender and open our hearts. A story that is being written one choice at a time.

Coming Home

To go within and excavate the things we spent our life numbing and burying is courageous work—it is the most important work. This journey home isn't only the remembrance of what love truly is, it is the remembrance of who we truly are through love.

As our systems thaw and our sensitivity is restored, we begin to come home not only to the world within us, but to the living, breathing one that surrounds and sustains us. We've heard our clients describe this shift as one from seeing the world in black and white to seeing it in vivid color. The world quite literally comes alive. Each passing person on the sidewalk is a universe of their own—souls walking home. The birdsong begins to catch our ear, the sunrise becomes a friend we greet each day, the trees become our teachers, and the animals a vital part of our community. We begin to see the sacred, the beauty within everything and everyone. As the truth of interconnectedness is embodied, the energy of love is naturally restored.

Simply put, liberated love is about coming fully alive. It's about restoring vibrancy to your cells and, in turn, everything around you. It's about being a living example of what is possible when you stop running from your pain and turn toward healing it, not just on your own but together with and through the love you share with another.

When you look back upon your life, the *only* thing that will matter is how you loved and how you navigated relationships. You'll ask questions like, *Did I love well? Did I answer the call of my heart's desires? Did I repair with the people I've hurt? Did I grow and change and create a legacy of connection that rippled through my community and will be remembered long past this lifetime?*

Liberated love is about being liberated from internal and external constraints that limit your ability to show up as the you-est you. And it will be through these constraints and limitations that you will continue to discover where your work lies. Your relationships will be the most potent and consistent reflection of where you are, and are not, in integrity with your potential, and what is possible for you in how you live and how you relate.

Don't waste this opportunity.

A Living Prayer

We've been blessed to walk parts of this journey home with so many beautiful, devoted, and fierce souls in the flesh, and now you, through these words. It is because of souls like you, the ones who came here to shake things up and choose a different story, that we are able to share this work and hold this prayer of healing and remembrance at this time.

We pray you remember that you are worthy, welcome, and a cherished part of the whole.

We pray you have the courage to continually choose love, over and over and over again.

We pray you feel safe to drop the armor, masks, and old stories, and share your unique medicine with the world.

We pray that you know, in your heart of hearts, that the world needs you in your wholeness. Those you share your big heart with need your voice, your thoughts, your feelings, your boundaries. They need all of you. And so do we.

As they say, "Heal yourself, heal the world."

Here's to healing, loving, and liberating.

Acknowledgments

Mark:

To my wife, Kylie, I am honored to be loved by you and to share the learnings of our love with the world. Creating this book was great preparation for bringing Jasper into the world and diving deeper into what it means to be two separate beings creating something that is the merger of each other. What a gift. Your heart bled into this book, and that is evident from how beautifully your words have found each and every page.

To Lauren Hall, our collaborator, this book would not have been possible without you. You brought so much insight, flow, and ease to the book-writing process. Thank you so much!

To our editor Elizabeth Beier and St. Martin's, thank you for believing in us and helping bring the vision of this book alive. We are forever grateful!

To my friends new and old, who have been on this wild adventure of transformation with me and held a mirror to where I need to grow and reminded me of what is possible for me when I step further and further into my heart and soul, thank you.

To my parents . . . boy, did I win the parent lottery. It is such a gift to be born through your love for one another, and that you have always been a soft place for me to land and held me in my deepest pains and shames.

You entertain all my desires for discussion, depth, and healing, and I'm so grateful for you both. This book is a testament to your love.

To my sister and brother, some of my dearest teachers and friends. I love you. Thank you for walking this path with me and demonstrating that we can hold difference with not only love but also reverence.

To Jasper, thank you for reminding me of the importance of living my life in congruence with my values and integrity. It is my greatest honor to take you on the adventure that is this world and teach you through both words and actions. You are my greatest creation.

To Jay and Jess, thank you for nourishing and caring for us as we birthed this book and Jasper. Love and appreciate you dearly.

To those whom I have shared love with and walked the journey of relationship, I am so grateful to each of you. You have such a significant place in my heart and the lessons and learnings we shared have helped me become the man I am today. None of this would be possible without each and every one of you.

To all the authors, teachers, guides, mentors who have supported me in getting to this moment, thank you.

To all of you reading, thank you for desiring to learn through me. I am so grateful that through stepping courageously through my suffering and into my purpose I have been able to touch your life, and you touch mine. We never know where an intuitive desire will lead us, and I am in awe that it has led us to this page meeting your eyes. Thank you.

Kylie:

Mark, my beloved, thank you for choosing to walk through the fire with me in this lifetime. Thank you for bringing my whole heart back to life, and for choosing love every single time. I love you.

Jasper, my sweet son, thank you for showing me the Way. The biggest blessing of my life is being your mother. You will always be my most beloved creation.

To my twin, Jess, this book—and liberated love—is only possible because of the unconditional love you've gifted me since day one. I thank God every day that I get to do this life with you. Thank you for nourishing me with yummy food and connection while I wrote this book. I love you. Thank you. Thank you. Thank you.

Mom and Dad, thank you for always choosing love over everything. It is because of the foundation you gifted me that I am the woman I am today. Thank you for being the most supportive, loving, and incredible parents. I love doing this life with you both so much.

Jason, my brother from another mother, thank you for always keeping it real with me. I am so grateful that we got to "grow up" together. I cherish that chapter, the chapter we're in now, and those to come.

Robbie, your loving heart, deep wisdom, and care is a gift I cherish more than you know. I'm so blessed to be your sister and friend in this lifetime. I love you.

Carsen, thank you for always being there, for loving me, and for gifting me with your nuggets of astrology wisdom. I love you.

Moses, thank you for making Titi take numerous breaks while writing this book to laugh, play, and adventure. I cherish you beyond.

Lauren Hall, thank you for being the riverbank to my creative flow and for supporting us in bringing this book into the world. You are hands down the most amazing book doula (collaborator) on the planet. It's been an honor to work with you, know you, and connect with you on *all the things*.

Elizabeth Beier and St. Martin's, thank you for choosing this book (and us), and for supporting us in birthing a new conversation—relational template—into this world!

To all of my mentors, teachers, and healers: Anahata Ananda, Steph Jagger, Janet Bertolus, Kendra Cunov, Elisha Halpin, India Dania, Mark Wolynn, Nicole Lohse, Sarah Soleil, Francis Weller, Nisha Moodley, and the Four Peoples. Thank you for being here, for walking your path, and for supporting me on mine.

To all of my seen and unseen allies: Mother Earth, the elemental beings, the mother tree in Tofino, Thunder Mountain, Tea, Cacao, Ancestors, and Guides—thank you will never be enough.

To Spirit, thank you for guiding me every step of the way.

To my sisterhood: Kate, Kelsey, Nicole, Kim, Anahata, Vienna, Mariana, Elisha, Laura, Christine, Jordan, Kendra, Courtney, Janne, Sarah,

Tanya, Jasmine, Sheleana, Ari, Selina, Tracy—my life is so rich in beauty, care, and trust because of each of you. Thank you for walking with me and holding me through it all.

To my beloved community, thank you for choosing liberation with and alongside me. I am humbled by the beauty you behold and the power within you. Keep holding the bar of integrity high—you're moving mountains.

To Mother Earth, it's a deep honor to be here. May we all continue to remember and walk gently upon you.

Appendix

Resources for Resourcing

FINDING A THERAPIST

Finding a therapist can be *daunting* (and may take a few attempts to find the right choice for you—just like dating!). Here are some tips for your search:

- Ask trusted friends and family for recommendations.
- Call a university psychology or psychiatry department to ask for recommendations for people trained in a specific program.
- Contact a larger clinic and ask for recommendations.
- Consult your insurance directory.
- Search a directory:
  - » Psychology Today
  - » Alma
  - » Zocdoc
  - » Monarch
  - » Headway
- Check your employee benefits (employee assistance program, or EAP, can connect employees with the right resources, and some offer a small number of free therapy sessions).
- Explore virtual options:
  - » BetterHelp

- » Talkspace
- » 7 Cups
- • Ask yourself after your session:
  - » Do I feel comfortable, calm, and safe with this person?
  - » Did they do/say anything that made me feel uncomfortable, agitated, and unsafe?
  - » Did they ask me what it is I wanted out of this experience?
  - » Are they really listening? Did they ask enough appropriate questions? Did they feel connected and engaged?
  - » Did their advice seem sound and did it resonate? Did it push me to places I needed to go?

FINDING A SOMATIC PRACTITIONER

There are many kinds of somatic, body-based practitioners out there. Finding someone who has a deep understanding of our survival physiology and our nervous system is key when you're looking for support in healing trauma and when wanting to reconnect back to your wholeness. A good practitioner is able to guide you into listening to and following your body's experiences and impulses and can also direct you into unknown territory as needed to shift the patterning you find yourself stuck in.

When looking for a practitioner, do research into the trainings they've done. Don't hesitate to ask them if they're doing their own personal sessions! A good practitioner understands the work through their own inner knowings versus simply applying a technique.

Lastly, listen to any hunches you get! If you're drawn to someone, there's a reason. Chances are you're drawn to them because something about them feels safe. Having someone who's able to hold space for you and your experience as an embodied, empathic witness is where true healing happens!

Here is a list of trainings that guide practitioners into deepening their practice in these ways:

- • Somatic Experiencing®, the work of Peter Levine
- • Trainings with Kathy Kain or Stephen Terrell
- • NARM (NeuroAffective Relational Model)

+ Internal Family Systems, especially when combined with Somatic Experiencing®

Directory of Practitioners: https://directory.traumahealing.org

Alchemical Alignment Certified Practitioners: https://alchemicalalignment
.com/findapractitioner

IDENTIFYING YOUR SAFE PEOPLE

We've all misidentified one or more people as "safe" only to find ourselves lost and destabilized in the process. Knowing how to identify a safe person is critical as we expand our community and golden net.

Characteristics of a safe person:

+ Can listen and receive truth
+ Takes accountability and responsibility
+ Recognizes and apologizes for mistakes (and then acts accordingly)
+ Is gentle, compassionate, and empathetic
+ Clearly and gently communicates boundaries, needs, and feelings
+ Communicates consistently and effectively
+ Encourages you to express your feelings and accepts them
+ Treats you as an equal
+ Respects your need for personal growth, privacy, and space
+ Accepts feedback well
+ Avoids destructive patterns

Characteristics of an unsafe person:

+ Dishonest (and avoids the truth)
+ Lacks self-awareness
+ Manipulative
+ Consistently withdraws without interest in accountability and repair
+ Apologizes but never changes
+ Unclear and inconsistent
+ Avoids important conversations

- Persuades you to adopt their own beliefs and views
- Controlling
- Overtly defensive and not willing to heal, or look at this pattern
- Dismissive

Overall, pay attention to your nervous system. Is it on high alert when you are around this person, or do you feel calm and internally relaxed and able to communicate openly? Do you feel able to let your guard down and show your authentic self? When the answer is "yes," these are your people!

EXPAND YOUR COMMUNITY

We've said it before and we'll say it again: *do activities you love and you'll meet people who are doing what they love too.* This can mean anything from taking a pottery class to volunteering to joining a hobby club or sports team.

Some other paths to expanding your community and golden net could include:

- Joining a recovery program (e.g., CoDA, a recovery program for codependents)
- Joining a container (e.g., the No Man Diet with Kendra Cunov)
- Attending a workshop
- Going on a retreat

Remember: Authenticity may move us away from some people, but it is always moving us *toward* others. This is the community that will celebrate our new way of being.

RECOMMENDED BOOKS

Here is a list of the books that have supported us immensely. We've broken them down into two categories: liberated love and somatic healing resources.

Books on Liberated Love

It Didn't Start With You by Mark Wolynn
All About Love by bell hooks
The Dance of Anger and *The Dance of Intimacy* by Harriet Lerner
The Power of Attachment by Diane Poole Heller

The Patriarchy Stress Disorder by Dr. Valerie Rein

It's Not Always Depression by Hilary Jacobs Hendel

The Wild Edge of Sorrow by Francis Weller

Belonging by Toko-pa Turner

The Origins of You by Vienna Pharaon

Loving Bravely by Dr. Alexandra Solomon

The Myth of Normal by Dr. Gabor Maté

Boundary Boss by Terri Cole

Iron John by Robert Bly

Women Who Run with the Wolves by Dr. Clarissa Pinkola Estés

No More Mr. Nice Guy by Robert A. Glover

When Things Fall Apart by Pema Chödrön

Codependent No More by Melody Beattie

The Gifts of Imperfection by Brené Brown

The Truth by Neil Strauss

Getting the Love You Want by Harville Hendrix

Hold Me Tight by Sue Johnson

Somatic Healing Resources

ReBloom by Rachael Maddox

Healing Developmental Trauma by Laurence Heller and Aline Lapierre

My Grandmother's Hands by Resmaa Menaken

The Body Keeps the Score by Bessel van der Kolk

Waking the Tiger by Peter A. Levine

Anchored by Deb Dana

Index